The Myth of M Globalization

The Myth of Media Globalization

Kai Hafez

Translated by Alex Skinner

polity

Previously published in German in 2005 as *Mythos Globalisierung* by VS Verlag für Sozialwissenschaften

First published in 2007 by Polity Press

Polity Press
65 Bridge Street
Cambridge CB2 1UR, UK.

Polity Press
350 Main Street
Malden, MA 02148, USA

ISBN-10: 0-7456-3908-9
ISBN-13: 978-07456-3908-6
ISBN-10: 0-7456-3909-7 (pb)
ISBN-13: 978-07456-3909-3 (pb)

A catalogue record for this book is available from the British Library.

Typeset in 10.5 on 12 pt Plantin
by Servis Filmsetting Ltd, Manchester
Printed and bound in Malaysia by Alden Press, Malaysia

For further information on Polity, visit our website: www.polity.co.uk

Contents

List of Figures and Tables

Introduction

Most of us would be hard pushed to imagine a world in which the process of 'globalization' had fully run its course. Will de-territorialization reign supreme, while jobs as well as products of every kind become interchangeable across national borders? Will the political borders that separate human beings fall away and societies be linked comprehensively by the media? The future of globalization is unclear, much as the egalitarian 'communist society' once was, but the contemporary period is characterized by profound upheavals. Politicians use globalization to justify reforms of the state while the private sector makes people redundant to ensure its ability to compete globally. Just the right social climate, in other words, for a 'myth'. This myth 'banishes the unsettling strangeness of its object, but generally retains the fascinating ambivalence associated with the inexplicable'.[1] It mixes facts with exaggerated projections and, whatever its potential to inspire fear, entails a utopian promise of a better world – it would hardly exist in the first place if it did not.

We need to start looking at globalization as a myth that fuses truth and falsehood. It must be subjected to critical scrutiny to minimize the risk of politicians and others misusing it as an unfounded ideology. From the outset, the notion of globalization has rested on two pillars. Human economic-material and intellectual-communicative productive power has supposedly escaped the constraints of geographical, cultural and national borders. It is said to be universally and globally accessible. This requires new forms of private and public cross-border communication. Globalization thus entails the assertion that international media relations are growing in importance.

However, the realism of this assumption has not yet been satisfactorily established. The globalization debate is typified by a downright anecdotal empiricism and by reasoning that inserts evidence and counter-evidence into visions of an allegedly globalized world from which there appears to be no escape. The anti-globalization movement also bears some responsibility for these visions. For regardless of differences of opinion about the advantages and disadvantages of a capitalist-driven globalization, 'optimists' and 'pessimists' share the same basic conviction, namely, that globalization is in fact taking place.

Both camps broadly agree that the symptoms of an Americanized global culture ('McWorld') and signs of cultural resistance in Asia, Africa and the Middle East ('McJihad') are *reactions* to the unstoppable advance of globalization. Everything in the world appears to be connected to everything else, for good or for ill. This 'network consensus' makes cross-border communication the core phenomenon of globalization. For while the opponents of globalization characterize it as an enormous culture annihilation machine working through the media, enlightened globalizers emphasize the advantages of cultural pluralism in a world in which world cultures can be accessed at will – thanks to the Internet, satellite television and modern mobile telephony. In his big-selling introduction to globalization, *All Connected Now*, Walter Truett Anderson, for instance, claims: 'In a globalizing society, all the world's cultures become the property of all the world's people.'[2] In this vision, more modest than the old notion of a universal culture uniting humanity, we can all remain as we are. The media allow us to understand what the other is like at any time. It is in itself entirely logical that this enlightened globalism is closely linked with the concept of 'Dialogue among Civilizations', which the United Nations elevated to its annual slogan for 2001. Yet this is exactly where the problem lies.

It was for long assumed that global interactions are increasing. In many fields of cross-border communication, this is in fact far less true than previously imagined. Media production and use are proving conservative cultural forces in many parts of the world. They are generating a reality which the 'globalization' approach struggles to cope with. What does it mean for example, if processes of cross-border communication on the Internet are increasing, but at the same time Internet traffic within national borders is growing far more rapidly? Does this make the Internet a 'global' medium or is it really a 'local' one? The existence of the technology of satellite radio and television is also a necessary but far from sufficient condition for global communication, for it tells us little about their actual reach and potential to change cultures and societies. How is one to interpret the fact that while nowadays a significant chunk of humanity has the technology to access foreign broadcasters at its disposal, it almost never makes use of it?

People refrain from engaging in global communication in this and many other ways. This is a far from trifling matter, for it casts doubt on the general concepts associated with globalization. How is the democratic 'public' to find expression at an international level? How is a global citizenry within a 'global public sphere' to have a debate about important issues of politics, social development and the environment, if the means of communication – the media – remain dominated by the nation and the state? In the field of so-called 'media diplomacy', how can transnational television networks bring a new, civil society element into international politics if there are no globally accepted networks and the only one which has ever played this role – CNN – has long since lost it? It would be simple to assume that the new Arab satellite television channels, such as al-Jazeera, provide yet more evidence that 'pluralism enriches globalization' and to point to the images which Western networks have borrowed from them. However, given the differences in these networks' world-views, one would also have to reflect upon whether CNN and al-Jazeera are not in fact merely the harbingers of an ever more divided media world, characterized not by *more*, but by ever *less* cross-border exchange.

The globalization debate has been marred by its almost exclusive focus on the 'new media' of the Internet and satellite television. We thus lack an overall appraisal of media globalization. The notion that the direct *one-to-many* or *many-to-one* communication of the epoch-making Internet would contribute to the 'end of journalism' has been proved wrong, as the growing literature on the 'myth of the Internet' lays bare.[3] People's media habits and how they organize their lives are not changing as radically as has frequently been assumed. In the field of international communication, traditional international reporting by the major national mass media continues to set the tone – above all during crises or wars. But what is truly global about international reporting within national media systems? When the *New York Times* apologized to its readers in May 2004 for its ill-considered acceptance of propaganda material produced by the American government during the Iraq War of 2003, this was seen as confirming the views of critics of war reporting. It was in fact far more than this. It was an admission that the 'global dialogue' of the media is in serious danger and that the media's political ties to their home countries are as strong as ever.

The question at stake today is nothing less than whether we have a functioning 'world communication system', allowing an undistorted view of the world, or whether we will have one in future and under what circumstances. Getting to grips with this requires us to analyse the ownership of global media and to take stock of media policy in a global framework. Has the state really become obsolete? Do transnational media companies dominate the media systems of the world?

In their well-regarded book, *Globalization in Question*, economists Paul Hirst and Grahame Thompson argue that the changes in the global economy are far less drastic than the vast majority of protagonists in the globalization debate have claimed. Even internationally operating businesses, they point out, tend to have a clearly recognizable home base or at least strong regional linkages.[4] This places a question mark over the assumption that there are entirely 'transnational' firms ranging freely across the globe and underpins the authors' conclusion that globalization is largely a myth.[5] Is the transnationalization of economic processes, which is often confined to the OECD countries, mirrored in the technological, political and economic integration of the media? Does this mean that a new north–south global division is in the offing?[6] Indeed, is it not the case that even in the OECD countries political and economic interconnections in the media field continue to lag far behind other economic sectors because international communication is closely bound up with culture, language and tradition? Cars may be universal – but this applies only to a limited extent to news, film and music.

A revisionist scholarly debate has begun to scrutinize the basic assumptions which have held sway so far. In media studies, critical voices have existed since the early 1990s. Marjorie Ferguson[7] has argued against the notion of the mass media as sites of cultural harmonization or even the Western-style democratization of the world. Joseph Straubhaar[8] as well as Georgette Wang, Anura Goonasekera and Jan Servaes[9] and John Sinclair, Elizabeth Jacka and Stuart Cunningham[10] have underlined how national and regional media systems are rapidly becoming more complex and consolidated. Global models often serve as 'templates' for new media formats, but differences in content and culture persist. Claude Moisy[11] has shown that since the end of the East–West conflict the extent of international coverage in the media and the consumption of foreign media are declining rather than growing. In his opinion, this gives the lie to the notion of a 'global village' in which the media report everything and reach all the citizens of planet Earth.

Silvio Waisbord and Nancy Morris[12] have pointed to the astonishing ability of the nation-state to assert control in the media sector, even under conditions of globalization. Daya K. Thussu[13] has described local resistance to global media empires. Colin Sparks[14] argues that the international and global use of satellite television has received far too much attention in academic circles, given that it has changed national consumption habits very little. While Anthony Giddens and others have propagated the notion that the era of the nation-state is at an end, James Curran and Myung-Jin Park[15] have warned against taking this for granted and making it the focal point of media analysis. Media developments beyond North America, Europe and Australia should, according to them, be paid more attention and integrated into theory building. Andreas Hepp, Friedrich Krotz and Carsten Winter advocate the globalization of media and cultural studies itself, its theoretical perspectives and research subjects.[16]

Such determinedly realistic and sceptical views receive little attention in the big disciplines of philosophy, political science and sociology, which set the tone for the globalization debate worldwide. Media and communication studies is a relatively small scholarly field. So far, it has been forced to watch more or less from the sidelines as the big subjects have 'expropriated' the concept of the media. To some extent, media research itself has also allowed itself to be infected by the euphoria of globalization, which appears to endow its own research object, the media, with such central cultural significance for the twenty-first century. In the wake of this maladaptation, media and communication studies still cling to naive concepts such as the 'global village', the 'networked society' or the 'glocalization of culture'. These are abstract models fundamentally resistant to description, measurement or confirmation by scientific means, which hinder rather than promote intellectual progress. Even within communication studies, it has been possible to claim, without provoking criticism, that countries and cultures are influencing each other culturally more than ever before,[17] that the integration of media systems has never advanced as rapidly and that the media's influence on politics has reached new heights.[18] But what is the evidence for this, and how can we measure other societies' influence on cultural change? This is all the more challenging if one takes into account the complex processes of indigenization and local adaptation which play a role in both the import of media and the construction of world-views within international reporting.

Again and again, attempts to systematize the field of globalization scholarship have shown a lack of empirical clarity and of a workable theoretical concept.[19] As far as empirical evidence is concerned, there are certainly 'harder' and 'softer' areas. It is a lot simpler to provide evidence of film exports than of cross-border media use. The cultural globalization of the entertainment industry seems more pronounced than that of political communication. The interpretation of empirical evidence is however theory-dependent. One's estimate of the influence of elites on the development of societies, for example, will determine how one assesses the significance of the 'info-elites' which have congregated on the Internet the world over. This determines whether the cross-border Internet truly has a significant culture-changing effect.

If 'globalization' is degenerating into an 'all-purpose catchword', as F. J. Lechner and J. Boli fear,[20] then we need to attempt a rescue mission, because the world probably needs positive myths of this kind. Ultimately, the Millennium Report by the United Nations on the cusp of the twenty-first century made it clear that a large part of humanity continues to live in poverty and ignorance. The media are a potentially important instrument of development. The division between normative givens and facts on the ground is the next challenge if we are to get the project of globalization on a sustainable footing. Technophilia and fictional utopianism are 'out'. The hard graft of gathering empirical evidence, vital to producing robust social and cultural studies, is 'in', as is precise modelling.

The present work tries, through theoretical systematization, to help take stock of the most important aspects of cross-border mass communication. The subjects of study, alongside international reporting, satellite television and the Internet, include imports and exports of films for the big and small screen, international broadcasting and international media use by immigrants. Chapters on the development of media capital and cross-border dimensions of media policy complete the volume. The book presents the author's original research findings, some of which have been published in other contexts over the last ten years and some of which are new; it also gets to grips with the work of other researchers. Alongside the North American and European media systems, particular attention is paid to the situation in Asia, Africa and Latin America.

1

Theory – Structural Transformation of the Global Public Sphere?

A clear theoretical model is vital if we are to take stock of the international and intercultural effect of media and forms of reporting of such different types as television, radio, print media, Internet, direct broadcasting by satellite, international broadcasting and international reporting. In the literature on globalization dealing with international communication, models of any kind are thin on the ground. Manuel Castell's famous three-volume work, *The Information Age*, does without almost any schematic models.[1] The same goes for multi-authored volumes in this field.[2]

The present work draws on systems theory to describe the globalization of mass communication. We may divide the key characteristics and conceptual tools deployed here into three fields:

- system connectivity
- system change
- system interdependence

Before discussing more closely the core concepts of 'connectivity', 'change' and 'interdependence' linked with the concept of system, it is vital to shed light on the frequently ambiguous concept of system itself. Cross-border communication is defined very unsystematically in the globalization literature, sometimes as inter- and trans*national* and sometimes as inter- and trans*cultural* communication. 'Cross-border' thus describes those processes of information exchange in the course of which system borders, of the nation-state *or* culture, are transversed. Almost all contemporary attempts to grapple with globalization theoretically that tackle issues of communication emphasize the nation-state or culture. The focus tends to be on the state, but sometimes it is on cultural areas, at times also labelled 'civilizations'. The idea of 'networking' is anchored in the assumption that the world features a number of poles which can be networked; a web is ultimately nothing without its nodal points.

The notion of network-like communication between actors who can be ascribed to states or cultures is problematic. This is apparent when one considers that these poles of the system are in principle equal. They can be regarded as subsets of one another depending on the situation. States may be parts of cultures – and vice versa. The resulting web of communication appears to resemble the kind of optical illusion whose content changes as one changes one's perspective. When the Uighurs, a Muslim minority in western China of Turkmen origin and thus related to the peoples of Central Asia, use media from beyond the national borders, should we regard them as actors practising inter*national* or inter*cultural* communication?

Quite obviously, it depends which aspect of the analysis we wish to focus on. A web emerges consisting of several dimensions. These complications are rooted in the fact that 'state' and 'culture' involve differing implications for communication, each of which has its own justification. In one case, communication between actors describable in terms of constitutional law or sociology (governments, NGOs, etc.) takes centre stage. In the other, the focus is on exchanges between subjects and groups in their capacity as bearers of linguistically and historically imbued norms, ways of life and traditions. Both perspectives may be important, as is apparent wherever state and cultural borders are not identical and cultural identity rivals the power of the state. Tribal cultures in Africa, for example, often extend across state borders, highlighting the advantages of scrutinizing both the international and intercultural dimensions of cross-border communication processes.

The existence of cultural areas such as the 'West', the 'Islamic world', the Indian subcontinent and Latin or German-speaking Europe is an additional factor making analysis more difficult. Such areas gain cohesion across state borders only with the help of mass media, adding a third dimension of regionality to the theoretical model. A debate on globalization restricted to the 'local' and the 'global' while neglecting the 'regional' would lack complexity. The immigrant cultures that we hear so much about, which communicate across borders and form 'virtual communities', provide further evidence of the value of examining international and intercultural communication as a unity. The division into the spatial levels 'global', 'regional' and 'local', intended as a heuristic and relevant to both dimensions of state and culture, is not contradicted by migration. Immigrants also communicate either locally, regionally or globally, even if the spatial parameters are the reverse of those of settled populations, as their local culture (their home country) is, so to speak, located in global space and they can develop a second locality only slowly.

System connectivity

Phenomena of system connectivity, sometimes called *interconnectedness* in the literature, describe the extent, speed and intensity of the international or intercultural exchange of information. Connectivity may be generated between entities, however defined, through various means of communication. Alongside mediated interpersonal communication (telephone, e-mail, letter, fax, etc.) we can distinguish the following fields of communication which depend on mass media (figure 1.1):

(a) direct access to the range of communicative services produced by another country/culture (Internet; direct broadcasts by satellite; international broadcasting (special television and radio services in foreign languages broadcast to other countries); imports/export of media);
(b) access to information and contexts in another country or cultural area conveyed by journalism (international reporting on television, radio, the press; corresponding media services on the Internet).

While this list makes no claim to completeness, it is clear that direct routes of access to cross-border communication are in the majority. One of the key factors shaping the globalization debate over the last decade was thus the fact that the number of means of transmission and the exchange of information beyond borders has increased dramatically. The 'new media' have set the overall tone of the debate since the 1990s, effectively distorting it, as the 'old media' have largely been ignored. In particular, the role of international reporting in the process of globalization has suffered a complete lack of systematic treatment. The technologically possible direct interleaving of national media areas, which people could previously experience only through the information conveyed by international journalism, has proven a fascinating and bothersome phenomenon for researchers.

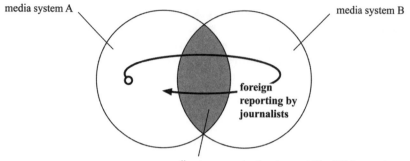

media system A   media system B

foreign
reporting by
journalists

direct communication (e.g. satellite TV, Internet)

Figure 1.1 Forms of cross-border mass communication
Source: author

However, it is far from certain that the new media, regardless of their many new forms, characterize the processes of globalization more than national journalism and international reporting. We therefore have to take both fields into account when designing our theories. Despite the rise of the new media and the mounting flood of information available on the Internet, the significance of journalism as intermediary has by no means diminished. Foreign media accessible via satellites and cables also represent a form of journalism, though one which arises outside of one's own media system. This means that the media user receives direct access to foreign journalistic cultures. Not only this, but the Internet has failed to oust even domestic journalism: journalistic mediation is in fact ever more significant to how people organize their lives at a time when the quantity of information is growing. If at all, online information services can replace the international reporting provided by national media only among small informational elites.

The concrete form of connectivity via the new media depends on a range of technological, socio-economic and cultural parameters:

Technological reach and socioeconomic implications of media technology. The nation-states and cultural areas of this planet are characterized by very different technological capacities for transmission and reception in the field of satellite broadcasting, depending on the prevailing political and financial parameters. The same goes for the Internet. Regardless of the strong increase in the number of connections, a 'digital divide' exists, above all between industrialized and developing countries, which restricts connectivity substantially.

User reach. The debate on the globalization of the media all too often fails to distinguish between technological reach and user reach. The number of those who use a technology per se lies below the technologically possible use – and cross-border use is of course only *one* variant of the use to which the new media may be put. We cannot simply assume that it is the primary form. Our eagerness to wed globalization to a normative agenda should not blind us to the fact that the Internet may be a misjudged medium that is contributing far more to intensifying local connections (e-commerce, etc.) than to creating cross-border networks.

Linguistic and cultural competence. To communicate with people in other states and cultural areas or to use their media generally requires linguistic competence, which only minorities in any population enjoy. To avoid dismissing cross-border connectivity as marginal from the outset, it is vital to distinguish between various user groups – globalization elites and peripheries. Connectivity is without doubt partly dependent on the nature of the message communicated. Music, image, text – behind this sequence hides a kind of magic formula of globalization. Music surely enjoys the largest global spread, and images surely occupy a middle position (for example, press photographs or the images of CNN, also accessible to users who understand no English), while most texts create only meagre international resonance because of language barriers. This issue is central to the evaluation of global connectivity as a more or less '*contextualized*' globalization. Images in themselves do not speak. They require explanatory text to transport authentic messages – and it is questionable to what extent such messages can overcome borders.

Connectivity in the field of international reporting also depends on the international department's printing or broadcasting capacities, the quality and quantity of technical equipment and correspondent networks. All these resources have an influence on the presence of other countries and cultures in the media of one's own country. Foreign reporting has always been a struggle because of lack of resources, particularly in terms of staff and funding. Even the largest Western media have, for example, no more than one or two permanent correspondents in Africa, a continent with more than fifty states. CNN, seemingly the exemplary global broadcaster, has no more than a few dozen permanent correspondents.

International journalism should be seen as a virtual odyssey. More than domestic journalism, it struggles daily to reduce the mass of newsworthy stories from the two hundred or so states of the world to a manageable form. In principle, the notion of a world linked globally through the media assumes that different media systems increasingly deal with the same topics. Moreover, the lines of reasoning deployed in this process would also have to 'cross borders'. Homogenous national discourses, with their quite unique ways of looking at international issues, would increasingly have to open up to the topics and frames of other national discourses (which does not mean standardization of opinion, as this would involve a more advanced form of cultural change and the development of a global 'superculture', which is another issue).[3]

To increase the connectivity of the journalistic systems of this world, the resources available to the media are just as important as the linguistic and cultural competence of the journalists.[4] In some ways, the issue of the connectivity of journalism appears in a new light under conditions of globalization. While media may compete in destructive fashion as described above, multimedia collaboration may help improve the quality of each individual medium. The Internet as a source for journalism is surely the perfect example. Yet here too it is crucial to distinguish theoretically between *technologically possible* and *actually practised* use.

Connectivity may ultimately occur within global communication not only between producers and consumers in various nation-states and cultural areas – that is, *inter*nationally and *inter*culturally – but also via a *trans*national (or cultural) media system. Here, media and media businesses would no longer have a clear-cut national base, but would emerge as 'global players'. The idea of a world linked through communication is anchored in the assumption that globalization is more than the sum of the links between its components. The structure of the system underlying the global media landscape would change if new supersystems similar to the United Nations or large NGOs such as Greenpeace developed in the media field. The media are in principle also capable of transnationalization, so that alongside national systems networked with one another, a second global system might also arise (figure 1.2).

Contemporary notions of what such a transnational media system consists of are however still very nebulous. Apart from a few global agreements brought into being by the major transnational trade organizations such as the World Trade Organization (WTO) (in the copyright protection field for instance; see chapter 8, p. 143), there are only a few transnationally active corporations which can be called 'global players' (see chapter 9). Regardless of the existence of such businesses, transnational media, that is, programmes and formats, are extremely rare. CNN, frequently mentioned as the perfect example of a leading global medium that encourages exchange of political

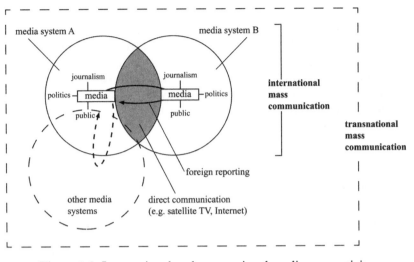

Figure 1.2 International and transnational media connectivity
Source: author

opinion worldwide, by concentrating on transnational programmes, seems to come closest to fitting this vision. Yet even this case is problematic, for CNN is no uniform programme, but consists of numerous continental 'windows'. There are many 'CNNs', but no complete global programme. Through the proliferation of satellite programmes in the last decade, CNN has lost its elevated position and is now merely a decentralized variant of an American television programme, whose country of origin remains easily recognizable in its agenda and framing. CNN tends to be a mixture of characteristics of the American system and the target system of the specific window; it is thus at best a multinational but not a global programme.

For want of concrete role models, a transnational media system remains largely a utopia. Individual large national media systems such as the American or binational services such as the Franco-German broadcaster Arte can supplement but by no means replace their national counterparts. The transnational media field is still largely devoid of formal diversity.

System change

In the second theoretical field, the focus is no longer on grasping the extent and type of cross-border communication through mass media.

The point here is to ascertain whether these processes of border cross-ing are significant enough to bring about changes in the political, social and cultural systems of the countries involved. Is the nature of these interactions such that they are not simply 'domesticated' by the receiving systems but influence and change them substantially?

For both the major realms of connectivity – direct communication through new media and mediated communication by means of jour-nalism – we need to clarify:

- whether receiving cultures are changed by transmitting cultures in the process of cross-border communication through the Internet, satellite broadcasting, international broadcasting or through media imports and exports;
- whether the media content of foreign coverage passed on by national journalism systems to their domestic populations is up to the task of changing the world-views and attitudes of the receiving cultures.

Three forms of cultural change are mentioned again and again in the globalization debate:

(a) the adoption of the 'other' culture (above all in the form of 'Westernized' globalization);
(b) the emergence of 'glocalized' hybrid cultures (Robertson),[5] which are influenced both by global and local elements;
(c) the revitalization of traditional and other local cultures as a reac-tion to globalization.

Theoretical concepts which lack a functional explanatory system and thus fail utterly to explain their own core concepts of 'global', 'glocal' and 'local' inevitably hinder rather than advance theoretical progress. Yet the tripartite division has taken hold as a kind of minimal con-sensus in the globalization debate because it attempts to grasp the role played by external influences in internal change. The biggest problem consists not in determining external global (a) or internal traditional (c) character, but in determining the content and dynamics of the hybrid category, 'glocalization' (b). How are hybrid cultures 'mea-sured'? How do we determine the significance of internal and exter-nal influences? Is Far Eastern pop music really evidence of a national or regional culture increasingly able to connect up to the wider world? Or is it an example of local modernization, certainly with recogniz-able global influences, but nonetheless primarily deployable at the local level and hardly 're-exportable'?

It is crucial at this point to take temporal dynamics into account. We must bear in mind that all societies and cultures pass through different epochs, characterized either by willingness to accept external influences or a tendency to seal oneself off from them. David Held, Anthony McGrew, David Goldblatt and Jonathan Perraton have for example quite rightly distinguished between forms of transparent and hermetic regionalization.[6] Global influences may be adopted by nation-states or regional cultures, then develop new forms of locality in processes of largely self-steered modernization. The resulting cultural forms often resemble global models to a certain extent, but in reality follow a logic of modernization present in all cultures, which is by no means inevitably compatible with globalization (Asian pop music, for example, may be the product of 'glocalization', but its acceptance levels are definitely higher in Asia than the US or Europe). In other words, glocalization may promote the local culture long-term and is not necessarily a step on the path towards a global 'superculture' (see Lull 2002).[7]

It thus makes little sense to subscribe to concentric notions according to which the national and the regional are merely constitutive subsets of the global. Popular political slogans such as 'Think global, act local' or 'Europe of the regions' are an expression of a myth of globalization which imposes a downright artificial order upon the processes of change worldwide. This ignores the fact that the local systems of this planet are engaged in competitive modernization, which *may be a long-term phenomenon*. It also fails to notice the conflicts between these systems. Yet these factors are as important if not more important than alleged globalization.

From a theoretical point of view, we must remember that it is as yet totally unclear to what extent cross-border mass communication is capable of representing societies and systems comprehensively in the first place. We can work from the assumption that each form of media communication represents only a limited slice of social developments and that special 'virtual' cultures are being created that may not be significant outside of the media. Other subsystems such as science, art, literature and 'everyday culture' as a whole, meanwhile, appear in the media to a much lesser degree. It is thus clear that change is occurring beyond the world of the media and, potentially, with quite different global or local implications. The cultural contact facilitated by mass media is based on a desideratum filtered and imagined through the media, whose significance can be elucidated only through a large-scale contextual analysis of globalization.

Yet media do have the potential to change systems, and here the individual media differ, sometimes significantly. The areas in which the Internet can work to change systems are diverse, because its form is untypical of the mass media. It represents individual and mass culture, science, art, business, entertainment and political information. The Internet features a high degree of cultural storage capacity and flexibility. It is fast, yet stores cultural knowledge long-term, unlike the fleeting medium of television. Highly complex knowledge cultures can cross borders in this way.

The Internet can generate alternative publics. It can unite political actors and oppositional landscapes worldwide to form a 'global civil society'. The CIA report *Global Trends 2015* (2000) predicted new challenges for national and international politics. The report assumes that while the nation-state will remain the most important political actor, its efficiency will be measured on the basis of how it masters globalization and how it comes to terms with an increasingly articulate and well-organized civil society worldwide. On this view, civil societies are often better able to solve problems than are governments and they will therefore take on more and more societal tasks. The report predicts that a growing number of international and national non-profit organizations in the educational, health and social sectors will increasingly break down the classical division of labour between the state, which sets the parameters of policy-making and represents the citizens, and society, which is restricted to a process of shaping public opinion without direct impact on political decision-making and to constituent elections.[8]

This prognosis by the American secret service, with its downright communitarian tone, experienced a setback as a result of the 11 September 2001 attacks on the World Trade Center and the Pentagon. Not least because of the shortfalls of the secret services themselves, which failed to notice that the attacks were being planned despite available information, across the world the state again interfered more vigorously in citizens' private lives (the Patriot Act in the US, etc.). The Internet, it could be argued, is becoming all the more significant as a platform capable of articulating and shaping the will of the citizenry, creating civil networks and even mobilizing people politically.[9] There is a certain absurdity in the fact that perhaps the most significant *transnational* movement identified with the Internet is none other than the so-called 'anti-globalization movement' (such as Attac).

In view of the structures underlying television and radio worldwide, which tend to be commercial, government-run or public, direct broadcasting by satellite is a downright elite medium in comparison to the Internet. It features formidable barriers to access, making it difficult to use it to articulate one's views, and highly developed journalistic selection mechanisms. Nonetheless, the comparative advantage of satellite broadcasting is that large publics can form rapidly, including cross-border ones. The Internet is fragmenting into countless sub-publics; in everyday life, these can be fused only by political organizations and networks. The international and intercultural use of television programmes, meanwhile, represents a genuine challenge to national publics. The structural transformation of the public sphere[10] in the nineteenth century has been outlined by Jürgen Habermas. He describes this as the formation of the bourgeois reasoning of developing democracies. It contains further – multinational, transnational, global – levels and may be growing beyond the narrow boundaries of the nation-state.

Is the media forming a 'global public sphere', as this popular and central concept in the globalization debate suggests?[11] The classic medium to which commentators so often refer to back up this thesis is CNN. As we have seen, however, with its strong links to the American system and to the target system of the regional window, CNN resembles a bi- or multilateral rather than a truly global discursive platform. How do things stand with the thousands of other programmes now receivable via satellite? Are they capable of functioning globally? What kind of user behaviour is associated with such services?

US scholars in particular have claimed that we are dealing here not just with a philanthropic utopia, but with a development anchored in real-world politics. The catchphrase 'media diplomacy' captures the capacity of media to act almost as representatives of the public and the peoples of the Earth, and to intervene in the traditional diplomacy between states, which is often stuck in a rut and conflictual in nature. Broadcasters that are clearly nationally based may perform such a function. Ideally, however, it should be taken over by formats of a transnational character. Media diplomacy has thus often been referred to as the 'CNN effect', joined in recent years by other models such as the 'al-Jazeera effect' (see chapter 2, p. 51 and chapter 3, p. 75). In all cases, the suggestion is that the media have global resonance and centrality, that is, within their specific spheres – Western or Arab – they enjoy a privileged position and thus have excellent prospects of changing the politics of international conflicts.

A concept of truly visionary force, the CNN effect suggests that there may at last be a way to respond to the old cliché that it is politicians rather than peoples that make war, by promoting the politics of peace through the media. An increasing number of NGOs, which engage in parallel diplomacy involving the organized public and lobbyists, are supplementing classic state diplomacy. What is more, the silent majority, represented by a journalism oriented towards public opinion and with a democratic conscience, could even intervene directly in conflicts. Yet the fact that the number of violent conflicts worldwide shows no sustained decrease casts doubt on the reality of this notion.

The entire academic world, more or less, has raved about this phenomenon for more than a decade. Where has it become a reality? The methodological problems involved in measuring media effects throw up numerous questions. The parallel and increasing tendency for the state to engage in public diplomacy does so as well. This has taken new forms since the second Gulf War of 1991 and the establishment of American and British information pools, up to and including the 'embedded journalism' seen during the third Gulf War of 2003. One wonders who will come out on top: television striving for independence and political influence or the state asserting itself through the media, and integrating every medium – the Internet as well as satellite television – into its propagandistic concepts. Will the media succeed in ending the era of reporting which separates political systems, in which every opponent is imbued with hostile imagery, which has accompanied every war, especially the world wars of the last century?

International broadcasting appears, at first sight, a typical vestige of pre-global mass communication centred on nation-states. Regardless of their often propagandistic character, radio and television messages intended for foreign countries, composed by many states in numerous languages, nonetheless have an undeniable charm. This makes them attractive even to a normatively laden globalization debate. They overcome the linguistic and cultural chasm that still marks direct satellite broadcasting (see p. 9). Classics of the Second World War and the Cold War such as Radio Free Europe were predicted to die away rapidly after the end of the East–West conflict. Reports of its death were exaggerated. International broadcasting is currently more vital than ever, though how it will develop in future is far from clear. In most countries, state support structures are still highly developed, so that international broadcasting is generally becoming a medium transferring *public diplomacy* to crisis regions.

Theoretically, however, the medium also lends itself to 'feedback loops' and dialogic forms of journalism.[12] Information on political developments in authoritarian states can for example be conveyed back to a particular public via the indirect route of international broadcasting produced by another state. International broadcasting may thus make up, to some extent, for the shortcomings of other media systems. Because it has strong linguistic capacities and is tailored to foreign broadcasting areas, it is in fact far better at reaching a mass audience than many new media. Dialogue may be established between the source and receiving country, though this requires some form of public broadcasting and a transformation of the model of state ownership.

Whether the international coverage of nationally based media can be part of a global public sphere is subject to dispute. Existing interpretations can be grouped very roughly under 'conversion theory' and 'domestication theory'. The *locus classicus* of conversion theory is Marshall McLuhan's 'global village' approach, according to which the mass media in particular are such a perfected form of the technological extension of the human sensory apparatus that a collective global consciousness is predicted to emerge in the twenty-first century.[13] McLuhan's work has left traces of conversion theory in late modernization theory. This assumes, for example, that as global communicative relations develop quantitatively, the level of information in the media increases, particularistic conceptions of foreign countries and the world as a whole are dismantled and international conflicts minimized.[14]

Critics of conversion theory have assailed it for overstating the globalizing tendencies of mass communication, by equating increasing technological networking and economic transnationalization with the universalization of media content. It also underestimates, critics suggest, the particularistic political, ideological and cultural influences affecting the international coverage produced by local, national and international media.[15] The assumption that international reporting undergoes 'domestication' has crystallized as the ideal typical alternative to globalization. There is plenty of empirical evidence that the same event, reconstructed on the basis of the same information sources, can end up being presented in highly divergent and sometimes even contradictory ways in different national media systems. This indicates that parochial political, social, organizational and religious-cultural influences on international reporting may be a profound stumbling block to the kind of homogenization of world-views that conversion theory has in mind.[16] From the perspective of conversion theory, the mediating role played by international reporting leads to conceptions of foreign lands that merge aspects of the country of origin and target country. From the perspective of domestication theory, meanwhile, international reporting reflects the influence of the journalists, media system and social system for which it is produced.

A global public sphere worthy of the name, which involved more than simply 'peering through the keyhole' at foreign programmes via satellite and included the *domestic media of specific countries* and their world-views, would have to unite a diverse range of national discourses. The technological prerequisites for bringing national discourses together in international coverage certainly exist. Media across the world are generally present on the Internet and it would thus be feasible for both media and perspectives to converge. Such projects, however, can easily come to grief as a result of linguistic barriers and lack of awareness and for want of the key resources of 'money' and 'time'.

It is crucial to take the resource base of mass communication into account as the third factor influencing system change. Here, the theoretical foundations include not only the actors of 'global civil society' and the nature of their discourse ('global public sphere'), but also the structural basis on which discourses can develop. Mass communication does not occur in a vacuum, but is anchored in the realities of market and political integration (see figure 1.3). For want of a more appropriate term and because the global media economy approach is overly economistic and thus best avoided, we may refer to the third dimension simply as the 'global media system'.

Film imports and exports, that is, trading links between national media systems, are the object of a global media system and form part of this system, which also applies to the activities of transnationally investing media companies such as Time Warner or News Corporation (Rupert Murdoch). The 'global players' of the media industry, rather like the creators of the Internet or the multiple, often national, owners of satellite television are at the centre of the globalization debate, in

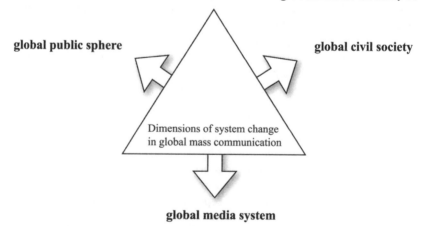

global public sphere   **global civil society**

Dimensions of system change
in global mass communication

global media system

Figure 1.3 Dimensions of system change in global mass communication
Source: author

sharp contrast to another category of actors, which appears only on the margins: media policy-makers. This imbalance, which crops up again and again, is undergirded by an implicit assumption that while the state is the main pillar of the old media, the transnational economy and the 'market' form the foundation of the new media. There is no theoretical justification whatsoever for refocusing the energies of media system research in this way. Alongside the media, such research has always taken the state into account and conceived the economy and society/public as influential factors.[17] Why should the economy alone emit cross-border impulses for system or cultural change rather than the state and its media policies? It is quite true that global regulatory policies created by nation-states have so far been rudimentary in the field of the media, while transnational firms undoubtedly have a major impact. Yet such arguments are skewed. Are transnational business cultures really having an impact and changing culture equally in all fields of connectivity? Are there in fact any major, irreversible interdependencies between media markets? If so, are they equally strong in all areas of content – in political news, entertainment products, cinema and radio?

System interdependence

The ability of mass media to change societies across state and cultural borders depends on a range of influencing factors which both *affect the media* and interact with them. A systems theory notion of international and intercultural communication would have to include the nation-state and its media system as a basic unit. Depending on the nature of the political system, there are differing relations of dependency with other societal subsystems such as politics, economy and society. In liberal-democratic media systems the mass media enjoy a high degree of autonomy as long as they continue to play their essential role within society, that is, identifying and debating issues and refusing to be dictated to by other subsystems in this regard. The other systems, however, form part of system environments. These do not exist separately from media systems and force them to adapt to some extent. Media and other social subsystems oscillate between autonomy and system survival, sometimes leaning towards internal system complexity, at others adapting to the external environment.

The notion of a world linked by communication extends and changes this model. It becomes increasingly difficult to demarcate the societal system within which the media operate. Publics can act transnationally, as can politics and the media itself. Alongside each national media system, there thus arises a second global system. To the extent that it becomes a component of the flow of information, it has great and growing influence. Interestingly, the emergence of this second global system not only has the potential to change the content of national media landscapes, but transnational developments may also occur, and, indeed, on all levels: transnational political systems (EU, UN) may come into being as well as transnational media (Arte, CNN, etc.).

Do these changes, however, allow us to speak of a communicative world system, as Emanuel Richter for instance has done?[18] More important than the mere existence of other entities beyond national media systems is a deeper understanding of their fundamental relations. Are foreign political systems really as influential as domestic ones? Do journalists feel as keen a sense of duty towards their foreign public as they do to their domestic one and does this lead to changes in the journalistic product? Are global, market and capital interconnections as strong as national and regional ones?

Cultural and societal change in a global system is not produced by *connectivity* alone, but is based on *interdependence*.[19] In an interdependent global system, autonomous national systems change into partly autonomous subsystems of a global macrosystem. One system can no longer exist without the other. The question is whether the global media and communication system has already become interdependent, whether international and intercultural communication processes have become so extensive and important that the individual (generally national) subsystems change each other and – this would be a further step – a new transnational media system is taking shape.

The present work probes a number of key issues central to answering such questions:

- How important are foreign markets to national television broadcasters whose reach extends to other countries via satellite? Who is winning the media policy battle over the opening or protection of markets – global capital or national media policy? The thesis that the state's regulatory powers are waning in the age of globalization must be proven before it can be deployed as the basis for theory building.
- Which political restrictions does the nation-state impose on new media such as the Internet or satellite television and how successful is it in this? Is civil society really succeeding, by means of international linkages, in enhancing the status of society–society relations, making them a component of international relations?

- Which policy approaches are concealed behind international broadcasting? Which interactions, mutual dynamics and feedback exist between national foreign policy, *public diplomacy* and international broadcasting on the one hand and the political and cultural target system of international broadcasting on the other? Are trust in and acceptance of the system becoming factors that change formats dialogically and which can thus influence both the system of origin and target system through new information policies?
- How can international reporting globalize as long as it is solely dependent on the home market and entirely detached from international markets, which represent the reporting countries without targeting them? What is the future of emerging transnational media use of the kind apparent in the Iraq War of 2003, when cross-border media use increased (Americans reading British newspapers on the Internet for example)? Are new forms of interdependence of global or at least regional scope developing here?

To explain the system- and culture-changing effect of the media, or their respective deficits, the key step is to analyse the political and economic interdependence of media at national, regional and global level and thus shed light on the true strength of global media policy and media economy vis-à-vis their local counterparts. The weakness of the interdependence approach, however, is that it is too focused on dependencies and fails to take into account accidental developments. System change, on the basis of cross-border mass communication, may also occur where interdependence does not yet run very deep. Here, the world functions as one big 'demonstration effect', a gigantic 'template' communicated by the media, sometimes featuring dysfunctional and anachronistic 'modes' extending around the world. It is chaos theory rather than functional systems theory that captures this best.

Nonetheless, the strength of systems theory lies in its comprehensive analysis, anchored in basic patterns of social behaviour such as the tendency to seek autonomy and adapt to the environment. To establish how realistic and significant the overall concept of media globalization is, it is vital to understand it better as a *process*, getting to grips with its dynamics and anachronisms. Ultimately, the key point is to lay bare the temporal disjunctions, variable pace and internal contradictions of the technological, economic, political and cultural developments characteristic of globalization; these have shaped all epochal paradigms from the Reformation through the Enlightenment to modernity.

2

International Reporting – 'No Further than Columbus . . .'

'International reporting' refers to the content and processes of media coverage of realities beyond the home state.[1] This is a form of communication mediated by journalism. It differs from direct forms of cross-border communication (such as the Internet) which can take place without mediation, but which lack programmes and only rarely have editorial departments or newsrooms to filter and process the growing quantity of information; these are generally not mass media in the sense of reaching large-scale publics.

Journalists and media play the role of intermediaries in the process of globalization. Their main task is to function as the central pillar of the 'global public sphere', processing facts, information and opinions from other countries for the public at home. They are responsible for elucidating information in the context in which it emerged, explaining the national and regional dimensions of the problem as well as how it connects with global issues. By presenting the perspectives of the 'Other' alongside one's 'own', as well as interpretations by third parties, international reporting has the potential, especially given the public's geocultural distance from the international event, to shift culture-specific values towards a global order of values. That is, while images of the familiar social world arise through a synthesis of primary and secondary socialization and direct experience, the consumer tends to lack direct experience when processing information about other nations or cultures.

What, though, does international reporting really involve? Does it in fact correspond, within individual media systems, to the ideal of a multi-perspective intermediary linking nations and cultures? There exists an enormous number of case studies on international reporting in individual states and individual media, which resist uniform interpretation. Nonetheless, one thing seems certain: global pluralism of content is just *one* facet of contemporary cultures of international reporting across the world. Much content continues to be lost in translation when news is transferred from one media system to another, giving rise to fragmentary world-views that are nothing less than grotesque. Only a small number of countries, topics and perspectives make it into the international reporting within a particular nation in the first place. Often, the only thing universal or global about the world-view of different media systems is that they all suffer from the same problem: the domestication of the world. Media content is distorted whenever international reporting more strongly reflects the national interests and cultural stereotypes of the *reporting* country than the news reality of the country *being reported about*.

American columnist Meg Greenfield's stringent lament, which appeared a quarter of a century ago in the *Washington Post*, on the failure of the American media, as she saw it, to explain the Islamic Revolution in Iran in 1978–79, continues to apply today. It is generalizable beyond the event itself:

> I think we are . . . witnessing the turmoil of a great civilization seeking to reassert and rediscover and – yes – ultimately reform itself . . . . And where are we in our ability to understand and to respond to all this? . . . Intellectually and emotionally we are about where Columbus was when he saw the natives and assumed that they were 'Indians' – except that we are sailing in the other direction.[2]

As a result of the shortcomings of international reporting, conflict-oriented world-views within international politics acquire societal embellishment. The famous 'CNN effect' thesis evokes the media as the conduit of a politics stuck in a rut and paralysed by special interests. On this view, the media function as agents of civil societies, de-escalating conflicts. This is a myth of a very special kind, which conceals several facts at once. When all is said and done, the mass media are not in the least oriented towards a 'world system', but in fact concentrate upon national markets, whose interests and stereotypes they largely reproduce. Moreover, the influence of the media on politics is negligible, particularly in relation to international conflicts that touch upon vital national interests. At such times, even in democratic states, the major print and broadcast media tend to take on the role of government propagandists over the short term, rather than de-escalating political conflicts. International reporting of this kind lags decades behind demands for a system-changing and interdependent globalization.

The world-view of international reporting

Sporting events such as the Olympic Games are transmitted simultaneously to many countries in the world. They enable the mass media to unite people the world over, beyond national, cultural or religious borders, as they watch the same images on television. Symbolic political events, such as the fall of the Berlin Wall, were media events of the first order, in which Marshall McLuhan's visions of a 'global village' seem to have been realized. In light of such images, who could doubt that Anthony Giddens, one of the guiding intellectual forces of globalization, was right to state that globalization is not only an economic process, but is determined by changes in the global information order?[3]

The content of international reporting is however often moulded by national viewpoints and stereotypes, that is, by particularistic rather than global perspectives. Rather than 'The Olympics', little 'national Olympics' are constructed on screens and in newspapers the world over, in which national sportsmen and women are the centre of attention. Anyone who has ever followed on television an entire Winter Olympics in Sweden knows how boring the national sport of 'curling' can become for non-Swedes after a while – about as dry as a whole Summer Olympics of Syrian handball for anyone unfamiliar with the players and teams in Syria.

Should these comments seem overly anecdotal, the complaints of experienced journalists such as Sonia Mikich, presenter of the German television magazine *Monitor*, must surely be taken seriously. In her contribution to the 'Tutzing Media Days' in 2002, she describes German international reporting as a bastion of 'intellectual provincialism' and its relationship to globalization as a paradox:

> Never have the Germans been so connected with other countries, economically and politically. Never has their need to understand world events been greater. The issue of global justice is becoming a question of survival in the twenty-first century . . . . Surely this is a period with much to offer correspondents and reporters. Not necessarily . . . The vivid reality of whole continents never or only rarely makes it into reports on Asia, South America, Australia (unless they have a refugee drama (Australia), a bankruptcy (Argentina) or a royal baby (Japan) as a peg on which to hang the story).[4]

The mainstream globalization debate regards globalization as a dominant force for change in the media industry and in media systems across the world. The Canadian communication studies scholar Marc

Raboy, for example, argues that the development of the media worldwide is influenced by two fundamental trends: technological change and increasing globalization.[5] His German colleagues Miriam Meckel and Markus Kriener, meanwhile, describe the globalization of the media as a process occurring on several levels. The level of technology and infrastructure has created the most significant prerequisite for the internationalization of communication. According to these scholars, on the second, institutional level, processes of economic concentration are driving forward the globalization of the media market. At the level of production, however, they state that only a small amount of transnational and multinational programming (such as that of CNN or the German–French television channel Arte) exists alongside the traditional national or local media. The fourth and final level, that of media content, is according to these authors characterized by the lowest degree of internationalization and represents, for the most part, particularistic perspectives.[6]

If we develop these ideas further, the process of mass media globalization resembles a tectonic shift that causes geological strata to move in various directions. The particularistic content of reports not only lags behind advancing technology and institutional globalization, the tectonics of international communication may even generate movement in the opposite direction. To talk sweepingly of globalization of the media, given the media system's seeming disorder, is to unjustly generalize the experience of technological global networks – and to become, imperceptibly, a 'techno-idealist'.[7]

In the early 1980s, within the framework of UNESCO, a debate was held on the New World Information and Communication Order (NWICO). In a 1978 UNESCO declaration on the media, at the instigation of the developing countries, the concept of the 'free flow of information' was replaced by the concept of a 'free and balanced flow of information'.[8] The political doctrines of the world organizations thus underwent a historical shift away from the right to seek, receive and disseminate information in unhindered fashion to the principle of 'balanced' communication. The majority of the developing countries in UNESCO rejected the dominance of Western news agencies and mass media within the international flow of information and communication. The NWICO project was consolidated programmatically in the so-called MacBride Report, commissioned by UNESCO, which appeared in 1980.[9] At a political level, the project of reordering North–South informational and communicative relations became bound up with the East–West conflict. The debate on NWICO has, however, recently been revived in academic circles.[10]

The advocates of a new world information order make certain basic assumptions, including the idea that the international flow of information and communication is not uniform, but features different zones and currents of greater and lesser intensity. On this view, a 'one-way street', or 'North–South orientation', marks the flow of 'data, messages, media programmes and cultural products' between the Western industrial and the developing countries. Information flows primarily from industrialized countries to developing countries and from Third World metropoli and elites to structurally weak regions and population groups with only limited participation in political life.[11] As a component of the 'one-way street' of information, the MacBride Report criticized the image of developing countries produced by news agencies and mass media in Western industrial countries: 'It has been frequently stated, in particular, that due to the fact that the content of information is largely produced by the main developed countries, the image of the developing countries is frequently false and distorted.'[12] The MacBride Report, however, regards the problems of international reporting as developmental problems found in *all* global media systems, that is, in the developing countries as well.

The report's comments on the quality of communicative content have also helped guide academic discourse. They can be divided into two categories:

- criticisms of the definition of 'news' and value of news;
- criticisms of the praxis of conveying news.

The definition of news based on core concepts such as topicality, novelty and universality (general interest) must, according to the MacBride Report, be expanded by additional criteria.[13] News within the global communication process is regarded as information intended to encourage awareness of and interest in issues, by informing people about events in the context of their emergence and development. News is also classified as a national informational resource and as a component of political education. The definition of news as factual information which deviates from 'normality', and which is up to date and relevant to the recipients of its messages, is not abandoned. It is extended by a complimentary concept underlining the sociopolitical relevance of the news to the social development of the country reported on.

Basic assumptions about the definition of news find expression in the critique of global news practices. This critique is also based on a comparison between media and the reality beyond media. On this view, a consequence of the 'a-normal' definition of news is that negative events (crises, catastrophes and conflicts) are over-represented as news is communicated at an international level. Meanwhile, everyday events across the world tend to be neglected. The following general shortcomings of the prevailing concept of foreign countries are also mentioned:

- overemphasizing (irrelevant) news;
- joining disparate facts to make an artificial whole (making news);
- misinterpretation by implication;
- the production of negative concepts of the 'Other' as legitimation and guide to action for individuals, society and politics;
- failing to examine significant developments and problems.[14]

The MacBride Report works from a complex model of how foreign countries are imagined. A list of criteria for determining the structure of the content of global mass communication arises only from the relationship between the individual and the whole (such as frame-topic-discourse); between events and their development; and between communicative content and communicated reality. Stereotypes are mentioned as subsets of the communication of news,[15] but the complex structural analysis of the conception of foreign countries communicated by the media is more prominent.

The largest international study undertaken so far is the 'Foreign News' study, carried out until 1980 by the International Association for Media and Communication Research (IAMCR) on behalf of UNESCO.[16] Research teams from 13 nations appraised press and broadcasting in 29 countries, which represented differing social systems and developmental stages. In recent years an attempt has been made to compile a new edition of the 'Foreign News' study. As yet, however, this has produced little that is new: the basic findings on international reporting appear not to have changed significantly.[17]

Attempts to generalize theoretically on the basis of research have so far come to grief because of fundamental differences of opinion on how to evaluate the empirical data.[18] Nonetheless, the following structural features of international reporting are theoretically significant:

- regionalism (and metropolitan leanings)
- conflict perspective
- political focus
- elite focus
- decontextualization

- failure to portray the structural problems that beset international relations

While the comparative findings of the 'Foreign News' study cannot be regarded as sufficiently secure to produce a ranking of the scale of international reporting in individual national media systems, the study provided information on the regional distribution of reporting about which the vast majority of the research teams agreed. In almost all the systems examined, stories about nearby countries in the region made up a particularly high proportion of reports, and *regionalism* (*geographical proximity*) can thus be described as a universal feature of international reporting.

Nonetheless, clear differences of emphasis are apparent in the 'news geography' of the Western industrial and developing countries. Media in the latter are clearly marked by regionalism, but also pay considerable attention to Western industrialized states. In other words, alongside regionalism, a strong focus on metropolises is apparent.[19] Western Europe and the US are paid more attention in the media systems of the world than continents such as Asia and Africa and regions such as Latin America, although these have the largest number of inhabitants, most of the states and the greatest territorial extent. Interestingly, a single exception emerges from the data of the 'Foreign News' study, though even its authors failed to acknowledge it. In the 29 media systems examined, more attention is paid on average to the Middle East than to North America. It is in second place behind Western Europe.

Table 2.1, an overview of the findings of the 'Foreign News' study, supplemented by an overall ranking, shows that Western Europe receives most attention in the media, followed by the Middle East, North America, Asia, Africa, Eastern Europe, Latin America and the superordinate international issues which resist attribution to a particular region. The strong presence of Western Europe and North America points to the North–South or metropolitan orientation of international reporting in most countries at the expense of South–South communication. This metropolitan bias is caused by a range of factors, such as the political and economic influence of Western Europe and the US, the ongoing influence of links from the colonial period, etc. Whether geographical, historical, political, economic or cultural factors are responsible for the fact that Asia, despite its population statistics and territorial extent, holds only a middling position, and that Latin America emerges as largely isolated in media terms, can be determined only through empirical studies on specific topics.

Table 2.1 Ranking of attention paid to world regions within foreign reporting

Subject region	North America	Latin America	Africa	Middle East	Asia	Eastern Europe	Western Europe	Overall ranking
				Reporting media systems				
North America	1	3	5	3	3	6	2	3
Latin America	6	1	8	6	8	8	8	7
Africa	5	6	1	4	5	7	5	5
Middle East	2	4	2	1	4	4	3	2
Asia	4	5	5	5	1	3	5	4
Eastern Europe	7	6	7	7	6	1	4	6
Western Europe	2	2	3	2	2	2	1	1
General international issues	8	8	5	8	7	4	7	8

Source: author, drawing on Sreberny-Mohammadi et al., *Foreign News in the Media,* p. 42

Almost all empirical studies of international reporting point to a highly developed *conflict perspective*. Reports focus relatively consistently on political and social crises, conflicts and wars, as well as natural and man-made catastrophes. The conflictual nature of an event is thus a significant factor in making it over the news threshold.[20] One might formulate the thesis that the conflict perspective of international reporting stands in diametrical opposition to the 'harmony perspective' in local reporting[21] and thus the construction of a negative-chaotic distant world correlates with the construction of a positive-harmonious familiar world. The empirical data, in any event, allow differing interpretations. The debate so far has been problematic. While a conflict perspective has frequently been asserted, the model of reality that undergirds this thesis – that is, the notion that it is genuinely possible to construct a conception of foreign lands true to reality and characterized by positive, neutral or negative dimensions – has scarcely been reflected upon. Yet we can only interpret a conflict perspective on the basis of data on media content if such data are related to a comparative theoretical foundation, that is, to a model of reality.

A model might plausibly entail various levels, including measurement of *how much of the coverage is negative*. The frequency and percentage of negative reports, often called 'negativism' in content analytical research, can be quantitatively determined for each individual country with the aid of event valences, word fields (wars, acts of terror, etc.) and other methods. The 'Foreign News' study has pointed out that it is not so much the absolute frequency of negative reports but rather the relative under-representation of positive reports in international reporting (particularly about the developing countries), which allows us to talk of a conflict perspective.[22] The study shows, for example, that the Middle East is particularly strongly connected in international reporting with military issues, criminality and other fields of conflict, while other realms of life remain 'invisible'.[23] Criticism of the above approach is frequently underpinned by the implicit assumption that 'reality' can be described by means of a tripartite parity model – one third negative, one third neutral and one third positive events – and that the mass media ought to strive to match this three-way division. Yet this is problematic. Such a three-way model of reality is too strongly trapped in epistemological and ethical premises to be of much use in social science theory formation, regardless of the fact that in what follows I assert that reality reconstruction is possible to some extent and is necessary to theory building. It is crucial that we avoid measuring the issue of media conflict perspectives according to an ideal three-way division. A flexible model that eschews dominance makes a better premise. If the three-way division of valences cannot ultimately be proven, we can nonetheless take it as read that the social reality of each country is complex enough not to consist exclusively or overwhelmingly of negative events. A value of more than fifty per cent of such events in the media would thus need to be explained in terms of a media conflict perspective.

Recent research reports by the international researchers' network Media Tenor elucidate in exemplary fashion the problems concealed behind the issue of conflict perspectives in the practice of international reporting. Figure 2.1 illustrates that in the period 2000 to 2002 inclusive, American television news in particular hit the absolute figure of 50 per cent negative reporting and that the cultures of reporting in countries such as the UK and Germany, though featuring a less developed conflict perspective, allow scarcely any positive news about the world through. Figure 2.2 points to the fact that between 2001 and 2003 German and American television news presented specific countries, such as Israel, as saturated by violent conflicts to such an overwhelming extent that viewers must have gained the impression, overdrawn at least for the Israeli heartlands, of a country wracked by civil war – an astonishing blow to Israel's image. Figure 2.3, meanwhile, shows that the presentation of violence in other countries clearly revolves around more than violent conflict as such, in fact privileging – from the standpoint of the reporting media – 'relevant' violence. A war-torn country such as the Democratic Republic of Congo, where huge numbers of people have

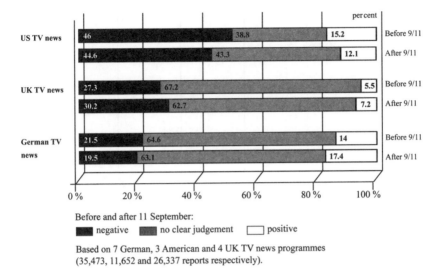

Based on 7 German, 3 American and 4 UK TV news programmes
(35,473, 11,652 and 26,337 reports respectively).

Figure 2.1 Trends in foreign news reports on television, 2000—2002
Source: Media Tenor 124, Bonn, September 2002 (based on original data set)

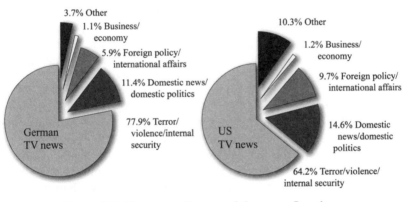

Figure 2.2 Terror as a feature of the news: Israel on
German television news, 2003
Source: Media Tenor 133, Bonn, June 2003

died, has simply been 'forgotten' by German television. It is of far
less relevance to the television news than the Iraq War, which features such explosive international resonance.

The *privileging of politics* represents a further structural feature of
international reporting. Media reporting regards the actions of political actors and systems as primary social driving forces. They thus

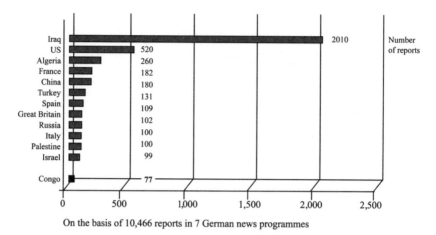

On the basis of 10,466 reports in 7 German news programmes

Figure 2.3 Coverage of conflict in German television news, 2003
Source: Media Tenor 133, Bonn, June 2003 (based on original data set)

represent a large chunk of the information communicated by those print and electronic media aimed at a general audience.[24] Like the privileging of elites (see below), the focus on politics is favoured by several factors. The limited capacities that typify international reporting has encouraged the privileging of the political; political events guarantee the necessary general interest which is the very definition of news; and strategic public relations carried out by political institutions make it easier to access information abroad.

Scholars have thus far failed to examine sufficiently the nature of the connection between the individual structural aspects of foreign newsmaking. We can formulate the hypothesis that, far from being phenomena *sui generis*, negative reporting and the conflict perspective are frequently due to the privileging of politics by the media. Concentrating upon the authoritarian political system of a country will almost inevitably entail a more negatively imbued media image than reportage with a more cultural or social emphasis. Once again, we are confronted here with the question of the model of reality against which media performance is to be evaluated. And again it does not appear useful to rely on a simple parity model, according to which all fields of life, from politics to sport, are of equal significance and may (or even – normatively – 'must') be conveyed by the media. If the political sphere dominates more than 50 per cent of international reporting, however, this may be regarded as the privileging of politics by the media.

Privileging of elites refers to the tendency of international reporting to concentrate upon official elites or counter-elites (such as rebels or coup leaders), while social groups and movements, political parties and the population as a whole are marginalized.[25] The combined privileging of politics and elites results in a consistent focus on political elites. At times, this means that the presentation of the Third World figures best known in the Western industrialized countries also features elements of entertainment (soft news) (the royal household of the Shah of Persia, the unpredictability of Muammar Gaddafi and the ruthlessness of Saddam Hussein are examples). Helmut Asche has pointed out that the concentration on elites in the reportage of Western industrialized states reflects the reality that the developing countries lack opportunities for political participation.[26] Yet there are political and other organizations in almost all developing countries, though the vast majority of them have a limited ability to articulate and pursue their political vision.

The event-centred definition of the news frequently leads to *decontextualization*, that is, neglect of political, economic, social and cultural relations of cause-and-effect. International reporting has often been criticized for this.[27] Contextual deficits are closely bound up with the privileging of elites and personalization of the prevailing vision of foreign countries; international reporting, according to the 'Foreign News' study, often reduces complex international processes to the psychological profiles of certain central actors.[28] Decontextualization occurs on several levels: it is the result of spatial, temporal and relevance guidelines laid down by the media organizations as well as the process of information acquisition and journalists' varying contextual expertise. It is, moreover, the result of the consumer's contextual knowledge of foreign settings, which is very limited as a rule: we can assume that people have a far greater need for contextual information in international reporting than in its domestic counterpart.

Structural conflicts within the global political and economic systems – such as links between progress and underdevelopment in the context of North–South relations – rarely form part of reports in the media.[29] This *failure to present the structural problems of international relations* is to a large extent a sub-aspect of the decontextualization typical of international reporting and the fact that media reporting is more event- than process-oriented. It thus comes as no surprise that in contrast to structural conflicts, violent conflicts between states (such as the Israeli-Palestinian conflict) have a major presence in reporting.[30] International reporting tends to seek, as empirical studies attest, a clear-cut geographical reference. Reports focus on a country or region or emphasize a given country's relations with another country. The spatial orders that mark political science or cultural studies – the 'First' and 'Third' Worlds or the 'Islamic World' and 'the West' – are analytical, partly ideologically imbued entities. They may appear in the framing concept of a text dealing with a specific geographical area, but only rarely define its central theme.

The emergence and effect of international reporting, distorted in many respects, can be related to a number of theoretical levels. At the micro-level of an analysis of persons, the journalist for instance brings competencies, world-views, perspectives, but also stereotypes and negative conceptions of the 'Other', all products of socialization, to the production of the text. A series of publications has presented evidence of ethnocentric conceptions of nations and people among Western foreign reporters.[31] The dearth of specific professional role models makes it all the easier for individual tendencies, anchored in socialization, to take on force. Debates on professional ethics within journalism pay little heed to questions about the intercultural and international function of international reporting as 'cultural intermediary' or 'contributor to foreign policy'.[32]

Central to the study of the influence of media organizations and the media system – at the theoretical meso-level – is the international flow of information. Ideally, through their access to local media and opinion leaders, foreign correspondents convey the self-images of the country being reported about. The existing networks of correspondents are, however, underdeveloped even in major Western media; individual correspondents often have responsibility for several countries. It remains unclear what impact alternative sources (such as the Internet) are having on international reporting. In any event, reporters are massively dependent on the major news agencies (especially Reuters, AP and AFP), which generally make up 50 to 80 per cent of the information sources used in international reporting. This promotes the development of a minimal global thematic budget in international reporting, which is effective across systems. Yet the central position of the agencies has also encouraged the standardization of international reporting, which tends to focus on conflicts and elites. It has also made it difficult (even for correspondents) to access information on unconventional topics and enhanced the reach of the public relations carried out by Western states in particular. News agencies too are cash-strapped institutions, which not only carry out research themselves, but also pass on the state's political PR to the media, which they in turn convey to the consumer.[33]

The overall picture of news across the world which emerges here is of a highly select and standardized spectrum of topics and types of topic. While these may be interpreted differently from one country to the next, major Western governments such as those of the US, UK and France exercise a significant influence upon the media of their home countries through their market-leading agencies. The 'trickle down' of government policies, driven by special interests, into the so-called 'free press' and the media is built into the structure of modern democracies, opening the door wide to the saturation of international reporting with propaganda. There are too many weak links in the informational chain of foreign newsmaking. Agencies are dependent on governments and often favour their own or 'friendly' governments in their reports. Media would often be unable to survive without massive input from agencies because they cannot afford to pay for a sufficiently large number of correspondents of their own. At the end of the chain of use are consumers. Because of their distance from events, they have little prospect of recognizing misinformation (see figure 2.4).

In recent years a counter-trend has become increasingly apparent. Key media in various world regions, such as Western television networks and the Arab broadcaster al-Jazeera, have begun to exchange news, enhancing the non-European countries' ability to present themselves to the world. However, sensitive issues of information security, such as independent media access to satellite reconnaissance, which has until now delivered static images censored by the military, have scarcely been tackled by media policy worldwide.

At the macro-level, to analyse why international reporting is beset with such problems, we have to examine its social embedding. From

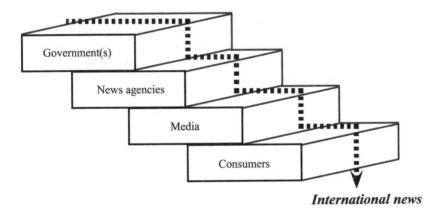

International news

Figure 2.4 The 'trickling down' of political public relations
into international news
Source: author

the perspective of systems theory, journalists, politics and social groups and organizations are social subsystems that compete for access to international reporting, while the media strive to achieve a balance between maintaining autonomy and adapting to the environment. International reporting is thus largely shaped by the mutual interaction of politics and media. While the political system, as the key actor within international relations, has much scope to shape international reporting, the elites and organizations interested in international issues tend to be small and exercise only minimal influence upon it. Moreover, media still receive relatively little stimulus from transnationally operating NGOs. 'Exceptional behavior',[34] up to and including terrorism, is considered a replacement for a successful media strategy by some social forces.

In terms of systems theory, it is apparent that the national political system exercises a strong influence upon international reporting, particularly at times of extreme crisis and war. Numerous case studies[35] have demonstrated the tendency for a patriotic consensus to emerge, even among media that generally maintain a critical distance from the actions of the government. The increase in interactions between national politics and international reporting applies not only to foreign and crisis policy, but also embraces the sphere of domestic politics. Spatial dimensions are crossed in the classic distinction between *foreign news abroad* (events in foreign countries), *foreign news at home* (for example, domestic events linked with foreign countries, such as demonstrations by immigrants related to their country of origin) and *home news abroad* (events in foreign countries connected with the domestic sphere). In addition, there exists a complex thematic networking of all fields of life.[36] Historical experiences, political cultures and current events in the home country may influence the extent and content of international reporting, and increase public interest, but also 'distort' the image of other lands. The American university system is often wrongly characterized in European countries as identical with 'Harvard', because role models for elite-oriented university reform are currently being sought in Europe.

While international reporting is thus fundamentally national, international interdependencies are generally thin on the ground, while markets, political opinions, organizations, media and culturally au fait interlocutors beyond the borders of one's own country have little influence. The media subsystem of international reporting certainly makes use of foreign countries as 'informational raw material'. It is, however, integrated into a communicative world system only to a very limited degree. Interdependent contexts are few and far between.

Most of the time, international reporting in media systems across the world is produced for a domestic audience, not for the regions in question themselves. This state of affairs has changed little, even in the age of satellite television (see chapter 3). Without such linkage, however, there is communication *about*, but not *with*, the countries involved. This makes it impossible to be sure of the quality of international reporting, as the domestic public is geo-culturally distant with little knowledge or ability to form an opinion. Influences on the news agenda are thus unipolar rather than multipolar. They cement the interpretative sovereignty of the particular national media system. In the 'global' world, the cross-border flow of information does indeed increase – but the mechanisms of local cognitive appropriation and domestication remain. The fundamental character of 'ego-centric' national media systems remains untouched. The ethnocentric apparatus informing most people's conception of the world has survived even in the age of globalization. While the perspectives of the 'Other' may make it through, ideologies, cultural stereotypes and national interests frequently function as a filter, from which only dialogic and interactive forms of international journalism could afford relief. In this connection, the media studies scholar and political scientist Hans Kleinsteuber has called for the antiquated concept of monologic international reporting to be given up. He advocates strengthening dialogic elements, above all by including journalists and more voices from the civil societies of the states being reported on.[37]

At present, however, there is no prospect whatsoever of such a reform of international reporting. What is being fostered is the exact opposite of a multicultural world. No shift is occurring towards a form of international reporting capable of resolving the fundamental contradiction between connectivity, system change and system interdependence that continues to hold sway.

One of the key paradoxes of globalization is that at present the preconditions for such a change appear unfavourable. Now that the East–West conflict is over, the producers and consumers of media are less interested in international reporting, which is often a marginal phenomenon. While such reporting enjoys a solid following among many proactive readers of national newspapers, it is a tall order to reach large numbers of television viewers, only some of whom are interested in politics. During the Cold War, international issues received greater attention than in the era of so-called 'globalization', which has in fact tended to promote regressive tendencies among the public.

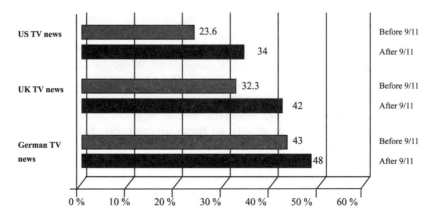

On the basis of 35,473, 11,652 and 26,337 reports in 7 German, 3 US and
4 UK news programmes respectively

Figure 2.5 Foreign reports as share of television news, 2000—2002
Source: Media Tenor 124, Bonn, September 2002 (based on original data set)

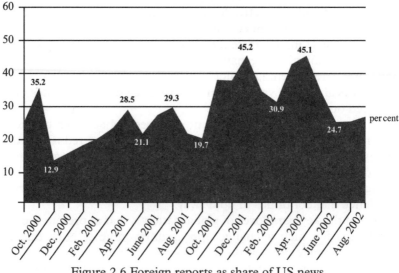

Figure 2.6 Foreign reports as share of US news
Source: Media Tenor 124, Bonn, September 2002

The world became a more dangerous place after the attacks on 11
September 2001. International reporting seemed to enter a new
phase, because for the first time in many years the decline in such
reporting within the media was reversed (see figure 2.5). This effect,
however, diminished soon after the events (figure 2.6). The increased

interest in foreign lands was in any case limited to issues of international terrorism and related matters. There was no clear indication of a new interest in global affairs, in the developing countries for example. While, for instance, the number of special programmes on international affairs on German television increased after 11 September 2001, regular time slots for international reporting have been declining or stagnating for years in the United States, Europe and elsewhere.

Private television companies are especially likely to regard international reporting as insufficiently profitable. Even in times of crisis, so runs the argument, advertising losses may do commercial damage. That profits can also be made from international reporting is however apparent in the story of CNN, the American news broadcaster, which moved into the black only as a result of the Gulf War of 1991. Commercial arguments are in any case somewhat out of touch. As yet, there are no solid studies of consumption and viewer figures are restricted to responses to existing programming, heavily focused on politics and crises and therefore, perhaps, of little interest to viewers tired of the seemingly 'chaotic' world beyond their national borders.

It is as yet unclear whether the current recession in international reporting is down to the range of services on offer or issues of use. What is certain is that international reporting features a number of fields that might benefit from reform, from education of journalists and training in the necessary intercultural competence through attaining resources and optimizing the flow of information to editorial crisis management and global networking.

The global non-dialogue of 11 September 2001

Following the terrorist attacks on the World Trade Center and the Pentagon on 11 September 2001, many observers expressed disappointment at what they saw as the strong tendency towards patriotism in US media coverage. Well-known newscasters such as Dan Rather of CBS allowed themselves to be cajoled into urging all Americans to support their president unconditionally.[38] Linguistic analyses show that the collective 'we' or 'our' dominated. CNN put its faith almost entirely in American government sources. It rapidly created the impression that war was the inevitable response to the events.[39] American television companies became the fount of political slogans urging the nation to unite and support President George W. Bush. More cautious commentators, who strove to achieve a balanced appraisal, were pushed to the margins.[40] Major American television companies reached agreements with the US government not to broadcast certain materials, such as video messages by the terrorists. Once again, democratic mainstream media, particularly television but also the press,[41] proved the plaything of the executive in times of exceptional crisis (see the following section). Every stirring, no matter how small, of a social dialogue on fundamental issues of war and peace was nipped in the bud.

The nation may thus turn in upon itself at times of extreme crisis. This is, however, not the only factor standing in the way of a global dialogue on international conflicts. German and Arab reactions to the events of 11 September in the media and the public sphere were, for example, almost mirror images of one another – though neither Germany nor most Arab countries were directly affected by the attacks. It rapidly became apparent that beyond the acute threat to the nation-state, international crisis may liberate cultural reflexes and modes of interpretation that hinder global dialogue and intensify awareness of cultural conflict. Many media reactions in Germany and the Arab world turned out to be differing perspectives on the same context, some of which expressed a downright irrational, false understanding of the 'Other'. Some perspectives, meanwhile, were clearly rational in origin, aspects of a meaningful critique of international relations. This critique, however, got through only to a few elites on each side. Especially in extreme crisis situations, an enhanced networking of publics would be of great significance. Media in the individual national language areas, however, often function as nothing less than 'critique filters', catching much of the material that might shake accustomed perspectives on world politics.

Immediately after the attack, German media began to look for explanations for what had happened in 'Islam'. Most of the major weekly newspapers, such as *Stern, Der Spiegel, Die Woche* or *Focus* devoted several cover articles to 'Islam as global power'. The distorted German conception of Islam, which presents it as a violent religion and ideology,[42] has been studied at length. In this respect, reports on Islam related to 11 September showed some progress. In contrast to earlier crises, such as the Rushdie affair of 1989,[43] the conflict in Algeria of 1991/92[44] or the Gulf War of 1991,[45] many German media made an effort to distinguish more clearly between 'Islam' and the peaceful Muslim majority on the one hand and violence-prone fundamentalists on the other. The magazine *Die Woche*, which has since folded, even warned in a leading article against the 'notion of Islam as the enemy'.[46] Print media tried to present a balanced picture of

Islam in cover stories and criticized widespread distortions and negatively loaded concepts of the Orient and of Islam.[47] A new generation of journalists, who had grown up with criticisms of one-sided views of Islam and the Orient, made their presence felt journalistically. Yet even after 11 September, we are still a very long way from a more balanced view.

It is difficult to prove, methodologically, that the media bear some of the responsibility for the fear and aversion which between 70 and 80 per cent of Germans feel towards Islam according to surveys.[48] Yet the connection does appear very plausible. Even in the more subtle contributions, Islam was almost exclusively of interest in its variant form as 'political Islam'. 'Islam' made it onto the media agenda only once it was linked with 'violence'. In the major illustrated magazines, downright blood-soaked imagery often stood in sharp contrast to nuanced texts. Even seemingly enlightened journalists did the image of Islam a disservice by mentioning it in the first place as a key factor in understanding terrorism, rather than researching the complex political and social causes (the collapse of the state monopoly on violence in the Middle East, conflicts rooted in the colonial period as in Palestine, etc.). Middle Eastern terrorism already existed in secular guise at a time when Islamic fundamentalism scarcely existed – in the form, for example, of the Palestinian attack on Israeli athletes at the Munich Olympics of 1972 or Palestinian plane hijackings. The Islamic rhetoric of fundamentalists is clearly often successful at steering attention away from the underlying history of structural violence.

Some authors have identified a general improvement in the image of Islam in the US media after 11 September.[49] While the German press made an effort to avoid stereotyping the 'Other', the image of Islam suffered from a politicization that has clearly become part of the German cultural heritage. This was defamatory without meaning to be, merely elevating a small slice of the reality of Muslim lives – radical fundamentalists and terrorists – onto the media agenda, while the 'peaceful Muslims' mentioned in passing hardly appeared in the media at all. Taken as a whole, the German media's approach to Islam after 11 September, a new fusion of complex analysis and structural failure to understand, creates the impression of 'enlightened Islamophobia'.

Time series analysis of German reporting casts light on the contrast with the response of Arab media. After the immediate reaction to the phenomenon of terrorism, from late September to late October 2001 many print media focused on issues arising where Islam and terrorism intersect. It was during precisely this period that the US began its military strikes, then war on Afghanistan, which broke out on 7 October. Only from the middle of November 2001, however, did fundamental questions of the point and aim of the war as a response to terrorism make the front pages of the German weekly newspapers.[50] The pacifism frame, as discourse analysis would term the counter-position on the war in the media,[51] was of course already present here and there in the German media during the preceding weeks. It was, however, not yet prominent on the media agenda and was of marginal significance. The fundamental issue of war and peace was thus only discussed consistently in German media after it was already far too late and no one could seriously believe it possible to create a climate of opinion that would influence political decision-making.

This 'phase displaced' pacifism was entirely different in nature from the contemporaneous response of the Arab media. Immediately after the attacks of 11 September 2001, Arab media, like their counterparts in the West and in other parts of the world, expressed sympathy for the victims and their loved ones and abhorrence towards the perpetrators. The closer it came to war in Afghanistan, however, the more Western and Arab publics drifted apart.

The attacks on the World Trade Center and the Pentagon were greeted with open sympathy by some in the autonomous Palestinian areas, in Lebanon or in the refugee camps of Jordan, that is, areas which had suffered repeatedly from Israeli violence in the recent past. The Arab public was, however, a far from uniform bloc. Most mass media, particularly the print media, took on the role of a connecting link between state anti-terror policies and the fragmented public. Abdel-Moneim Said, writing in the largest Egyptian newspaper, *al-Ahram*, added his voice to the support for New York and its citizens: 'The attack on the World Trade Center was certainly an attack on one of the most recognizable symbols of American financial might. But it was also, if less obviously, an attack against the whole world, an assault on all those peoples, colours, faiths and races that combine to make the mosaic that is the city.'[52] Arab newspapers printed numerous photographs of memorial services for the victims of the terror attacks, particularly in cases where Muslims were involved.[53]

No one was keener than the press in authoritarian states of the Maghreb, such as Algeria and Tunisia, which have pursued a particularly hard line against the Islamist opposition in recent years, to stress that fighting terrorism has to be a common goal of Arab and Western states. Here, the West was accused of making a 'strategic mistake' after 11 September (*El Watan*, Algeria). Many people in this part of the world believed that Islamists might be absorbed as asylum seekers and that a political deal might be struck with them. Great Britain in particular was referred to as a hotbed of Islamism.[54] Close allies of the US such as Pakistan, Saudi Arabia and the United Arab Emirates were regarded as 'vassal regimes', which had encouraged terrorism by recognizing the Taliban and by providing financial aid to the Algerian Front Islamique du Salut (FIS).[55]

Immediately after 11 September, the response of German and Arab media, which emphasized a universal humanism in relation to the victims of the attack, was still very similar. In the weeks that followed, however, many differences between the two public spheres developed apace, throwing up serious questions about the state of globalization. 'Reporting on Islam' was centre stage in Germany. Commentators asked how 'Islamic terrorism' could be dealt with, while points of view opposed to American military action in Afghanistan were poorly represented and gained momentum only when events had advanced to a point where such a public response was politically irrelevant. In Arab media, meanwhile, anti-war stances had taken on force earlier and with considerably more vehemence. While media and publics in most countries of the Maghreb reacted in comparatively sober fashion because of the relative distance from the trouble spots of the Middle East, Iraq or Afghanistan, a well-known newspaper such as the Franco–Arab magazine *Realités*, published in Tunisia, unequivocally condemned the war in Afghanistan in its review of the year. It described it as a war that destroyed the very values it claimed to defend. Francis Fukuyama's notion of the 'end of history' made him widely popular in the US and worldwide following the end of the East–West confrontation. His vision evoked a global society both liberal and just. In the view of *Realités*, it was clearly apparent that this idea could now be interpreted only as a new design for an imperial world order. The war in Afghanistan, in the magazine's opinion, symbolized the total subordination to Washington's decision-making power.[56]

Intriguingly, this widespread view of an unjust war in Afghanistan was linked with a critique of 'globalization', with negative consequences for the civil population. The war, so the argument went, laid bare the limits of 'globalization'. War and terrorism were regarded as direct symptoms of a world order characterized by a widening chasm between poor and rich countries.[57] Such comments were not only made in the Middle East after 11 September, but were also discussed in identical fashion at founding summits of the anti-globalization movement Attac.[58] In the West, the primacy of the politics of security and stability was clearly reinforced by the events of 11 September. Commentary in the Near East, meanwhile, increasingly pointed up the lack of political concepts aimed at reordering the political and economic relations between the US or Europe and Islamic countries.

One might have thought that the age of globalization would reduce conflict by networking civil societies. If we look at the responses of German and Arab media and publics to the terror attacks of 11 September, however, there can only be one conclusion: the tendency was to erect barriers. The West and the Arab world cultivated highly insulated media discourses. These lacked the capacity, in key areas, to integrate the response of the 'Other' and come to meaningful conclusions about international relations. Dialogic international reporting as evoked by Hans Kleinsteuber? Not a chance.

Consensus did more or less prevail after the attacks in that the terrorism was roundly condemned, but each side tended to view the terrorism perpetrated against itself – here the World Trade Center, there the Israeli occupation, etc. – as more serious. And while one side called for a thoroughgoing revision of American policy on the Middle East to ensure a more just solution to regional conflicts, the other side shirked this challenge by indulging in a downright speculative discourse about the links between Islam and violence. This behaviour led in turn to a steady increase in anti-American and anti-Islamic sentiment and to chain reactions that distorted perceptions worldwide. Public perception within the 'Orient–Occident' construct consists in large part of compulsive thematic fixations and conspiracy theories. Such discourses often have less to do with rational deliberation than with public rituals through which people affirm and reassure themselves.

It is little wonder, given these enormous obstacles to communication, that the Arab media was saturated with pessimism about the state of the world: the 'end of pacifism', the 'end of globalization'. Have we really arrived at such a sorry pass?

The Iraq War 2003: war reporting in the far from obsolete nation-state

Like the Gulf War of 1991, the Iraq War of 2003 also brought in its wake a large number of scholarly analyses on the role of the media in the outbreak and execution of the war. The great majority of studies so far have concentrated on the main belligerent party, the United States.[59] Comparative studies of international reporting before and during the war would in fact have been ideally suited to uncovering whether nationalist war propaganda continues to hold sway in the age of globalization. The following comparison of media reporting on the Iraq War 2003 in the US, Great Britain and Germany once again suggests that the system of international reporting remains subordinated to national interests and political actors – though the British press does in fact provide grounds for hope.

Data produced by the major American public opinion research institute, Gallup, show that public opinion in the US before, during and after the Iraq War of 2003 developed in textbook fashion (figure 2.7). The public, quite ready to criticize before and after the war, flocked to support President George W. Bush, giving him high levels of support during the acute phases of the war – what communication scholars call *rallying round the flag*. Before the war there were more sceptics, while afterwards concerns about the heavy human and financial costs of the occupation depressed spirits.

There is broad agreement in the literature that much of the major American mass media exhibited marked patriotic and pro-government tendencies in response to the Iraq War. The American watchdog

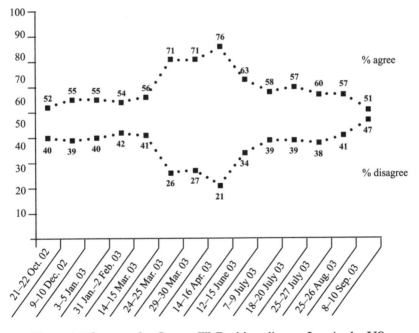

Figure 2.7 Support for George W. Bush's policy on Iraq in the US
Source: <www.gallups.com/poll/releases/pr030912.asp> (15 May 2003)

organization FAIR (Fairness and Accuracy in Reporting), for example, complained that the major newspapers the *New York Times* and *Washington Post* scarcely allowed opponents of the war any space to express their views.[60] American television broadcasters fired up the public mood with special reports such as 'Countdown Iraq' and 'Showdown with Saddam'. The then director-general of the BBC, Greg Dyke, criticized this one-sided pro-American stance and the latent war propaganda of American radio and television programme makers. Fox News, the leading news broadcaster at the time in the US, openly expressed sympathy for the neo-conservative agenda of President Bush. Dyke assailed the largest chain of radio stations in the United States, Clear Channel Communications Inc., for actively mobilizing people for war throughout the country.[61]

The list of offences against the principle of objectivity by American media before and during the Iraq War 2003 is almost endless. This is confirmed in a study carried out by FAIR during the war in March and April 2003.[62] According to this study, from the start of the invasion, government actors were in the majority on the major networks ABC, CBS, NBC, CNN, Fox and PBS, while opponents of the war were under-represented. More than 70 per cent of all invited interviewees spoke in favour of the war, merely 10 per cent against. Official voices, whether members or former members of the government,

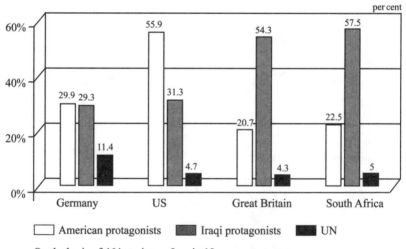

On the basis of 464 stories on Iraq in 19 news programmes

Figure 2.8 Protagonists in television news reports on Iraq, 2001–2002
Source: Media Tenor 124, Bonn, September 2002 (based on original data set)

made up more than half (around 60 per cent) of all guests, the military enjoying twice as much representation as civilians.

These research results are confirmed by the international research network Media Tenor, which also estimates the presence of American government representatives on American television screens at 60 per cent. That this truly was a national reflex of the American media is shown by comparison with Germany and the UK (figure 2.8), where far fewer American government representatives and many more of their Iraqi counterparts were given airtime. In the media of the chief actor in the Iraq War, the United States, its own elites and thus national interests and justifications clearly took centre stage.

Public opinion in Great Britain was more critical of the war than in the US, but less critical than in almost the whole of the rest of Europe (with the possible exception of Poland). When the war began, support for the government rose to more than 50 per cent in Britain, peaking when allied troops won the war.[63] The images of the toppling of Saddam Hussein's statue in Baghdad and of cheering Iraqis brought Prime Minister Tony Blair public support for his pro-war policy, which had previously wavered. The fact that the statue's destruction involved the mise-en-scène of only around one hundred Iraqis, encouraged by American troops in an otherwise deserted capital city, was neither here nor there. Most consumers of media trusted international reporting in this regard – quite wrongly, as soon became clear.

The tabloids owned by media tycoon Rupert Murdoch, the *Sun* and *News of the World*, had got behind Blair's war plans from the very beginning.[64] When George Galloway MP called for sanctions against the United States during the war, the *Sun* pilloried him as a 'traitor'.[65] The serious daily broadsheets the *Guardian*, *The Times* and the *Independent*, meanwhile, remained relatively objective. When the war broke out, Robert Fisk, the *Independent*'s star reporter, spared no detail in reporting how a taxi driver was hit by an allied bomb, and attacked the Blair government's lack of humanity. Headlines such as 'Night of Terror'[66] or the description of the bombing of a marketplace in Baghdad as 'obscene' were clear-cut, but criticism of the war diminished during its course with the growing success of the British forces, until even the *Independent* covered its front page with the 'Final Countdown for Baghdad'[67] and the collapsing statue of Saddam Hussein without a word. While critics got the chance to air their views in *The Times* and the *Independent*, at least in their later pages, the imagery deployed in *The Times* was strongly militaristic: press briefings from the army, soldiers in action, soldiers being handed flowers, etc. *The Times* used unambiguous pro-war language in its headlines: 'We are liberating a country that is enslaved by a lunatic',[68] 'The blitzing of Baghdad'[69] and 'Ruthless despot who can't resist a gamble'.[70]

While the British press as a whole thus fluctuated between patriotism and neutrality, British radio and television were markedly more distanced and sober than their American counterparts, though even they were accused of providing too little airtime to opponents of the war, of whom there was no lack in the country.[71]

The German public clearly opposed the war in Iraq, as did its counterparts in states such as France, Spain, Portugal, Italy, Denmark, Sweden, Finland, Belgium, the Netherlands, Russia and Turkey. In some of these countries the government supported the war.[72] In contrast to public opinion, however, the German press was far less determinedly anti-war.[73] Liberal and conservative publications such as *Die Zeit* or the *Frankfurter Allgemeine Zeitung* criticized Chancellor Schröder sharply for his undiplomatic refusal to support the war and for damaging German–American relations. Papers on the liberal left such as the *Frankfurter Rundschau* were predominately pacifist, but many programmes on German television strove to provide a platform for supporters as well as opponents of the war.

How can this empirical reality of war reporting in the United States, Great Britain and Germany be interpreted against the background of the globalization debate? The examples of the US and, to a lesser extent, Great Britain, confirm that 'rallying round the flag'[74] is a widespread mechanism and that modern democratic states, as 'fortress societies', function no differently than any authoritarian propaganda state. It is not so much that governments actively influence the people. Rather, through their belligerent behaviour, they set the scene for the triggering of defensive instincts among members of the public, who come to see themselves as a defensive community. It is thus utterly false to assume that in the present era global opinion – in this case the overwhelming rejection of war by the vast majority of states and publics in the Middle East – can influence or even mould the media and public opinion in states prepared to go to war. In the special case of international reporting in states involved in war, the national government sets the tone. The arguments put forward by governments and institutions in other countries, or even by the 'world system' of the United Nations, have little impact. The informational raw material of the news may come from outside, it may contain correct (and incorrect) facts and reports from countries such as Iraq, but the 'story' of the war is a domestic production, and when push comes to shove it is as particularistic and belligerent as it ever was.

Interpreting this situation through the prism of systems theory, international reporting in wartime is clearly thrown back upon its structural deficits in the field of global interdependence. Most media do not operate and are not anchored transnationally; they do not serve different markets and thus contrasting landscapes of opinion and national spheres of interest. Regardless of all the discussions about the United Nations and the Security Council, political influences on the media and publics are not globalized in such a way that the belligerent national government's strong media presence is balanced out. In wartime, the media have to adapt profoundly, over the short term, to these 'harsh' internal and external national environments. When the war is over, things may become more relaxed. This is apparent in growing pluralism and a new openness to the world.

How, though, can we explain the extraordinary resilience of sections of the British media and television? At certain times, the so-called 'home front' of the media in a country at war was shaken. Was this globalization?

It is at least apparent that under favourable conditions even a 'narcissistic' system such as that of international reporting can resist monopolization by national politics and assert the norms of multinationalism and global peace. In 2003, these conditions included the fact that a country such as Germany was not involved in the events of the war and the national pressure on the media was slight. The British public, meanwhile, as part of a confederation such as the European Union, was exposed to a range of political influences. These found expression in the media and slowly relativized the primacy of the media's wartime fixation on the national. This last development in particular suggests that there is a close connection between the rise of a transnational political system and the emergence of transnational cultures of international reporting. Only when forces beyond the borders of the nation-state exercise an influence on publics, which is viewed as legitimate, do they have the chance to establish themselves in the media – not the other way around. There is as yet no sign of a political world system, given the weakness of the United Nations. The influence exercised by the vigorous system of the European Union is thus an example of regionalization rather than globalization.

The myth within the myth: the 'CNN effect'

The 'myth of globalization' rests upon several stories that authors have often adopted from other authors without scrutiny and which have then been subject to constant repetition. This has not made them any more correct. In the thematic field of 'media and globalization', several myths are combined. Globalization as cross-border force of mass communication is interwoven with the myth of the 'mediatization' of politics and society[75] and the notion that the media's impact is constantly intensifying.[76] The story of the American news network CNN, which rose rapidly to the status of leading global medium during the second Gulf War of 1991 and which seemed to represent a new type of television, is symbolic of how an event can be mythically imbued.[77] CNN operated more quickly than traditional media, and was, above all, globally available and accessible via satellite. For the first time, the principle of *national* international reporting was undermined. In the 1990s, CNN also seemed to become increasingly relevant to politics as a result of these outstanding qualities. The broadcaster created the impression that it was capable of influencing the foreign policy of the United States. It seemed to have overturned the dictum that in international affairs, largely because the consumer is so distant from events, politics can make the most of its empirical headstart and dominate events. Almost overnight, many observers worldwide came to believe that here a medium had succeeded in using its global advantages in production, information gathering and viewer reach to its own ends, giving international politics as a whole a more cosmopolitan face and leading it out of the narrows of national interests. Over the course of time, the term 'CNN effect' was applied to other media such as the Arab network al-Jazeera (see chapter 3, p. 75) and became an important slogan in the globalization debate. Had the dream of a global public sphere been realized?

As the book progresses we shall see that transnational television viewing via satellite, upon which the attractiveness of CNN was largely based, has *not* diminished the interpretive sovereignty of international reporting within the nation, because it is not a mass cultural phenomenon (see chapter 3, p. 57) . The criticism of international reporting and American reporting on the Iraq War of 2003 outlined in the previous chapter provides evidence that the second aspect of the so-called 'CNN effect', its power to change politics, has also been subject to a high degree of myth-making. How can media that allow themselves to be influenced by politics and patriotic sentiments in this way influence politics, guiding it towards global consensus, no less?

It will come as no surprise that there has been a critical reappraisal of the CNN effect in recent years. Piers Robinson declares large parts of this complex a 'myth', and various authors have produced studies showing that the effects of television and the media on foreign policy tend to be apparent, if at all, at the margins of international politics.[78] This also fits in with earlier analyses, on the key role of German media in ending the so-called 'critical dialogue' between Germany and Iran in the mid-1990s for example.[79] Royce J. Ammon and Piers Robinson have produced independent studies of international political issues such as Kurdish autonomy after the Gulf War of 1991 or the conflicts in Somalia, Bosnia and Kosovo, which the media is frequently claimed to have influenced, and have come up with similar findings. In almost all cases, political decisions for or against Western intervention had already been made before larger-scale media reporting.

If these authors are correct, the media can exercise an effect on foreign policy above all in places suffering humanitarian crises (such as Somalia or Rwanda), and even here, they can do so only when the following factors come together:

- There must be a vacuum in the field of political decision-making, characterized by disagreement within governments, ruling parties or other institutions (such as parliaments) about foreign policy;
- The crisis must be 'suited' to television, that is, it must produce emotionally moving images accessible to the media that the public finds touching (which did not apply, for example, in the case of the civil war in Rwanda);
- There must be a consensus about the evaluation of the political situation. This tends to apply to humanitarian catastrophes and genocide, but less to 'simple wars', albeit the border between the two is often blurred and may be manipulated to political ends.

Ammon and Robinson remark, with differing emphases, that the American media had a certain influence on the establishment of no-fly zones to protect the Kurds in Iraq (after the war of 1991), air strikes by the Americans in Bosnia in the mid-1990s and in Somalia. In the case of Somalia, however, Robinson points out that the more far-reaching decision, to dispatch ground troops, had already been taken before extensive media reportage. Robinson thus comes to the conclusion that the 'CNN effect' is subordinate within world politics:

> [T]his book suggests a strong CNN effect in relation to air power intervention during humanitarian crises. However, the research here into instances of ground troop intervention during humanitarian crises indicates that media coverage is not a major factor in producing these high cost, risky operations. The widespread assumption that these

interventions were media driven is a myth . . . . [C]laims by communication theorists such as [Ingrid] Volkmer that there now exists 'a
worldwide homogeneously time-zoned bios politicon, instantaneously
affecting worldwide political action . . . or public resolutions transmitted around the world by CNNI' appear vastly overstated. Despite the
radical claims of some, new communication technologies have not
transformed world politics and media-state relations.[80]

Here, Ammon in particular brings out how the speed of television and
the access to images do in fact have the potential to make the media
an actor in politics. He too, however, recognizes that even then, many
favourable circumstances have to come together. The armed forces,
moreover, have also shown, especially during the Gulf Wars of 1991
and 2003, that they have learnt from their 'failure' during the Vietnam
War. They now manage access to images either restrictively (censorship) or proactively (information pools, embedding, etc.). The Civil
War in Rwanda with its one million dead produced no images of
victims, and even the rapidly growing number of reports failed to
bring about humanitarian intervention. Given that international
reporting is currently strapped for cash, and is increasingly degenerating into 'leftovers' (Meckel), there is no prospect that the media will
triumph over the armed forces or foreign policy.[81]

In vital issues of national foreign policy, the same rule continues to
apply: the media *follow* rather than *lead*. The true strength of the
media consists not in its capacity to influence politics, as evoked in the
'CNN effect', but in the affirmation and legitimation of national
politics. This is bound up with the risk of encouraging 'jingoistic
patriotism', as in the US during the Iraq War of 2003, and making
international conflicts worse. Scholars who have probed in more
depth the issue of the media's potential to promote peace worldwide,
such as Robinson, drawing on Noam Chomsky, have come to the conclusion that the production and maintenance of the political consensus (*manufacturing consent*) on the 'home front' have been two of the
key tasks of the media and of international reporting since the First
World War at least.[82] The risk, to which the former chief executive of
major news agency Agence France-Presse (AFP) Claude Moisy also
refers, is that inadequate international media reporting promotes dangerous political decisions, particularly during crises and under pressure of time.[83]

In terms of technology, institutions, production and content, the
development of the media is enabling people to communicate more
and more and across an ever larger area, but not necessarily in a more

meaningful way or with greater understanding. Getting the euphoria about globalization in check in light of the insights of media content research does not mean disputing the globalization of the media entirely. It would however be illusory to believe that in the age of mass democracy media no longer produce propaganda or that media discourses are always pluralist. Increasing communication and communicative connectivity not only have the potential to solve problems but also to make them worse, by providing visual embellishment for pro-war policies for example. As long as international reporting and national media systems fail to enter into more far-reaching interdependencies through, among other things, the integration of media markets, conflicts between nation-states will continue to set the tone in the media world. Until then, there is a danger that media, far from pursuing global 'media diplomacy', will in fact cement conflictual political cultures that strengthen the national identification undergirding the nation-state, encouraging cultural conflicts (as happened after 11 September 2001). They may even reinforce tensions between majority populations and religious, ethnic and cultural minorities. The prevailing conceptions of foreign countries and of the world found in the media may imbue the public image of minorities, especially during periods of large-scale migration.[84]

3
Satellite Television – the Renaissance of World Regions

One of the utopias central to globalization asserts that direct broadcasting by satellite can break through the ethnocentrism of nation-based international journalism. On this view, overcoming the limitations on media use imposed by the nation-state would be a significant step towards broadening national horizons and forming a global identity.

However, the communicative networking of the world by means of direct broadcasting by satellite, either television or radio, is as yet no more than a myth of globalization. A small portion of the public at most regularly watches television programmes from other countries. The character of 'television without borders' is determined by cosmopolitan information elites who watch international broadcasters based in other states or well-known networks such as CNN, by overlapping television use in linguistically homogenous regions (as in the German-speaking countries of Europe) and by the special interests of immigrants. There is no question of there being a comprehensive global network of consumer habits. Direct, authentic access to the cultural production of other states, unfiltered by the journalism of one's own country, remains an enormous, unused resource of globalization.

Language barriers are proving almost insurmountable, and national media discourses are of negligible interest beyond national borders. The deficits of international reporting, which treats international issues as easily manipulated leftovers, are dispatched to the world indirectly via satellite television. They prevent such reporting from generating much social resonance. Western international reporting, while claiming to be anchored in the spirit of democracy and asserting its leading role in globalization, ignores oppositional elites battling to achieve democracy in other parts of the world. Even in the age of supposed globalization, apart from a small number of historical moments such as the fall of the Berlin Wall, the Western media remain in a pre-global 'spiral of silence'[1] of enormous dimensions.

It is thus no surprise that, paradoxically, the age of globalization has seen national programmes proliferate and regional media empires develop. The technologically possible and seemingly effortless access to unfamiliar televisual worlds remains the exception – the rule being the reproduction and further evolution of national and regional media cultures, now that digital media have eliminated the shortage of terrestrial frequencies.

The growth of national and regional television markets, especially in the former colonial spheres of Latin America, North Africa and the Middle East, as well as in Asia, is currently the primary factor changing media systems – and its relationship to globalization is ambivalent. Is regionalization a staging post on the path from national to global television cultures? Or is national and regional growth proving so dominant that it is functioning as a bulwark against the global networking of the media? Are nations and major cultural-religious regions such as the Chinese sphere, 'the West' or the 'Islamic world' sealing themselves off from one another? Is Samuel Huntington's 'clash of civilizations' really a 'lack of communication'?

The range of issues thrown up by current developments is exemplified in the case of the Arab satellite broadcaster al-Jazeera, based in the emirate of Qatar on the Persian Gulf. It became world-famous following the attacks on the World Trade Center and the Pentagon on 11 September 2001 because it broadcast video messages by Osama bin Laden, supposedly behind the attacks, on several occasions. It subsequently became the leading source of opinion critical of America in the Arab world. This network fuses conventional international reporting, mainly made for an Arab audience, with a clear pro-democracy tenor. The latter conveys the universal values expressed in human rights and corresponds to a global values-based culture of the kind many advocates of globalization have in mind. Whether we will see globalization worthy of the name, which not only interlinks hemispheres technologically but changes media, media users and their societies and cultures, depends in large measure on how these leading regional media develop.

Cross-border media use and the triumph of the monolingual middle classes over cosmopolitan elites

A well-nigh endless number of commentators views the development of a global televisual landscape as the key factor bringing the world

together. Key programmatic meetings of the United Nations such as
'Forum Barcelona 2004', organized by UNESCO, have established a
link between the decline of state borders and the globalization of the
television audience, above all as a result of the growing popularity of
transnational networks.[2]

Intellectual pioneers of globalization such as Anthony Giddens,
Director of the London School of Economics and Political Science for
many years, have described the introduction of modern satellite communications technology as a *dramatic break with the past*, because
simultaneous communicative relations are possible between different
parts of the world for the first time.[3] One of the sociologists and cultural studies scholars setting the tone of the globalization debate, John
Tomlinson, regards television as the medium of globalization *par
excellence* because of its wide popularity.[4] Communication studies
scholars such as Stephen Dahl also think that the industrialized states
at least have moved closer together through the Internet and satellite
television.[5] Other leading scholars such as David Held and Anthony
McGrew express related ideas. They describe the speed, scale and
intensity of world-spanning communication, made possible by satellite television among other things, as evidence of the hegemony of
'corporations' and the ousting of the historic forms of domination –
the state and 'theocracy'.[6]

Even politicians use the myth of satellite television linking the world
to get across their political messages. During a visit to Morocco in
2000, for example, Evelyn S. Lieberman, Under Secretary of State for
Public Diplomacy and Public Affairs, made the daring prognosis
that the country would, like almost every state, be 'fundamentally
changed' by globalization, especially given that there are already more
than 40,000 Internet connections there and satellite televisions even
in the most modest homes. The Internet, satellite television and economic globalization, the Under Secretary of State concluded, constitute the three key forces influencing not only everyday life, but also
American foreign policy, which is being catapulted into an 'era of new
realities, new problems and new chances'.[7] This vision is as cryptic as
it is far-reaching, evoking the sustained influence of satellite television
on such differing fields as everyday life and foreign policy in such
different countries as the US superpower and the peripheral Arab
state of Morocco. It endows this particular medium with the same significance as profound upheavals in the global economy.

Given the enormous significance so often attributed to satellite
television by different governments, organizations and experts over
the last two decades, it is all the more astonishing that, as yet, no one

has subjected the international use of satellite television to remotely satisfactory and comprehensive scholarly examination. All we have are empirical building blocks, making it difficult to come to theoretical conclusions – one could be forgiven for thinking there was nothing worth studying here at all. Academia thus leaves it largely to the broadcasters themselves to draw up statistics on reach and use in the field of television. They are keen to show these in a positive light due to market position and competition factors. This in turn caused Matthew Engel, a journalist working for the British *Guardian* newspaper, to remark: 'There are lies, damned lies and global television statistics.'[8]

In recent years, an increasing number of scholars have in fact striven to bring a new realism to the debate on the globalizing effect of satellite television. In his analysis of the European satellite television market, Richard Collins has produced an unsparing appraisal of the flawed media policy assumptions inherent in pan-European television projects such as 'Eurikon' and 'Europa'. The PETAR study (Pan European Television Audience Research), which repeatedly examined Europeans' response to commercial satellite broadcasters such as Super Channel from 1987 to 1995, revealed not only poor viewing figures but also enormous discrepancies in culturally imbued viewer preferences. Collins describes as illusory the assumption that the same national or even pan-European range of programming could find acceptance in all the countries of the European Union.[9] The renowned British communication studies scholar, active at the London School of Economics and Political Science among other institutions, identifies 'unresolved contradictions between a television market which is formally integrated but which in fact is profoundly divided by the linguistic and cultural differences of its television viewers.'[10] This phenomenon, Collins argues, is the main reason for the low level of European demand for cross-border television.

If the available statistics are to be believed, things have changed little since the PETAR study. Uwe Hasebrink and Anja Herzog are right to argue with reference to Europe that the technological internationalization produced by satellite and cable television has not as yet been matched at the level of media use, as neither programmes from other countries nor transnational networks have met with much response.[11]

The situation in Europe is mirrored in most other regions of the world[12] and constitutes a 'global trend'. Cross-border television use is still the absolute exception and is restricted to special situations (countries where the same language is spoken and international broadcasting) and special groups (immigrants and global elites):

Crossing borders in homogenous language areas. In homogenous language areas separated by state borders such as German-speaking Germany, Austria and Switzerland or the English-language area taking in the United Kingdom and Ireland, people have been watching television across borders for many decades. Here, it is above all viewers from the smaller states with fewer broadcasters who can expand their choice of programmes by accessing those of neighbouring countries. While for example a German-Swiss receives up to two-thirds of her programmes from other countries (Germany and Austria), in the Netherlands the figure is a still substantial 10 to 20 per cent (depending on which study you read),[13] but in Germany well under five per cent.[14] Border crossing in homogenous language areas may have been intensified by satellite television, but has been known since the days of terrestrial television broadcasts and is thus far more an expression of regionalism (see p. 69) and minor televisual border traffic than of world-spanning globalization. For those who support the idea that satellite television and globalization are interrelated with the forces transforming politics and everyday life – forces set free by the removal of borders between televisual worlds – use within language areas is irrelevant, as it is overly traditional and remains largely restricted to specific, extended cultural areas.

Multilingual international broadcasting. International broadcasters have also been a familiar feature for decades. Following the attacks of 11 September 2001, many countries rediscovered the radio and television programmes produced for international broadcast as a key instrument of communication (see chapter 6). These media are also far older than direct broadcasting by satellite. The spread and reception of radio programmes has hardly been touched by satellite, as radio continues to be received primarily by terrestrial technology. The range of programming offered by providers of international broadcasting, however, increases the size of the potential audience – technologically speaking. Such offerings, however, merely augment television use worldwide, and the actual number of viewers tends to be very limited. The news journalism that is one strand of international broadcasting increasingly finds itself in competition with new television services in the receiving countries or their neighbours in the same language area (see p. 69). Because of its multilingual nature and access to large numbers of people in many countries, international broadcasting does have great potential for the future. It cannot, however, simply be described as one of globalization's winners, and should certainly not be regarded as evidence of the global consumer's internationalized television use.

Cross-border media use by immigrants. The rise of satellite television has made it possible for immigrants all over the world to remain in touch with the media of their home states and regions (see chapter 7). Many studies demonstrate that the media use behaviour of immigrants has changed substantially. This is a major reason why they are so often evoked to back up claims of a broader tendency towards global television use – a tendency which, however, to repeat, does not apply to the majority population of the states in which the immigrants have made their home.

Media use by global elites. If we adjust the figures on cross-border television use by factoring out regional and language area effects, the latter intensified by migration and multilingual international broadcasting, and scrutinize the reality of global television use, it continues to be extremely low in most countries. It certainly makes up no more than one to five per cent of television consumption as a rule.[15] A large portion of this use is by 'global elites'. The study 'Europe 2004' by the IPSOS Institute has carried out a representative examination of media use among 3.8 per cent of the European population, who can be counted among the global elite because they have a high income and frequently go on business trips. Transnationally oriented networks such as CNN make up a larger portion of media consumption than among average users. No less than 24.7 per cent of the 3.8 per cent interviewed watch CNN at least once a week, and 14 per cent watch international news daily.[16] Even this finding, however, must be interpreted in context. The 'travelling' European elite members surveyed often *have to* fall back on English-language and transnational formats when they leave their home countries, as their usual European programmes are not available in their hotels. The major Western television companies such as CNN and the BBC have achieved incomparable spread in the cable systems of the world. This situation should not be confused with globalization in its original sense of a total removal of barriers to media use, which would allow these elites to take advantage of the numerous national television services existing worldwide, far less with increased use of foreign programmes by the broad mass of television viewers.

The assumption of advancing globalization often resembles a 'hotel thesis of globalization', in which globalized media use is extrapolated

from the mere technological existence and availability of satellite television. Western scholars and experts appear particularly enthusiastic
about the possibility of finding a small number of transnational programmes and a handful of American and European networks in hotels
for the middle classes the world over. They mistake their own curios-
ity with large-scale use in the countries in which they experience these
things. Yet the fact that mobile elites fall back upon transnational
media, among other things, tells us little about the global position of
these programmes.

The fact that the world market for satellite television has been
growing, since the early 1990s at the latest, has often been interpreted as a sign of the globalization of the media.[17] In many countries
in Asia, Africa and Latin America, however, people tend to want
satellite dishes not in order to receive Western programmes but to
watch new satellite channels based in their own country or the
extended language area. Regular consumption of European and
US programmes remains limited to small elites in most countries.
Financial hurdles to the acquisition of satellite-receiving technology,
language barriers or lack of interest in media offerings tailored to
a Western audience stop the lower and lower-middle classes in particular from making regular use of Western programmes.[18] Use
analyses show that even in acculturated regions such as the Franco-
phone Maghreb – in Morocco, for instance, mentioned by Evelyn
Lieberman as an example of globalization – the regular consumption
of Western television programmes tends to be restricted to small sections of the upper-middle and upper classes. The consumption of
Western media by the dominant upper classes is highly unlikely to
boost significantly the prospects of system change, that is, political
transformation and democratization.

Media studies scholar Larbi Chouikha talks about a social 'chasm'
between the consumers of foreign and national information. In the
Arab world, for example, language barriers, feelings of cultural
unfamiliarity and scepticism about Western reporting on the Middle
East have helped ensure that the very section of the population that
determined the political dynamics in the Arab world through
national, Islamist or other movements over the course of the twentieth
century – the lower-middle classes – watches national or regional programming the vast majority of the time.[19] Yet in the postcolonial era,
the lower-middle classes, including students, teachers and petty
traders, were the key political force in many developing countries, due
to the combination of a relatively high level of education, social depri-
vation and political exclusion from their own society. The low degree

of cosmopolitanism and lack of money to travel characteristic of this group are reflected in low levels of foreign language knowledge, making them the monolingual middle classes, who rarely choose to watch foreign television channels.

In reality, one of the key reasons why non-European viewers of networks such as CNN form a small and fluctuating group is because many people distrust it. Uwe Hasebrink and Anja Herzog's assumption that most television consumers remain loyal to the news programmes of their home country[20] is confirmed by the example of such consumers in the Middle East. While 61 per cent consider the pan-Arab network al-Jazeera trustworthy, only 10 per cent have the same view of CNN,[21] a degree of trust which inevitably condemns any medium to a marginal position within society.

The 'fate' of the attention paid to CNN and its worldwide acceptance epitomizes how the boom in the technology underpinning direct broadcasting by satellite, far from bringing about a concentration upon certain leading global media, has in fact achieved precisely the opposite. Networks linking nations and regions have largely failed to materialize. During the second Gulf War of 1991, CNN was *the* default medium for international affairs, a pioneer among transnational news channels enjoying high levels of trust even in the Middle East. CNN was the reason why many people purchased satellite dishes in 1991. Step by step, however, as time passed by and native satellite broadcasters were established in Europe, Latin America, Asia and the Middle East, the pioneering American network fell further and further behind. Today, it is hardly perceived as a global medium, but rather as a reasonably enlightened form of American self-presentation. CNN merely sparked off the awareness of programme makers (and politicians) worldwide that satellite technology provides a new medium which can be exploited to political and commercial ends. It triggered the subsequent boom in regional and national satellite networks on almost every continent.

John Sinclair, Elizabeth Jacka and Stuart Cunningham underline that neither in the Middle East, nor Asia, nor even in Latin America, where American influence is often described as very great, do Western television programmes dominate.[22] It was wrong, these authors argue, to regard the strength of the American television film economy during the early stages of the development of television, in the first decades after the Second World War, as a permanent state of affairs. It in fact marked a transitional phase only, quickly brought to an end by autonomous developments.[23] According to these Australian scholars, global television is now influenced more than ever by regional centres such as Brazil, Mexico, Saudi Arabia, Egypt, India, Hong Kong and Taiwan, and to a far lesser extent by global contexts.

Global television and the 'spiral of silence' afflicting democratization

From the early 1990s on, satellite television was central to many debates expressing the hope that this new global medium would have a positive effect on the spread of democracy worldwide. In the era of globalization, it was thought, authoritarian censorship could be got round and rendered unworkable to such an extent that foreign media could balance out the deficits imposed upon the domestic mass media. Global political information and mobilization was to replace nationalistic-authoritarian misinformation and stagnation. Nothing less than a 'television revolution' was expected.

Patrick H. O'Neil is just one of a large number of authors who have described the persistent influence of cross-border news flows upon world politics and 'political change'.[24] O'Neil mentions two pieces of evidence to back up this claim: the Chiapas Rebellion in Mexico, which was influenced considerably by its international echo, particularly by the campaign of solidarity on the Internet, and the collapse of communism in Eastern Europe. The demise of the Soviet Union has often been regarded as the consequence of a television revolution, because the collapse of the old regimes spread in a domino effect across such states as Hungary, Czechoslovakia, Poland, etc. and pre-occupied media across the world.

As attractive as this idea may appear, however, it is riddled with shortcomings. First of all, the reportage was limited to the period of upheaval itself. It cannot, therefore, have triggered the events which ultimately caused the regimes to collapse. Mikhail Gorbachev introduced his policy of openness in the mid-1980s, and he himself engaged systematically in public relations in pursuit of his aims, joining forces with the Soviet media to oppose the party bureaucracy of the Soviet state.[25] Citizens of the GDR fled to the German embassy. These and many other developments and events preceded the media representation of the upheavals.

We are left with the argument that the global media provided the political events with indispensable reinforcement, without which the political dynamics that finally caused the Soviet Union and the Eastern bloc to disintegrate may not have arisen. This notion, however, fails to recognize that almost no households in the Eastern bloc were fitted with satellite dishes at the time. In point of fact, foreign media could influence things, if at all, as a component of 'minor border traffic', in other words terrestrially, or through Western international broadcasters. Thus, if Western media did indeed play a role in Eastern Europe, this occurred less against the background of global conditions than European-regional ones and on the basis of broadcasting technology as old as the Second World War, deriving from a pre-global era.

The political transformation in Eastern Europe thus had nothing to do with satellite broadcasting and the new media, if mass media were in fact a decisive factor at all. In any case, the effectiveness of interpersonal political communication, that is, word-of-mouth propaganda, public gatherings and demonstrations, should not be underestimated. The thesis that the mass media promoted revolution in 1989–90 is impossible to prove, as other channels of communication cannot be ruled out as intervening factors. What is more, this thesis also fails to take into account the fact that revolutionary upheavals are fixed components of history and also took place during periods in which our 'global' media did not yet exist. An event such as the French Revolution had social consequences throughout Europe. It was emulated in Germany, Poland and as far as the Eastern Mediterranean region, despite the fact that radio and television had not yet been invented and the impact of the press was inevitably minimal because of high rates of illiteracy and strict censorship.

The 'Third Wave of Democratization', described by Harvard political scientist Samuel Huntington, also abated before direct broadcasting by satellite and the Internet was introduced into media markets. The 'Third Wave' began with the political changes in southern Europe (Greece, Portugal, Spain) in the 1980s and continued in Latin America and some Asian countries, reaching the former Eastern bloc countries in the late 1980s. Since the spread of the new media central to 'globalization' in the early 1990s, meanwhile, global democratization has stagnated (see chapter 8, p. 149).

It would of course be wrong to assume that the development of the new media is causally responsible for political stagnation. However, reversing the chain of causality by pointing to the supposed power of the new global media technologies to boost democratization is equally out of the question. We as yet lack evidence of this. At least in the short term, enhanced technological conditions for access to cross-border radio and television have failed to produce political revolutions.

None of this means that 'media' play no role in processes of democratization. They do so in a range of ways: as underground and alternative media, through repeated criticism in the major televisual and print media and the dissidence among journalists worldwide identified by human rights organizations in their annual reports. These are all media-based contributions to democratization, evidence of which can be found in every example of the 'third wave' – but they have little to do with the new media so central to globalization.

To enhance globe-spanning links through satellite television, strengthen cross-border television use and thus bolster shared political discourses and the global spread of democracy, many television programmes on every continent would require both reorientation of content and internationalization.

To elucidate this thesis, let us turn to the example of the cross-border role of media in processes of democratization. It is first essential to establish the fundamental distinction between 'big' and 'small' media.[26] Small underground media (pamphlets, etc.) are of great significance in authoritarian periods because of their potential to support social and political movements. The big media which, like television, reach the masses can make a meaningful contribution to democratization only from outside the state in question. As far as the use of democratizing mass communication by means of satellite television goes, before the establishment of a democratic order, the ball lies in the court of opposition groups living abroad. Yet they are unable to take action without help from the state, as they tend to lack the money, licences and access necessary to take advantage of satellite technology. Alternatively, the much-vaunted 'global public sphere' may take on this function.[27] Individuals and opposition groups, denied access to television in their own countries, can increase public pressure on local politics indirectly via a presence in international media, which can be received by satellite in the country in question. Such a 'boomerang effect' (Sikkink and Keck 1998) would constitute evidence of a globally networked world.[28]

However, the news which consumers in authoritarian states currently receive via television produced in democratic countries, above all in America, Europe and a few countries in Asia and Africa, only rarely goes beyond the informational content of their native censored media, putting a dampener on the euphoria surrounding globalization. Western international reporting is only suited to producing effective boomerang effects to a very limited degree, because the limited time slots for international news and background reports cannot guarantee continuous reporting beyond moments of crisis (see chapter 2).

Studies of the international reporting on German television news programmes and in the German national press have shown that there is only a very limited amount of space for foreign political actors, particularly for the organized democratic opposition across large parts of the world. This predicament cannot of course simply be assumed to apply to global media, but nonetheless suggests an alarming initial picture. An analysis of German television news carried out by the major broadcasters ARD, ZDF, RTL and Sat 1 revealed that in reports on the Islamic world only around a third of actors represented was from the Islamic world.[29] The overwhelming majority was from the West, testimony to the great significance of such news-related factors as 'Eurocentrism' or 'involvement'. The more strongly the news event is linked with Western interests, politics and persons, the greater the likelihood that it will make it into the media. This does not however apply to the presentation of the victims of violence, who comprise a large part of the actors, reflecting the focus on violent conflicts in international reporting.[30] It is no doubt important to the global exchange of information to show the victims of war and violence, especially as they are frequently invisible in the media of the countries in question themselves. It is however problematic that the relative over-representation of politicians and victims or citizens leaves almost no space for social organizations and the forces of the democratic opposition.[31] It is precisely such groups which had high hopes of globalization. The end result is that of the short time slots available on German television, almost nothing is left over for the democratic opposition, because most of the organizations presented are nationalistic or radical, often terrorist groups.

This tendency becomes even clearer in existing nuanced studies of the German press, but most likely applies equally to German television. It provides an indication of the state of other media systems the world over. International reporting in the German press differs from German television in certain respects, as foreign politicians are more strongly represented here than Western ones. Moreover, from the 1980s on, the presence of foreign social organizations and (opposition) parties has grown.[32] Yet even this tendency, positive at first glance, occurred in parallel with a radicalization of the prevailing conception of foreign countries and the ousting of non-violent opposition groups from German media. The German press rarely focuses on the democratically oriented forces of the opposition, tending to privilege those with radical, terrorist or religious-ethnic leanings; in short, the extreme opposition rather than the moderate opposition.[33]

This also means that radical forces have an easier time making an impact on their countries via the global public sphere (satellite television, Internet, etc.) than does the moderate opposition. This indicates that a functional symbiosis exists between democratic Western media and radical forces in the developing countries, between the tendency to report conflicts and radical forces' propaganda priorities. The history of both the PLO and the Kurdish PKK, which largely modelled itself on the PLO, should be seen as a more or less conscious strategy designed to get their political demands onto the agenda of the international media by means of violence.

The shortcomings of research in this field can be remedied only by large-scale comparative projects including case studies of the composition of actors in the foreign news. Nonetheless, we have to assume that regular national television programmes the world over – other than during revolutions and similar upheavals – are incapable of presenting political events in distant lands with enough subtlety to render them of interest to the countries themselves and local processes of democratization and development. People may well watch foreign broadcasts to learn more about the world ('demonstration effect').[34] With the exception of special crisis situations, in which global television may function as a catalyst, however, they would certainly not be advised to watch television from other countries in order to learn more about the situation in their *own* country.

One exception to this depressing assessment is foreign-language international broadcasting, one of whose key tasks is often to provide opposition forces with access to the airwaves (although this is not always the case, as the example of the American Arabic-language broadcaster al-Hurra demonstrates; see chapter 6). The cross-border transmission of television programmes produced by opposition forces in foreign countries has also increased over recent decades.[35] Both within the large-scale international framework, through US broadcasters who transmit to Iran for example, as well as minor border traffic from neighbouring countries, the opposition abroad has found new ways of communicating with the home population. On closer inspection, however, it is evident that we are generally dealing here with phenomena limited to a homogenous language and cultural area, often in fact to a sub-region of the world (see p. 69), though it must be acknowledged that oppositional cultures are often able to evolve more freely in the consolidated democracies of the large industrialized countries of North America, Europe and Asia than elsewhere. Against this background, the question remains: is the influence of the opposition abroad significant? Theoretically speaking, can this form of global interlinking truly change political cultures? Positive examples of this – above all the Iranian Revolution of 1978–79, which was organized from Paris – point to such potential. Even here, though, the coups succeeded not with the aid of the technologies of globalization, such as cross-border satellite television broadcast to Iran, but through the video and audio cassettes featuring the speeches of Ayatollah Khomeini smuggled into the country.[36]

Leaving aside foreign-language international broadcasting and the television networks of the opposition abroad, it is at present impossible to speak of a general, direct 'democratization effect' exercised by cross-border satellite television. For the relatively small sections of the population who regularly make use of satellite television to watch foreign programmes, the main impact probably consists of a 'demonstration effect', which is difficult to grasp or describe. This involves an insight into other life-worlds and political contexts made possible by television, and undoubtedly broadens the cultural horizons of relatively small elites: no more, but also no less. The moderate democratic opposition, which exists in every country, benefits from this only very indirectly. It may place its hopes in the mobilizing effect of broadcasts by the opposition abroad, but surely not in the global cacophony of television broadcasts beamed into the country from foreign parts. The technology of direct satellite broadcasting has eliminated the problem of lack of frequencies and facilitated the differentiation of national and regional television cultures in homogenous language areas. Satellite television, meanwhile, has contributed practically nothing to the processes of globalization.

The regionalization of the media in geo-linguistic areas: 'Huntington' on the small screen

American television researcher Joseph D. Straubhaar objects vigorously to suggestions that globalization is the core paradigm informing the development of communication and the media. Straubhaar refers to Marjorie Ferguson's contribution to the myth of globalization (see Introduction): '[A] more significant phenomenon than [the] idea of globalization, per se, may well be the "regionalization" of television into multi-country markets linked by geography, language and culture. These might more accurately be called geocultural markets, rather than regional markets, since not all these linked populations, markets and cultures are geographically contiguous.'[37]

This qualifying remark points out that, for example, immigrants can also use the satellite networks of the home country and we are thus dealing with a geo-cultural rather than regional phenomenon in the sense of cross-border media use within world regions (see chapter 7).

Basically, however, authors like Ferguson and Straubhaar have turned the conceptions of globalization traditionally associated with the media on their head. In their view, globalization is little more than a pipe dream of Western media capital – while regionalization of the media is the reality throughout the non-European world. This thesis is in fact backed up by many empirical indicators. Yet while 'globalization' has exercised minds the world over, only a small number of researchers occupied with the international and comparative development of television has been initiated into what is practically occult knowledge. It is not these scholars, but their colleagues in the major disciplines of political science and sociology, who are setting the tone of the globalization debate the world over. Despite the fact that the media, alongside the economy, is viewed as the central feature of globalization, scholars fail to pay sufficient attention to media studies scholarship (see Introduction).

Because international audiences extending across linguistic boundaries are often too small and elitist to be significant, the indirect consequences of globalization are still more important than the direct ones. The key development of the contemporary era is not the tuning in of Asia, Africa and Latin America to Western programmes (or vice versa). Instead, the technology and style of the modern Western television industry have been emulated and developed further in other countries and regions of the world.[38]

For around a decade, social scientists have been preoccupied with the phenomenon of 'new regionalism'. This refers to the increase in informal, non-hierarchical, comprehensive and multi-dimensional interactions in various fields of economy and society.[39] While 'old regionalism' was clearly dominated by relations between governments, the new regionalism is based on networks and interactions between societies within the various world regions. This includes political networks between NGOs as well as the transmission and use of media beyond state boundaries.

Australian media studies scholars John Sinclair, Elizabeth Jacka and Stuart Cunningham assume, as does Joseph Straubhaar, that the growth of regional media markets is more significant than the advance of (mainly English-language) globalization.[40] They argue that while Western cultural influences are indeed absorbed and integrated via media in geo-linguistically homogenous regions such as South Asia or Latin America, they are ultimately transformed into new national and regional products. An autonomous culture of television news and native film and television productions has worked to resist the 'cultural imperialism' of Western globalization (see chapter 4, p. 83).

The number of television and radio stations in Asia, Africa, Latin America and the Middle East, most of them privately owned, has in fact increased greatly over the last ten to fifteen years. Modern media cultures have developed in the various world regions, in societies often authoritarian in character but featuring spaces of liberalism, through a mixture of Western news *formats* and indigenous news *content*. The 'regionalization of globalization' is thus palpably different in nature from what Roland Robertson calls 'glocalization'. Far from being an equal mixture of internal and external influences, national or regional matters dominate content, a straightforward consequence of the fact that the makers and consumers of the new regional media remain within their own particular worlds.

While many small languages are dying out worldwide, the major world languages such as English, Chinese (Han), Arabic and Spanish are spreading and becoming increasingly influential. In India, dozens of television programmes in Hindi, transmitted across the national borders, have been made in recent years. The Arab world, Latin America and South Asia are undergoing a similar regionalization of their televisual landscapes. Europe is far ahead of these regions as far as political and economic interconnections are concerned, but European media exist only in rudimentary form, as the linguistic differences are too great. Both Latin America and the Indian sub-continent have the notion of democracy in common, are integrating rapidly into the world economy, and cross-border media networks are far more advanced than in Europe. The countries of the Arab world also have much in common in terms of political culture, and although they have not yet achieved democracy, here too powerful forces are working to achieve a common media landscape. How this will impact on democratization is as yet unclear (see p. 75).

The numerous television programmes of one of the largest providers in South Asia, Zee TV, are at present popular in countries such as Pakistan, Nepal, Bangladesh and Burma. The Pakistani advertising industry uses this Indian network to ensure advertisements reach customers in Pakistan.[41] Other Indian networks such as those of Asianet target the Malayalam-speaking consumers of South India or the Indian diaspora in the Arabian Gulf region.[42] One might be tempted to consider Indian television a purely commercial phenomenon. Manas Ray and Elizabeth Jacka, however, have pointed out that the government of Bangladesh, for example, which represents a very small segment of the country's super-rich, is extremely concerned about the influence of middle-class consumerism, reflected with particular force in Indian television films, because it may encourage social unrest in the poverty-stricken country.[43] Indian television is a challenge to the Islamic ideal of equality and justice, through which the upper class in Bangladesh, which used to dominate the country's public television, attempts to paper over class differences.

Latin America and the Caribbean are further examples of advancing regionalism in the field of satellite television. The English-speaking Caribbean has been a testing ground for regional cross-border radio and television broadcasts for decades. Long before the age of satellite, states such as Cuba had significant problems stopping terrestrial radio and television signals, unwanted from its point of view, from penetrating its borders. Cuban media users have always had access to broadcasts prohibited for reasons of state.[44] In contrast to the situation in South Asia, the media on offer in the Caribbean has long consisted of a mixture of news and entertainment; there is a very long tradition in this region of accessing information about one's home country via regional media interconnections.

In Latin America, the regionalization of the media industry has taken very different forms, which often tend to resemble the entertainment-centred media culture of South Asia rather than the situation in the Middle East or even the Caribbean. The central trend in this world region consists of the commercialization of Latin American television by the big media enterprises Globo and Televisa. Their strong focus on profits, but also their close connections with ruling elites, have tended to make independent and controversial news and information programmes a scarce commodity. Small alternative media try to keep up with the commercial sector through regional cooperation, but this is almost impossible, especially in the field of television, because of the high production costs. Radio ventures are thus the main actors in this field.[45]

Commercial motives are a significant factor in the production and use of television in all the world regions described here. To the extent that capital flows in the world's media sectors cross state borders at all, they usually remain – leaving to one side Euro-American 'giant mergers' between media enterprises – within a regional milieu characterized by linguistic and cultural ties (see chapter 9). If we can make out a new border-crossing trend in the field of satellite television, it is 'new regionalism', which is advancing far more vigorously than large-scale globalization. National television broadcasters are as a rule still more popular than foreign, even those from close regional neighbours.[46] They are being supplemented, however, by a visible and rapidly growing use of networks based in regional neighbours – a development which, as we have seen, does not apply to those from 'far-away lands'. While there is no direct, scientifically proven connection between media influence and identity, it is highly likely that the current state of satellite television markets across the world tends to favour national and regional rather than global identities. The European and US television markets remain largely within national contexts of consumption, though small-scale regional border traffic is also common in Europe and Canadian television viewers watch American networks. Yet openness to foreign satellite networks remains very limited and is typically 'undermined' in Europe by a strong fixation on dubbed or subtitled American film and television film imports which seemingly hinders European consumption of foreign language television (see chapter 4). Border crossing is for the most part limited to linguistic sub-regions.

The much-vaunted reversal of the North–South global news flow by means of networks such as the market-leading Arab news channel al-Jazeera remains the exception, limitation to national or at most regional media discourse the rule. The media and media empires of satellite television unleash their culture-changing force, if they have any, where they are understood: in a specific region (and among the associated 'diaspora'). From the point of view of globalization, this new regionalism is thus a double-edged sword. New points of resistance to a global culture (for the sake of simplicity let us characterize it through terms such as 'human rights' and 'democracy') may develop, rooted in the new dynamics of regional interaction conveyed by the media. Is satellite television thus a kind of catalyst for Samuel Huntington's 'clash of civilizations'?

In the early 1990s, Samuel Huntington produced a thesis which has enjoyed much prominence since then. He predicted that following the end of the East–West conflict the world would no longer be dominated by the ideological struggles of earlier times, but by a 'clash of civilizations'. Its key characteristic would be the collision of 'the West' with 'Confucian China' and the 'Islamic world'.[47] Huntington's views are reminiscent of the earlier theory of cultural areas produced by Oswald Spengler. Despite its popularity with a broad public, Huntington's theory has received a mainly critical reception in scholarly circles.[48] One of the key criticisms asserts that Huntington sees cultures as determining world politics, rather than grounding his analysis in concrete actors and socio-political conditions. These create the real conflicts by using cultures, which are generally very heterogeneous and which can be understood in various ways, as the ideological building blocks of one-sided interpretations.

Despite all the criticisms of Huntington, scholars have as yet made little progress in explaining the relationship between the thesis of the 'clash of civilizations' and the actually observable phenomenon of 'new regionalism'. The relations between culture and communication in this new regionalism have been comprehensively neglected. Does advancing globalization refute Huntington's views or are they confirmed by regionalization with an anti-globalist tenor? The American political scientist is surely right to point to language, culture, religion and civilization as the breeding grounds of political ideologies. Huntington, however, misinterprets the salience of these things, seeing complex political and social processes merely as products of a particular culture. Yet at the end of the day culture – a dimension embracing the values, norms and modes of thought and behaviour characteristic of groups – is itself the result of many social, economic and political processes. Cultures do influence these processes, but in their entirety, as complexes of often contradictory subcultures, not as distantly perceived stereotypes à la Huntington.

Communication and the mass media are constitutive elements in the formation of culture. Writers such as Antonio Gramsci and Hannah Arendt, whose work on Italian fascism and German National Socialism emphasized the evolution and effects of ideology and propaganda,[49] and more recent cultural studies authors such as Stuart Hall, suggest that those political and social forces with the power to impose their definition of culture have a crucial impact on the course of political development.[50] The communicative character of culture consists not only of processes of encoding and decoding of cultural signs, that is, of the definition or construction of culture, but also of the more or less successful dissemination and public enforcement of certain definitions.

It is no coincidence that Islamists representing conservative values, whose popularity increased in the 1980s and 1990s in much of the Islamic world at the expense of Islamic reformers and modernists, are also skilled media tacticians. They use so-called small media such as video to propagate their aims while evading state censorship.[51] Notably, they deploy Western media and the global public sphere in order to raise their political profile in their own countries as, supposedly, the only alternative to the existing systems. They dominate the traditional communicative fora such as the marketplace and the mosque.[52] The ethnicization of politics in the former Yugoslavia was also encouraged, if not induced or even caused, by the vigorous communicative proliferation of particularistic ideologies.

At bottom, Huntington's apodictic of a conflict rooted in innate differences between world cultures and religions such as Islam, Confucianism and the West denies the communicative character of culture, its capacity for interpretation and change. Huntington fails to recognize that many of the anti-Western tendencies in the Islamic world are anchored in misperceptions. In this sense, the 'lack of communication' between cultures is more striking than the 'clash of civilizations'.[53] Cultural globalization will depend to a great extent upon how the cultural balance of power, which is itself largely identical with the communicative balance of power, develops.

The nation-state remains at the heart of the media. At the same time, broadcasting and televisual spaces of a regional and geo-cultural hue are increasingly vigorous. While these traverse national boundaries, they come to a stop at the borders of the linguistic, historical and cultural past. They have the potential to reinforce the formation of nationalistic and 'civilizational' identities. Old political loyalties continue to dominate the new regional televisual settings, as Sinclair, Jacka and Cunningham correctly state.[54] This is apparent not least in the fact that the regionalization of television, at least according to such observers as the human rights organization Freedom House, has failed to increase the number of free media systems during the last fifteen years (see chapter 8, p. 149). Once again, regional proximity leads media organizations to avoid criticizing the authoritarian governments of neighbouring states. Media empires in Latin America, South Asia or the Arab world[55] represent an initial expanding of horizons beyond national media. They impart knowledge of new lifestyles and showcase a media pluralism that promotes democratic ideas.

At the same time, however, something quite different is happening. The regional level of media functions to stem the flow of influences from globalization. Experience worldwide shows that overfeeding the public with a skyrocketing number of native-language television channels, transmitted and received via the various means of distribution (cable, terrestrial-digital and satellite), has blunted if not destroyed the great majority of consumers' hunger for truly global programmes and utterly different discourses and perspectives, which could play such a key role in optimizing the cultural and political progress of a given country. Satellite technology has contributed to a renaissance of national television and a 'new regionalism' within geo-cultural areas. Whether this regionalism can be penetrated by globalization or will oppose and neutralize it is as yet uncertain.

The case of al-Jazeera: an 'Arab CNN'?

The development of the Arab satellite television station al-Jazeera is a prime example of the differing forms and effects of the 'new regionalism' characteristic of satellite television. Having started life as a small broadcaster based in the emirate of Qatar on the Persian Gulf, al-Jazeera became the leading news network within a few years of its foundation in 1996 in a booming satellite television market of more than twenty Arab states. Al-Jazeera is both a product of globalization and a quite independent development. It has largely adopted the aesthetics of American news and talk-show formats and adheres to a thoroughly Western media ethics privileging veracity and pluralism, making it a trail-blazer for democracy. As an Arab network, al-Jazeera nonetheless operates primarily with Arab sources, tackles Arab topics and is preoccupied with the perspectives of an Arab audience. In terms of content, it is also biased to some extent towards the modes of perception typical of Arab political culture, particularly in cases of regional or international conflict, without making enough effort to include a diversity of standpoints from around the world.

Al-Jazeera has been described as the most significant 'Arab party'. Given the lack of functioning democracies and institutions, some commentators assume, Arab cross-border satellite television is taking on the function of intermediary between state and society. Authoritarian Arab governments have frequently intervened over the last ten years after receiving an earful of unaccustomed and unambiguous criticism from al-Jazeera. Liberal intellectuals and above all average television consumers were and are enthusiastic about the network, viewing it as the greatest breakthrough in the media world so far for freedom of speech, the democratic agenda and a wide range of views critical of governments.

Al-Jazeera is an example of how, in the new world of cross-border satellite television, the smallest of changes may have major effects. The decision by the Emir of Qatar, Sheikh Hamad bin Khalifa al-Thani, to take on a large chunk of the editorial staff of the BBC Arabic service and offer them the chance to run an independent station in Qatar in 1996 was probably an attempt to promote the image of Qatar as a modern country. Before long, al-Jazeera, which eluded direct censorship by other states, reached the entire Arab world. Following the attacks on New York and Washington on 11 September 2001, the network became the most important informational bridge between the Arab world and the international public. An Arab medium succeeded in breaking into the global public sphere, still dominated, decades after the great UNESCO debate on the New World Information Order (see chapter 2, p. 26, and chapter 8, p. 143), by the major Western news agencies and media. Al-Jazeera reversed the North–South news divide. It transmitted pictures of terrorists, theatres of war and victims – while the global top brass talked politics on its programmes. The leading contemporary statesmen and -women and many figures from public life have had and continue to have their say on the network, considered the key point of access to more than 200 million Arabs worldwide. Al-Jazeera is a star in the firmament of global media interconnectivity. The network fits all the criteria of the new era. Above and beyond system linkages, it visibly influences information cultures in the Arab region and worldwide and thus appears to embody an almost prototypical form of 'glocalization'.

Though it is mainly images and video material from al-Jazeera that are re-transmitted in the West, and less often editorial content, an Arab medium is at least now frequently quoted as a source. The global dialogue appears to have got off the ground at last. Al-Jazeera is even taking a step further. Not only has it contributed to connectivity through satellite broadcasts and to system change by means of a changed regional and global news culture, it also wishes to promote system interdependence. At any rate, the network has a comprehensive and up-to-the-minute English-language news website, and plans to furnish its programmes with English subtitles in order to tap global markets. This, however, is where the problem starts.

For even its English-language online journalism can hardly conceal the fact that al-Jazeera is increasingly becoming the voice of pan-Arab resistance to the United States and Israel. Its global leanings have been suppressed in the wake of the crisis sparked off by the events of 11 September 2001 – the 'War against Terror', as the government of George W. Bush calls it – in favour of a new pan-Arab nationalism. In view of al-Jazeera's particularly impressive contributions to the liberalization of the Arab public sphere, criticism of the network was long limited mainly to the US government. Increasingly, though, the possible ideological distortion of Arab satellite television is also a matter of controversy among scholars and Arab journalists. In reality, the epithet applied to al-Jazeera of 'CNN of the Arab world' explains little, especially given that American media proved extremely biased during the Iraq War of 2003 (see chapter 2, p. 46).

The international perception of al-Jazeera, the leading Arab news network based in Qatar, can be divided into two phases. Before the attacks on the World Trade Center and the Pentagon on 11 September 2001, al-Jazeera was praised in the Western world as a democratic breakthrough in television; after the attacks critics increasingly attacked the network for directing propaganda against the US and Israel and bolstering terrorism. Turning first to the democratic agenda, it is striking that there are almost no robust academic content analyses of the network, and none at all dealing with its treatment of the topic of democracy. Since its establishment in 1996, al-Jazeera has without doubt made pathbreaking contributions to democratization in the Arab world. It was the first broadcaster which dared to criticize Arab governments. The conflictual style of debate characteristic of many programmes has been singled out for praise as a major step towards a public political culture.[56]

A recent analysis and evaluation of the English-language *aljazeera.net* has however turned up some sobering findings.[57] It claims that on *aljazeera.net* the issue of internal political development towards democracy is largely drowned out by a focus on the problems of American and Israeli foreign policy. Contributions dealing concretely with democratization in the Arab world can be counted on the fingers of one hand. The issue of 'Arab reform' has a more central position, but there is a failure to link it concretely with specific countries and to a political programme and vision. The medium's ideological fixations, which enable the airing of a range of opinions, are less striking than the limited scope and lack of sophistication of the democracy agenda, which remains only loosely connected to the problems of the individual Arab states. Even in the key field of human rights, as another analysis has revealed, in recent years *aljazeera.net* reported a good deal more about American, British and Israeli than about Arab torture, though it has published at least some articles critical of countries such as Morocco, Tunisia and Bahrain. In its current form, *aljazeera.net* is certainly in no position to call itself an 'Arab party of democracy'.

Al-Jazeera's programming certainly includes a large number of discussions in which Arab governments are criticized, and this continues to represent a special potential of the broadcaster to bolster democratization. It must also be admitted that we lack thorough empirical analyses, so that we can only identify trends. The current trend suggests that after 11 September 2001, both in al-Jazeera's programming and its Internet presence, the democracy agenda is increasingly being overlain by the occupation agenda.

Repulsing the external 'enemy' from two Arab lands in particular – Iraq and the Palestinian areas – clearly unites forces within the Arab world with differing views of democracy in a kind of journalistic moratorium. As far as the international reporting of al-Jazeera and the other satellite networks is concerned, since 11 September not only the US and UK, but also independent Arab journalists and scholars, among others, have been persistently critical. Commentators identify the

Arab network's chief merit as its ability to make images of Palestinian, Iraqi and other victims of the American-British and Israeli occupations, which rarely appeared in Western media, accessible to a global public. Its capacity to represent authentic counter-positions through interviews with, for example, the American or Israeli government, also comes in for praise. Dissenting opinions are being aired for the first time on Arab television, and here al-Jazeera in particular has distinguished itself from the leading American news network Fox News. During the Iraq War of 2003 for example, Fox failed to interview politicians and commentators from the Arab world and instead openly supported the stance of the American government.[58]

Al-Jazeera is however considered less objective in its privileging of a pan-Arabist agenda in the selection of news. The vast majority of editorial contributions, while rightly criticizing the injustice of Israeli and American policies, vastly understate the role of Arab states and regimes and of privatized violence (terror). They devote too little airtime to Israeli victims and stir up emotions in partisan fashion. Most scholars agree on these matters – though they draw quite different conclusions from them. The French Panos study has shown that *aljazeera.net* is one of the media in the Arab world most critical of the US.[59] Mamoun Fandy argued as early as 2000 that al-Jazeera, with the exception of its news programmes, embodies the views of a novel alliance consisting of nationalist Baathists and Islamists[60] – a criticism still being made by Arab journalists.[61] Muhammad Ayish states that al-Jazeera is failing to uphold professional objectivity whenever it becomes the mere reflection of a pan-Arabist consensus.[62]

Mohammed El-Nawawy and Adel Iskandar accept that the network is biased, but call this 'contextual objectivity': al-Jazeera has to be pro-Arab to make up for the pro-American and pro-Israeli tenor of Western media.[63] Nawawy and Iskandar are right to underline the sense of relief and fascination which al-Jazeera has inspired in the Arab world as partisan of the Arab cause. The West's hegemonic control of the information flow, embodied in the large news agencies and broadcasters, has been broken for the first time. Salameh Nematt suggests that the Arab television stations represent, through their one-sided imagery of the victims of American and Israeli violence, the continuation of a pan-Arab stance, which has increasingly diminished in recent years along with the Arab League.[64]

This analysis is however insufficient, for the new pan-Arabist momentum is more than a mere continuation. Traditional pan-Arabism was anchored in the opportunistic stance of Arab nation-states vis-à-vis the Palestinians. The national interests of states such as Egypt frequently predominated, diminishing their solidarity with the Palestinians, any remnants of which were finally swept away by the Camp David peace treaty between Egypt and Israel of 1979. The sympathies of the Arab peoples with the Palestinians, meanwhile, remained unbroken; any peace with Israel was a 'cold peace' as long as it failed to find a workable answer to the question of Palestinian statehood. The reportage of al-Jazeera and the other Arab satellite broadcasters, all of which are similar in tone, though some couch their reports in less dramatic terms than others, captures the people's emotional views more clearly than the old institutions of pan-Arabism. In this sense, the Panos study is quite right to describe the Arab media as a 'platform for collective identity and imagination'.[65]

Hazem Saghieh, a journalist at the Arab daily *al-Hayat*, is one of those to argue that following the decline of the major institutions and unions of the Nasser era, Arab satellite television functions as an intermediary between state and society and represents a new stage of the pan-Arab project. He also believes, however, that crossing the fine line between objectivity and partisanship, which is theoretically necessary, at least in relation to the conflict in the Middle East and Iraq, has failed. The network's media populism, which involves 'regurgitating' the views of citizens, has, he suggests, brought about a high degree of politicization but reinforced the stagnation of political ideas.[66]

We can provisionally conclude that the establishment of al-Jazeera in 1996 was in many respects an at least indirect consequence of globalization. The network furnished a mass Arab audience not only with a Western aesthetics of news, but also a pluralist and sometimes controversial anti-authoritarian understanding of the media as a 'fourth estate' vis-à-vis the Arab state. It also helped beat a path, along with other news networks founded later, out of the one-way street of the international news industry, dominated by the US and Western Europe and by networks such as CNN or the BBC, in which the global news agencies hold such a hegemonic position.

At the same time, it is evident that the network is tied to the Arab market and – despite having an English-language website – to the Arabic language and the ideologies, perspectives, opinions and stereotypes found in mainstream Arab culture. This renders the network's output the polar opposite of the often equally one-sided reports produced by Western networks (see chapter 2). What is new about the current situation, in comparison with the era before the introduction of satellite television, is the technological-spatial overlap in the reception of television broadcasts featuring quite different ways of seeing the world. In principle, the consumer can access these at the touch of a button without leaving the sofa. It is becoming clear that this 'pluralist patina' of broadcasts in various languages is insufficient to justify the euphoria about the globalization of television. Small, sometimes minuscule information elites are the only ones who do in fact access these various channels, a group which in principle has always been capable of informing itself of differing perspectives on world politics.

The task which remains is to make perspectival diversity in the global age a concern of individual television cultures and broadcasters, that is, to encourage internal rather than external pluralism. The capacity of a long-standing pioneering network such as al-Jazeera to connect up to the wider world has clearly diminished in recent years. The regional pressure exercised by markets and political cultures has increased. Clearly, the 'new regionalism' is at times quite impervious to globalization.

4

Film and Programme Imports – Entertainment Culture as the Core of Media Globalization

Entertainment culture is the central feature of contemporary globalization. In contrast to the media provision of news, which entails the exchange of information and opinions of a mainly political nature, imported films, music and literature impose strict limits upon local attempts to domesticate globalization. While a news report within the context of international reporting may be adapted to national political preferences almost at will (see chapter 2), imported films, for example, are near-impossible to manipulate. Meanings may be changed by cutting scenes, dubbing or subtitles, but the film's core messages still reach consumers in the importing country. Music is fundamentally resistant to alteration.

Entertainment culture is almost universally popular because of its capacity to compress and aggrandize the quotidian (love, sex, violence, action, etc.). It is one of the core elements of media globalization because its content is fairly resistant to manipulation in the process of international and intercultural transfer. In the words of the Hamburg media studies scholars Anja Herzog and Uwe Hasebrink, 'entertainment is more international than information'.[1] From the standpoint of globalization theory it may be argued that the combination of universal appeal and resistance to local manipulation endows entertainment culture with the greatest potential of all cross-border communicative system linkages to bring about cultural change. This is why both public and scholarly discourse tends to look to this sphere for evidence of globalization effects: American pop music is considered evidence of the trend towards a uniform global culture and Hollywood films a portent of the Westernization of global cultural settings.

The aim of this chapter is by no means to deny the significance of a global entertainment and consumer culture, but to relativize and evaluate it. American and Western entertainment culture is not the all suppressing and dominating force often portrayed by both advocates and opponents of globalization. Nor can the processes of change and transformation shaping the cultures of this world simply be understood as adaptations to an encroaching Western culture, though these imports often accelerate cultural change. Certain aspects of what appears to be the globalization of culture in fact constitute the modernization of traditional cultures. The seemingly global 'Other' is the modern 'Self'.

Who's afraid of Uncle Sam? Relativizing American cultural hegemony

Much criticized, seemingly outdated and yet hugely vital, the thesis of 'cultural imperialism' has survived every shift of theoretical paradigm, from modernization and dependence theory to globalization theory. Rare is the debate on the globalization of communication and culture that manages to do without the term, and the point of reference is almost always the asserted and assumed influence of American cultural exports on the other cultures of the world. The media, so it sometimes seems, are merely the conduits of a US hegemony operating with cultural rather than military means. The monopolization of 'minds' is evoked as a neo-imperial strategy of domination – films instead of armed force, entertainment rather than dollar imperialism.

The notion of thoroughgoing US dominance and global significance is taken for granted in conservative circles in the US. The words of the well-known *Washington Post* columnist Charles Krauthammer are representative: 'We dominate every field of human endeavor from fashion to film to finance. We rule the world culturally, economically, diplomatically and militarily as no one has since the Roman Empire.'[2]

A pertinent indication of the hegemonic position of the United States is the European television and feature film market. In the field of television, the exchange of European films is almost non-existent. In multilingual Europe, with its small and medium-sized markets, the exchange of European films has to be promoted 'artificially', that is, through political intervention by the EU. American films meanwhile make up a large portion of programming in most European countries (see below).

What could be more natural than to assume that globalization, at least in the cultural sector, far from developing according to the model of concentric circles – from local through (European) regional to global – and involving equal exchange of local and regional cultural goods worldwide, in fact means the step-by-step erosion of local and regional cultures as a uniform American global culture spreads across the world. The principle of decentralized globality is replaced in this unipolar cultural model by that of the village-like omnipresence of the hegemonic culture. In the age of spaces shrunk by media technologies and of increased cultural contact as borders fall away, American entertainment dominates culture in the 'global village'. This is surely not what Canadian communication studies scholar Marshall McLuhan, who invented the concept, had in mind. As early as the 1960s, he described the mass media as a perfected form of the technological extension of the human sensory apparatus and predicted the rise of a collective global consciousness.[3]

The United States indubitably leads the world in many realms of culture – one need only think of the fact that around 75 per cent of current Nobel prize winners come from the US. American cultural products are more globally available than those of any other national culture. Yet we cannot simply take it as given that this hegemony produces an imperial suppression of indigenous cultures. These two features – leading position and hegemony – are often confused. Certain studies, now considered classics of communication research, on the effect of American film exports in other parts of the world, point to the power of peripheral cultures to resist the seemingly hegemonic culture.

In their studies of the reception of the soap operas *Dallas* and *Dynasty*, Tamar Liebes and Elihu Katz have shown that media use is an active process, enabling media information to be embedded in local systems of reference and meaning. On this view, systems of use vary between individuals as well as between cultures.[4] The social 'effects' of media representations are not regarded solely as linear processes of manipulation of input and output, but as processes of 'negotiation' between the symbolic resources of the audience and the symbolic components of the text.[5] Media content is not inevitably decoded as intended by its producers, but is subject to a process of negotiation over symbolic meanings.[6] Regardless of the textual parameters (topics, frames, etc.) media users may generate discourses that pick up from where the media product left off and develop its concerns further. For the most part, these are not generated in the original foreign context of the international media product, accessible only with difficulty because of the vast distances constraining the consumer, but in the local or national milieu. An international comparative study of the use of soap operas such as *Dallas* – the epic about a family of Texan oil barons – identified differing associated social discourses.

The assumption that media users' reference systems are thoroughly entrenched within homogenous sociopolitical cultures has proven characteristic of comparative research on media use in different cultures. Observations of and interviews with viewers of *Dallas* in the Netherlands, the Federal Republic of Germany and Algeria in the 1980s have shown that the content of discourses triggered by identical media products of foreign origin may be diametrically opposed. In the Netherlands, *Dallas* was positively valued as a counter-pole to the loss of family and community values in Dutch society.[7] In the German Federal Republic, the series functioned as a projection of still highly patriarchal German family structures[8] and in Algeria as an affirmation of the patriarchal extended family and as a warning against the gradual dissolution of these structures.[9]

In other realms of the entertainment industry the product for export is less resistant and it is possible to adapt it to foreign markets in a more targeted way than with film exports. Sports advertising is an example. In such sectors, significant changes are starting to emerge in the process of import and export, even at the level of production. Are Western sports stars such as Michael Jordan, David Beckham or Oliver Kahn really the same media personalities in Asia, where they are utterly idolized, as in their own countries? No, for numerous quotidian stories and scandals taken up by the media in the West – Kahn's divorce, Beckham's indiscretions – are lost on the way to Asia, where these personalities function as pure idols and advertising icons. Does the fact that some people in China have recently begun to celebrate 'Christmas' mean that the country is on the verge of a major wave of Christianization? Hardly. The end of the year is celebrated in rhythm with the world economy, but with culture-specific interpretations of meaning.

In sum, Western cultural goods are nothing other than raw material, which the various forces of the market – from Western traders to the non-European individual – more or less do as they like with. While, however, decontextualization à la Liebes and Katz may significantly temper the effect of cultural imperialism, it cannot entirely undermine hegemonic system change and suppression of culture, as it is impossible to prevent the original meaning from being transferred in many cases. 'Context' is not everything – facts matter too, even if this means fictional content.

If, for instance, the death penalty is imposed for murder in an American film, this is a cultural message that cannot be dubbed away. When all is said and done, the import and export of films is a combination of the authentic presence of a particular culture, such as that of the United States, in global space, and a local reinterpretation, though this cannot eliminate narratives entirely. Even universalia such as love, sex and jealousy, core features of all entertainment cultures, take on shifting normative forms in different cultures at different times; these enter into competition in processes of cultural import and export. Who can state with any certainty that the local context of interpretation always exercises a more powerful effect than the messages presented in the imported film? It is rather more likely that imports sometimes promote a shift towards global values, while at other times cultural absorption holds sway. It is precisely this combination of circumstances which makes Roland Robertson's notion of 'glocalization', the mixing of global and local cultures (see chapter 1), a useful theorem for grasping the processes of cultural import and export.

The polarity that marks the debate on cultural imperialism, which fluctuates between the omnipresence of American (or Western) culture and the omnipotence of the user (Liebes and Katz) requires us to take a sensible theoretical middle course. Liebes and Katz cannot exclude the possibility that the cultural exporter will leave an indelible impression on his product, which is comparatively resistant to manipulation. Just as it is vital to get to grips theoretically with manipulation itself, we cannot afford to neglect the manipulation of the manipulators by means of an intercultural deconstruction of the media text by the user. The dissatisfying but realistic conclusion must therefore be: Western imports do not necessarily but *may* work to change cultures. Their messages may take on force and suppress indigenous cultural achievements, depending on the individual, social and cultural state of affairs in the receiving country; their universal validity is by no means guaranteed.

In light of this, it seems paradoxical that one of the key secrets of the success of American films in the international context in fact consists in their low level of cultural attachment and tremendous potential for universalization. Hollywood stories are often structured in a complex and exciting way, but require only a minimum of cultural knowledge. Michael Thiermeyer explains this by claiming that Hollywood adopted this style in the highly multicultural milieu produced by immigration to America in the 1920s and 1930s, when the US film industry was booming, in order to survive commercially.[10] On this view, American films' suitability for globalization is the long-term consequence of an early multicultural and democratic experience, which had a culture-shaping effect, and indeed to a greater degree than elsewhere.

How, though, even from a purely theoretical point of view, can a de-cultured film export industry suppress culture in other countries? Is it possible for American film exports to be globally successful and at the same time to have little influence on culture? The apparent logic of this idea fails to capture how de-cultured commercialization may also work to suppress culture. Here, the main effect is not Americanization, but the economization and de-differentiation of world cultures in the process of globalization.

That the spread of cultures is determined in part by economic as well as cultural strength is all too often forgotten in the globalization debate. While the globalization of the economy does take centre stage in this debate, it is carefully kept separate from the issue of cultural development. Anyone that assumes, however, that cultures, especially entertainment cultures, interact *in themselves* is ignoring the field of activity of the 'cultural entrepreneur', as Lebanese political scientist Ghassan Salamé calls the producers, distributors and cultural policy leaders of the world.[11] American film and programme exporters in the film and television industry simply have at their disposal the largest amount of capital and the best apparatus of distribution and advertising agencies. This enables them to position their films and music as effectively as possible on the world market through advertising campaigns and an offensive market policy.

The Hollywood film industry, moreover, has the invaluable advantage that its productions have as a rule already paid for themselves on the large domestic market and are making a profit. A variable pricing policy featuring affordable prices can thus be calculated when exporting films, even to the poorest countries. Nonetheless, the export sector is increasingly important to many major American film production companies. Again and again, the academic literature dealing with the reasons for the export success of American films has placed emphasis on comparative competitive advantage. As a result of the enormous size of the US market, willingness to invest and product quality are on the up.[12] This advantage is economic, not cultural in nature, and it conceals more or less effectively the fact that even many consumers are showing signs of weariness with American mass-produced goods. Hollywood has its crises too.

In many states, on the other hand, authoritarian governments, ethnic-nationalist and religious-nationalist movements are all 'cultural entrepreneurs'. All are struggling for what Italian Marxist and theoretician Antonio Gramsci described as cultural hegemony (see chapter 3). The American entertainment industry is probably less concerned with the classic issue of the installation and maintenance of ideology as an instrument of domination, which was Gramsci's focus, than with creating a broad cultural consensus for the sale of products. This intention can, however, be made politically useful, as shown by the significant role of American films in US international public relations.

American political scientist Robert J. Lieber and cultural studies scholar Ruth E. Weisberg see the spread of American cultural products as evidence of America's 'soft power'. The United States, they suggest, forces no one to consume its cultural exports – people do so of their own free will, and this is the best evidence of the special magnetism and appeal of American culture.[13] The concept of 'soft power' comes from Joseph S. Nye and was developed by this Harvard political scientist to complement the concept of US military 'hard power'.[14] In the context of the Iraq War of 2003, for example, Nye called for a shift, certainly valid in principle, away from the Bush administration's privileging of the armed forces and a return to a politics emphasizing the cultural appeal of the United States and its way of life. This would build on voluntary alliances. Nye's notion is that a superpower that produces compelling cultural ideas has an attraction for other cultures and societies; it is thus more likely to find favour with others when it comes to upholding its national political and economic interests. Such a power has far less to fear from centrifugal forces and cultural resentment, as exemplified by Islamists, than a purely exploitative power.

This is an attempt to come up with a set of normative and strategic objectives in order to safeguard future American pre-eminence, without massive confrontation and risk, into the twenty-first century. It should not necessarily be regarded as a description of the present state of affairs. Doubtless, much of American culture appeals to consumers in other countries. It is also clear that the United States' economic and political power makes it culturally pre-eminent, in line with the motto: 'Power makes you interesting.' The concept of 'soft power' is however not entirely correct. At present, as during all historical periods, American culture not only involves spontaneous appeal, but also requires the industrial production of fascination on a huge scale. This 'fabrication' of cultural allegiance is a profoundly communicative process based on adroit agenda-setting (who and what is 'in'?) and advertising campaigns, which no Hollywood film could do without.

If, however, we assume that the potential for cultural imperialism exists in theory, however diluted and economically based it may be: how influential are American film imports? It is striking that supporters of the thesis that American culture holds a dominant position tend to offer a very select range of evidence to back it up. As evidence of Hollywood's cultural power, Robert J. Lieber and Ruth E. Weisberg mention, for example, the large American share of European cinema markets, as high as 70 to 80 per cent in Germany and Italy.[15] The UNESCO World Culture Report 2000 confirmed that, in most countries, the United States is the major country of origin of cinema film imports.[16]

Authors like Lieber and Weisberg fail to acknowledge, however, that the number of American films on television is often significantly smaller. It is true that American feature films quite often make up from 50 to 80 per cent even of European television films.[17] Yet this state of affairs is due in significant part to the high production costs of feature films, which the individual European countries try to avoid by showing US productions. The situation with regard to television series and dramas is quite different. As a result of comparatively low production costs and high demand, most European television systems clearly favour national productions.[18] In almost a quarter of European countries the top ten is made up exclusively of national productions. The same applies to Arab television, where the average share of foreign films is very low, with the exception of a few, albeit popular, channels (MBC, ANN etc., see table 4.1).

Significantly, American market share in the states of Asia, Africa and Latin America is only rarely mentioned in the globalization debate, perhaps because the available figures ultimately fail to support the thesis of an American-dominated globalization. The available data is not satisfactory for all countries and some of the relevant comparative research projects are already more than ten years old. Nonetheless, it is apparent that, apart from states with an unusually high proportion of American films on television (for example Canada, Jamaica and many other Caribbean states), the share of US productions of total daily production tends to lie below 20 per cent. In many states in Asia and the Middle East it is even well below 10 per cent.[19] Hollywood exports have obviously failed to destroy Chinese, Indian or Arab film culture. In these parts of the world, home to half the global population, native productions dominate. Latin American states tend to import American television production ideas and genres more than Asian and Middle Eastern ones. Yet here too native adaptations and national productions utilizing these formats predominate – American programmes are bought in far less often.[20]

The process of globalization, limited here for the time being to the American export of entertainment culture, is obviously not a zero-sum

Table 4.1 Program production in Arab television organizations

Channel	Production in %		
	Local	Arab	Foreign
Jordanian Satellite Channel	80	18.5	1.5
Emirates Media			
1. Emirates Channel	40	40	20
2. Abu Dhabi Channel	70	30	10
3. Abu Dhabi Sport	30	35	35
Bahrain Satellite Channel	40	50	10
Tunisia's 7	70	30	0
Algerian TV	75	25	0
Saudi Channel (1)	53	47	0
Saudi Channel (2)	73	n/a	27
Sudan TV	79	15	6
Syrian Satellite Channel	100	0	0
Oman TV	50	25	20
Palestinian TV	n/a	n/a	n/a
Qatar TV	60–70	20–30	5–10
Kuwait TV	64–78	30.98	4.4
Jamahiriya Satellite Channel	70	30	0
Moroccan TV	61.5	19.9	18.6
Egyptian Satellite Channel 1	100	0	0
Egyptian Satellite Channel 2	100	0	0
Nile TV (International)	99.5	0	0.5
Nile News Channel	100	0	0
Nile Drama Channel	98.2	0	2.8
Nile Sport Channel	98	0	2
Nile Culture Channel	97.2	0	2.8
Nile Family and Children	98.5	0	1.5
Nile Varieties' Channel	99	0	1
A1 Manara Channel	60	0	40
Nile Higher Education Channel	100	0	0
Nile Educational Channel	100	0	0
Nile Information Channel	100	0	0
Mauritania TV	n/a	n/a	n/a
Yemen TV	60	30	10
A.R.T. NETWORK			
1. Varieties Channel	90	10	0
2. Sport Channel	10	30	60
3. Children's Channel (America)	30	10	60
4. Children's Channel (Europe)	45	10	45
5. Movies Channel (America)	30	70	0
6. Music Channel	70	30	0

Table 4.1 (Continued)

Channel	Production in %		
	Local	Arab	Foreign
7. Movies Channel	30	70	0
8. "As you like it" Channel	70	20	10
9. Iqra Channel (Riad)	70	15	15
10. Pedagogy Channel	95	5	0
11. Open Channel	90	10	0
12. ART Europe	75	25	0
13. ART America	85	15	0
14. ART Latino	85	15	0
15. ART Africa	70	15	15
MBC	43	18	39
LBC Sat.	82	5	13
LBC Europe	88	5	7
LBC America	87	9	4
LBC Australia	87	9	4
Sharjah Sat. Channel	30	55	15
Dubai Television	n/a	n/a	n/a
Ajman Channel 4	30	55	15
Orbit Network	n/a	n/a	n/a
Al Jazeera	80	5	15
Al Mustaqbil TV (Future)	n/a	n/a	n/a
ANN (Arab News Network)	65	0	35
Iraq Channel	95	5	0

Source: Arab States Broadcasting Union, 2000 (cited in Ayish 2003, p. 105 f.)

game, in which one party's profit (US) is the other's (the rest of the world's) loss. Native cultures may change, but they also often grow in a dynamic way, and they can use the new global sphere as an export market and thus massively increase their cultural radiance. People in countries such as China, the most rapidly growing military power with a high rate of economic growth, are not only anxious in the face of globalization, they are also gaining a new self-confidence. Cultural and film scholar Wang Ning, for example, reminds us of the tradition of Chinese films which have found success and acclaim in the West too, such as *Red Sorghum*, and regards the advance of American films on the Chinese market, now that China has joined the WTO, as a challenge, involving risks but also opportunities:

> [W]e cannot neglect the increasing penetration of weak (Third World) cultures, which finds particular embodiment in the current penetration

of Chinese film by the American film industry. [. . .] [B]ut on the other hand, more and more Chinese films are interesting the Western audience, thus highlighting and even globalizing the Chinese cultural and aesthetic spirit. [. . .] Since China is a large country with a splendid cultural heritage and film production, China ought to make greater contributions to the world, not only economically but also culturally.[21]

What the Chinese mean to do, the Latin American states have already succeeded in doing with their television soap operas, which are not only well represented on regional markets, but have also arrived in countries such as Russia and Germany. This is an indication of the potential for a non-American, non-Western form of globalization in the field of entertainment.[22] Even in the South, entertainment production may be globalized; at the very least, it cannot easily be driven out of native markets.

The Indian market, as open and capitalist as it is, has not as yet allowed American films to dominate on the big or small screen – quite the opposite. In India, 'Bollywood' – a hybrid term consisting of 'Bombay' and 'Hollywood', referring to the country's enormous film industry – has enjoyed decades of acclaim. 'Bollywood' now produces roughly as many films annually as the Hollywood original. Most Indian films are certainly far less globalizable than their American counterparts, because they tend to be closely bound up with national ways of life, clothing, myths and other cultural peculiarities.[23] Nevertheless, 'Bollywood' is a cultural bulwark for the south Asian sub-continent with its population of well over a billion. Its displacement by a foreign competitor is unimaginable.

Much the same applies to pop music markets and even the culture of food, part of entertainment culture in a certain sense. In cities such as Cairo, New Delhi, Beijing or Moscow there are certainly fast food restaurants such as McDonald's, and the international media lavishes a great deal of attention on every opening in a new location. Yet in comparison to native fast food chains, the American restaurants remain marginal. Eagerly frequented by well-off middle-class children, they ultimately remain no more than islands in the sea of native cuisine.

Under such circumstances, who's afraid of Uncle Sam? The case of South Korea shows, in paradigmatic fashion, how strong, yet at the same time how weak, America's position within the worldwide entertainment industry can be. While less than 10 per cent of prime time programmes are imported from the US,[24] in 1993 a record 84 per cent of takings from cinema ticket sales was generated by imported (overwhelmingly American) films.[25] Even in South Korea, however, the film industry, largely destroyed by the Second World War and the American occupation, has shown clear signs of revival over the last decade. It is not only new indigenous films that are enjoying great success. There is also strong resistance to American cultural imperialism in South Korea, sparked off, among other things, by aggressive competition from American film distributors.

It may be that Europe, because of its historical proximity to US culture, is more receptive to or at risk from its hegemonic tendencies. Or perhaps non-European cultures are subject to ever greater Americanization as they develop into industrial societies. At present, however, this utopia is very far from being a reality. Even if it is closer to being realized in the film industry than in television, cinematic culture can scarcely be regarded as representative. Data on the film industry should certainly not be referred to selectively to back up the globalization thesis.

The globalization of entertainment no doubt has relatively great potential to go beyond mere (technical) connectivity and induce societal and cultural changes. Yet 'glocal' adaptations at the level of production and consumption and an at least partial decline in the United States' economic pre-eminence are just as likely as further displacement of indigenous entertainment sectors, given that new centres of global cultural production are being established in Latin America and Asia.

Commentators have been too quick to proclaim the global victory of American culture, underestimating the vitality of many cultures, particularly in Asia, Africa and Latin America. What is more, the selectivity characteristic of their arguments rests upon the at least implicit assumption that American culture is simply superior, taking no account of the culture industry supporting it. Moreover, the approach is fixated on entertainment and consumer culture, above all film and pop music, while 'edifying' culture, that is, arts, literature or even humanities, is a mere footnote in the globalization debate.

The distortions of the globalization debate include the total lack of a balanced assessment of the inputs and outputs of globalization based on the various cultural sectors. Analysing the relationship between the complex subsystems of national and regional cultures and American culture would be a gargantuan task. Even leading scholars frequently subject the issue of globalization to a species of anecdotal empiricism which is incapable of clarifying theoretical concepts. The phenomenon of globalization is indisputably producing a well-nigh inexhaustible quantity of data, which academia, applying the methods of empirical social science, will need a decade to come to terms with. The failure to develop a systematics anchored in cultural theory seriously hampers debate and should be rectified as soon as possible.

One need do no more than glance at the best-seller list of the German magazine *Spiegel* for confirmation that, while American authors and publishers are strongly represented in Germany, they are far from dominant. In the up-market commercial literature business, they make up around a quarter of best-sellers at present.[26] The same certainly applies to the field of classical music and much of the plastic arts, in which American culture is strongly represented but by no means hegemonic. The United States has the most Nobel Prize winners in the natural sciences[27] because its universities enjoy the best equipment, pay the highest salaries and can buy in competence from around the world. The US has not, however, managed to produce the largest number of Nobel Prize winners for literature;[28] when all is said and done, in many fields of culture, quality cannot be planned, even when backed by economic power.

American cultural exports are strongly represented above all in highly commercial sectors of entertainment culture. Here, as in the commercial film and pop music business, cultural traditions play little role; attaining large profit margins and the power to produce and distribute are key. The issue of the global interactions between an American culture of globalization and indigenous cultures may thus arise only on certain cultural fronts. Before mulling over the 'for' and 'against' of American cultural hegemony, it is vital to produce an empirically robust foundation capable of undergirding such reflections.

How the globalization of entertainment culture helps permeable national cultures modernize

The extent to which the globalization of media and communication has the capacity to change cultures is an issue extending far beyond the problem of the market position of American entertainment exports. The *indirect* effects of the cross-border transfer of film and television on national and regional cultures may be more significant to assessing the cultural consequences of globalization. Is the content of indigenous cultural production changing under the influence of the new global connectivity, particularly through the increased import and export of films for the big and small screen? Can we discern a global influence even in places where native productions appear to exist and are in fact on the increase? Are these being brought into line with Western cultural models?

Bearing in mind the tripartite theory of possible cultural models of behaviour within globalization – adoption, rejection or adaptation of the imported cultures (see chapter 1, p. 9) – the key issue is clearly not simple forms of adoption of imported cultures, which usually means imitation of Western fashions. The challenge is to come to terms with the knotty issue of rejection or adaptation, in other words with localization and 'glocalization'. Roland Robertson's theorem of 'glocalization' has too often been trivialized. It in fact strives to explain the cultural processes involved when cultures come into contact. It is not, however, a magic formula for analysing any form of cultural development. Even in the age of globalization, many relatively autonomous developments take place in the countries and regions of this world.[29]

If native film and television productions are to avoid being throttled by imports, and perhaps even grow, the minimum requirement is that the culture be literate in the Gutenbergian sense. Total displacement of cultures through Western dominance, bringing them to the verge of obliteration, appears to be possible at most among so-called Indian or indigenous cultures, but not among book cultures such as the Chinese, Japanese, Persian or Arab. The MacBride Roundtable, an institutional successor to the intensive debate led by UNESCO on the 'New World Information Order' until into the 1980s (see chapter 2; and chapter 8, p. 143), noted that 'the lives, languages and cultures of indigenous peoples are at great risk of extinction amidst today's revolution in communication technologies'.[30]

Globalization proceeds on a quite different basis in literate cultures. Here, traditional forms of culture may persist, stored in the collective memory through an extensive body of written works.[31] Traditions may even experience a boom in the midst of globalization, as apparent in the comprehensive re-Islamization affecting many parts of the Islamic world. Headscarves were hardly to be seen in the Cairo cityscape of the 1960s, but are once again omnipresent, even among youth and at universities.

When we look more closely, however, apparent resistance to globalization is a complex process. Are we really dealing with the straightforward preservation of tradition and resistance to external forces? Or can we make out modernizing and even glocalizing elements? A daring thesis might assert that re-Islamization is an expression of glocalization, that is, an apparently anti-Western counter-culture into which elements of Western culture are mixed more or less through the back door.

This is quite obvious in the political sphere despite all the conflicts and contradictions. The 1979 Islamic Revolution in Iran was unable to eschew Western institutions such as a constitution and parliament. The fact that the majority grouping of the Muslim Brotherhood in Egypt and elsewhere has come out in favour of introducing a multiparty system, formerly regarded as an attack on the unity of Muslims, also indicates that the seemingly local or even anti-global may entail elements of the global. Absurd as it may sound, political Islam, the driving force of re-Islamization, in its various manifestations, from the moderate Muslim Brothers to Islamist terrorists, is a special form of the modernization of a stock of traditions. By no means does it involve the straightforward preservation of tradition.[32]

The relationship between many traditional or conservative social practices and modernity is marked by ambivalence. Wearing the Islamic headscarf may be either an expression of male repression and patriarchal subordination or an indication of a new form of feminism, which differentiates itself both from men and from the Western idea of emancipation, its model the 'new Muslim woman'.[33] These paradoxical combinations arise because the modern Islamist movement is in fact no longer at home in traditional, usually rural circumstances, but in the urban periphery of cities such as Cairo. As a result of the rural exodus to this bloated metropolis of almost 20 million people, old cultural paradigms remain fresh, while simultaneously synthesizing with the modern urban economy and the sociocultural movements taking shape in the city.

However, even if most Islamists are open to the use of modern information technology and are brilliant media tacticians[34] (where would Osama bin Laden be without his satellite telephone to organize the al-Qaeda network?), the anti-globalist and 'traditional' cultural sector is sceptical about cultural imports and every palpable expression of a 'Western' culture that challenges the definition of local authenticity, one of the key features of re-Islamization. The revisionist cultural and political movement in the Islamic countries, but also in much of Asia and Africa, is focused on a stock of traditional and quite often religious symbols. Western films, Hollywood, Western literature and music mark the boundaries of what it is willing to accept. Globalization of the economy, technology, including certain political technologies – all these get the green light. Globalization of cultural norms, values and behaviours, which have been components of the production of art and culture since time immemorial, even globally accessible entertainment culture – all are rejected out of hand.

It is of course profoundly simplistic to suggest that non-European societies merely wish to preserve a traditional identity. Differences in the understanding of culture are highly developed within each national culture. In a large number of developing countries, it is from the outset difficult to accurately assess the cultural situation because authoritarian governments impede the opening up and development of culture. Thanks in part to modern information and communication technologies, most national cultures have become more transparent. They are more open to external influences, which they then subject to a process of cultural assimilation. 'Islamic rap music' is hardly likely to develop but there is such a thing as Arab rap. Arab music has been characterized by cultural syncretism since the Second World War at the latest. Even famous musicians such as Egyptian singer Abd al-Halim Hafiz (1929–77) gave this the seal of approval, creating Euro-Arab fusions in both instrumentation and composition.[35]

Indian or Arab pop music show how a global cultural 'raw material', such as Hip Hop, the origins of which are 'Western', yet at the same time 'African', is taken up by non-European cultures and inserted into local contexts. Texts and music are altered and developed further in ways expressive of the local area or region. In this case, the main effect of Western imports consists not in how people deal with the imported product itself, but in the indirect effect of the import sector upon the native production of entertainment culture.

The mark of cultural globalization, rather than the transfer of cultural goods through import and export, is its influence on the indigenous entertainment industry, which it stimulates, generating new variations in form and style. In short, globalization ushers in comprehensive modernization.

As yet, very few of the commentators participating in the globalization debate have recognized that these processes of modernization are not, as often assumed, an expression of Westernization. Joseph S. Nye, one of the guiding intellectual forces of dependence theory, is an exception: 'People sometimes attribute changes to globalization that are caused in large part simply by modernization. [. . .] The global information age may strengthen rather than weaken many local cultures. [. . .] Economic and social globalization are not producing cultural homogeneity.'[36]

Modernization can breathe new life into local cultures by providing a new diversity of forms and stimulating dynamic cultural developments, which is the best insurance against Western cultural standardization. This is apparent if we reverse our perspective. Only a few of the newly emerging products of Arab or Indian pop music are re-exportable. Turkish singers such as Tarkan have made a name for themselves – but a large portion of Turkish pop has never received international recognition. If modern cultural forms across the world were merely Western copies, internationalization of every kind would be easier. Non-European pop music processes Western influences. It forms unique musical styles, characterized by indigenous rhythms and sounds and texts imbued with local flavour that would be incomprehensible elsewhere.

Much of the time, what appears at first sight to be a form of homogenizing globalization, featuring adoption of Western culture, is in fact the modernization of a particular culture. This culture retains 'its own' character despite assimilating external influences. This kind of modernization, stimulated at a global level, thus has a tremendous capacity to preserve cultural particularities, insofar as this is the producer's aim. It is also possible to develop strategies enabling a cultural product to pursue a global career comparable to American and Western products. At the end of the day, cultural globalization indirectly makes local cultures more flexible in their adherence to local and global identities, both old and new.

Globalization does not mean the levelling out of cultures but in fact bolsters the modernization of cultures worldwide, a process generated by cultural contact. It thus assists the comprehensive and pluralist renaissance of national and regional cultures. Cultures can clearly become interlinked; they are open systems. Predictions of a 'clash of civilizations' (Samuel Huntington; see chapter 3, p. 69) apply at most to the traditionalist and particularist aspects of a culture. Even here, as we have seen, modernization is unavoidable, although it is often monopolized and re-interpreted by anti-globalist forces. Even the modernist and more open cultural fields, meanwhile, have their own special features.

This complex relationship between globalization, tradition and modernity is captured in postcolonial cultural studies, as exemplified in the argument of Mbye Cham, Professor of African Studies at Howard University in Washington DC:

> Are we witness to an increasing melting away of the local in the face of the American superpower's narcissistic nationalism, hidden behind the mask of the global norm? It may seem this way in many fields, but in cultural practice, in my opinion, the issue is far more complex, because it touches the core of the persistent creative tension between the local and the global. I do not believe we are dealing here with two mutually exclusive entities which, reflecting the nature of such concepts, see tradition and modernity as opposite poles and which erase the dynamic which these opposites entail when they tie Africa down to the static and traditional and the Western world to the dynamic and modern.[37]

Modernity is neither the key identifying feature of a single epoch nor the prerogative of a state or cultural area. It is a style particular to each culture. Depending on the historical circumstances, this style exhibits varying degrees of development.[38] Both advocates of Western-style modernization and many critics of cultural imperialism make the same basic assumption. They regard non-European cultures as weak. Depending on their circumstances, they must either be modernized through external globalization or their survival must be ensured by means of anti-imperialist, traditionalist cultures of resistance. Few observers have grasped the process of cultural 'renaissance'. This facilitates internal reforms set in motion by external stimuli, which themselves have great potential for autonomy, but also enhances a culture's capacity to connect with the wider world.

This is all the more astonishing given that European cultural development would be unthinkable without the vital impulses emanating from early Arab–Oriental 'globalization' in the Middle Ages. The northern Italian city-states such as Florence and Venice, where, among other things, the first universities in Europe were founded, were in particularly close contact with the great Islamic-Oriental empires at the height of their efflorescence. The launch of European modernity was made possible only through the Arabic translations of, and commentaries on, Greek philosophical and scientific classics.

It would surely occur to no one to describe what followed – European merchant capitalism, the Industrial Revolution, the Enlightenment – as the 'Orientalization' of the West. By the same token, the contemporary modernization of the non-European world in the process of globalization is not 'Westernization', or is so only to a very limited extent. In every historical epoch, cultures which spread on the basis of economic and political power served as a universal matrix and thus contributed to the reconstitution of other cultures. Persians, Greeks, Romans, British and French: all have performed this bridging role for one another and for others, without causing literate cultures to die out. The title of 'world capital' is a kind of 'challenge cup' which has travelled from Athens to Rome, then, via many staging posts, to New York. It may be in Beijing by tomorrow.

5

The Internet – the Information Revolution Which Came Too Late for the 'Third Wave of Democratization'

It may at first sight seem deluded to deny that the Internet, particularly the World Wide Web, this 'network of networks', has a globalizing effect. Yet a number of phenomena place a question mark over both the quality and quantity of virtual border-crossing. Rather than having sparked off a revolution in international communication, the Internet is a technology on the basis of which a global culture *may* unfold and become established in evolutionary fashion – in a process that may extend over many decades, perhaps centuries. Yet even this developmental prognosis rests on as yet shaky foundations. One might also argue that in terms of actual use the Internet, despite its potential to network the globe, has never been a primarily *global* system of communication. The tendency for national and regional interconnections to increase more rapidly than international ones with the help of the Internet may be intensified. Cultural peculiarities may even be reinforced; cultures may move further apart.

In any event, one piece of evidence that supports this thesis is the fact that the Internet, which has spread across the world dramatically since the 1990s, has as yet failed to fundamentally open and democratize media systems across the world. The information revolution has been left untouched by the 'Third Wave of Democratization', postulated in light of the democratic transformations in Latin America and Eastern Europe (see chapter 8, p. 149).[1] The reasons for this are complex and by no means solely anchored in the gaping 'digital divide' between industrialized and developing countries. The key factor is in fact the chasm between increasing international interaction and the Net's meagre political relevance and power to mobilize. This web creates a virtual world which often lacks a corresponding real-world counterpart.

The medium of the Internet has taken centre stage in the globalization debate because it differs from the classical media in many ways.
The Internet is not necessarily market-oriented. It is in principle
beyond the reach of authority and has enormous potential to link societies, as opposed to merely politics, the economy and institutions or the
odd cosmopolitan individual, communicatively across borders, by
eliminating the separation between sender and recipient of communication. The study *Global Internet Geography 2004*, published by the firm
PriMetrica, points to rapid growth in international Internet traffic over
the last decade.[2] Despite the implosion of the 'new market' for information technology at the turn of the millennium, the international
exchange of data via the Internet has steadily increased. It is currently
doubling every sixteen months, and indeed both in terms of technological capacity to send information (supply) and actual use (traffic).

The central artery of exchange via the Internet is the transatlantic
axis between the US and Europe, the flow of information being asymmetrical in that more of it reaches Europe than the US. In any case,
the level of transatlantic data traffic in both directions still lies far
above that of transpacific exchange, another major axis of Internet
traffic (figures 5.1 and 5.2).

Does the sheer extent of Internet traffic allow us to speak of a globalization of Internet use? There are clearly very different geographical
foci. Global Internet traffic does not entail a symmetrically woven
web, but a transatlantic 'data highway', next to which many other

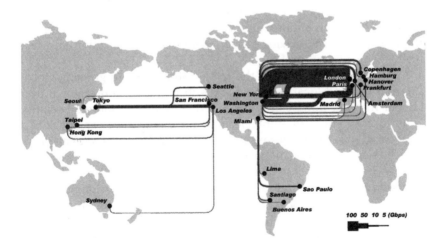

Figure 5.1 International Internet routes
Source: PriMetrica Corp., 2003 (<www.telegeography.com>, 30 July 2004)

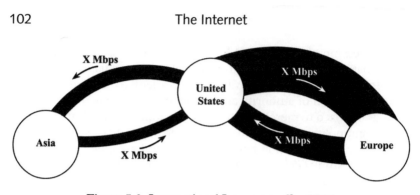

Figure 5.2 International Internet traffic, 2003
Source: PriMetrica Corp., 2003 (<www.telegeography.com>, 30 July 2004)

links between continents and countries look like poorly developed country roads, some of them full of potholes.

The quantity of data, moreover, tells us nothing about *who* uses the Internet; whether, for example, it is used as much to social as to commercial ends or whether the latter predominate. Business Internet use can change the world via the indirect route of economic processes, by moving production plants and jobs. It does not, however, automatically produce a networked and globally informed world, in which politics, economy and civil societies have sufficient knowledge of the 'Other'. If the economic sector dominated cross-border communication via the Internet, other sectors of society could be globalized at a significantly slower pace, generating an unbalanced form of globalization with consequences that are far from clear. A world coming together materially is by no means one in which global knowledge increases. Misperceptions and conflicts may be reinforced. Is the Internet a machine driving global economic centralization and featuring explosive cultural force?

Another problem: what is the relationship between growing global Internet use and local (national and sub-regional) and regional use? Global Internet flows can be regarded as both absolute and relative quantitative indicators of increasing connectivity. One can speak of a clear trend towards increasing global connectivity only if one can prove that the sub-regional, national and regional rate of growth in exchange via the Internet is *lower* than that of international Internet traffic. Otherwise, the key trend characteristic of the Internet might be the stimulation of local rather than global relations. Is the Internet a local medium? A study of the structures of interconnection by Alexander Halavais has shown that international links are far rarer than national. In the United States around 90 per cent of all hyperlinks remain within the national borders. In Europe the figure is 60 to 70 per cent at least, and around 70 per cent of cross-border European links lead to the US, which is evidence of successful transatlantic relations rather than genuine globalization.[3]

The Net as Tower of Babel

One of the most interesting developments in the realm of the Internet is its increasing multilingualization. The hegemony of English as transnational *lingua franca* persists but is rapidly diminishing. Around two thirds of all Internet users are *not* native speakers of English, but of Chinese, Spanish, German and French (figure 5.3). The increasing internationalization of the Net entails a diversification of users' linguistic abilities. The content of the Net also appears to be increasingly multilingual.[4] As the creation of websites is not limited to Western industrialized countries, in the foreseeable future it may no longer be only the users of the Internet who are multilingual; its content may be as well. Gert Raeithel, the American studies scholar based in Munich, proceeds on the assumption that none other than computers and the Internet will bring the linguistic dominance of English to an end.[5]

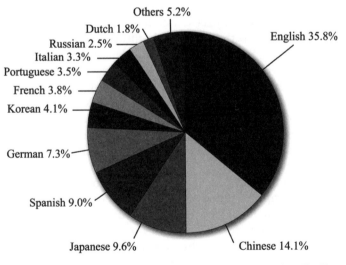

Others 5.2%
Dutch 1.8%
Russian 2.5%
Italian 3.3%
Portuguese 3.5%
French 3.8%
Korean 4.1%
German 7.3%
Spanish 9.0%
Japanese 9.6%
Chinese 14.1%
English 35.8%

Percentage of world online population 2004

Figure 5.3 Native speakers online
Source: Global Research Project (<www.glreach.com/globstats>, 25 February 2006)
Courtesy of Global Research Project and Media Tenor.

Table 5.1 Distribution of languages on the Net

Language	Share of websites, 2001	Language	Share of websites, 2001
English	52.00%	Portuguese	2.81%
Spanish	5.69%	Romanian	0.17%
French	4.62%	German	< 6.97%
Italian	3.06%		

Source: The Fifth Study on Languages on the Internet, Networks and Development Foundation, <http://funredes.org/LC/english/L5/L5overview.html>, 28 February 2006)

Today, languages are already in competition on the Internet, with various organizations worldwide propagating further development of the multilingual Net.[6] Between 1998 and 2001 the proportion of English fell from around 75 to 52 per cent. Other European languages made up around 20 per cent of languages on the Net (table 5.1).[7] The proportion of non-European languages, above all languages such as Japanese and Chinese, currently amounts to around 30 per cent – and given the huge population of countries such as China, this segment has particularly great potential for growth. Some observers even expect that the number of Chinese Internet users will increase to the point that Chinese, after English, may have the second largest spread of any language on the Net within the foreseeable future. The share of languages such as German, Spanish, Chinese and Japanese currently lies at around the same level. Other important languages include Russian, Korean, Dutch and the Scandinavian languages, though these are used significantly less. Hundreds of languages have a modest but growing Internet presence; the number of languages on the Internet is steadily increasing. The Internet, dominated for years by the technological power of the US and by English, is evolving into a 'web of Babel'.

The ongoing development of Universal Networking Language (UNL) is a trend running counter to the Net of Babel; it is intended to enable direct computer-aided translation of Internet content.[8] However, systems using it are not yet fully mature.

One of the main reasons for the tendency towards multilingualism is the introduction of non-Latin characters in the addresses of the World Wide Web. On the one hand, the move away from ASCII code as general standard has made it easier for large parts of the world to access the Internet. Around 90 per cent of people in the world do not speak English as a native language and can use it as a second language only to a very limited degree. In this sense, the Internet is slowly breaking away from its attachment to Western elites. On the other hand, the Internet threatens to disintegrate into linguistic sub-communities, which runs counter to the notion that it is helping to globalize knowledge. The 'Babel' variant of the global knowledge society will do little more than create a highly compressed version of cultures anchored in their national languages, rather than promoting the exchange of global knowledge. The multilingual Internet, moreover, can rapidly become the vehicle of a reinvigorated nationalism, as for example during the Sino–American spat over colliding jets above the South China Sea in 2001, when thousands of Chinese expressed their displeasure at the American government on the Internet.[9]

The digital divide

The Internet's development into a multilingual tool used equally by all parts of the world is being hindered by the striking asymmetry in global Internet connections. While the level of Internet use is high in the industrialized states on the basis of a solid technological infrastructure, a high pro capita income and advanced media competence, the situation in most developing countries looks very different. NICs (newly industrialized countries) such as China are increasingly catching up with the West and are using the Net in ways that conform to their political systems.[10] The Middle East, Africa and large parts of Asia, however, in which the growth of Internet connections and Internet use is restricted to urban elites, are falling further and further behind the rest of the world.

Even continental comparison (figure 5.4) fails to fully convey the true global divide. It is evident that Africa and the Middle East are very far behind, but Asia appears to be in a strong position, with about the same number of users as North America or Europe. The fact that Asia is home to a population several times larger than North America and Europe together must of course be taken into account. If all sections of the global population were equally networked, there would be far more Asian Net users. It is also striking that the vast majority of Asian users are from Japan, South Korea, Taiwan, Hong Kong and China. Most other countries on the continent have a user rate of less than or around one per cent of the national population – compared with at least 50 per cent in developed industrialized countries such as Germany or Japan. China, with its roughly 1.3 billion inhabitants, is indeed home to more than 50 million Internet users – but this is only around 3.5 per cent of the population.

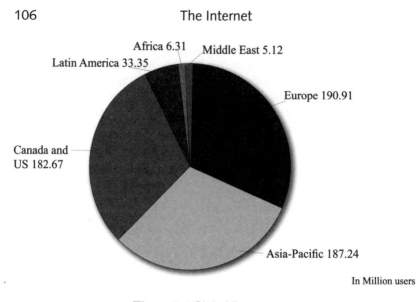

Figure 5.4 Global Internet use
Source: estimated user statistics based on the NUA index (<www.nua.ie>,
25 August 2004)

The term 'digital divide' thus has two different meanings today. It describes the deficits in the development and use of information and communication technologies on a global scale, that is, when comparing highly industrialized and developing countries. 'Digital divide' also describes imbalances between informational elites and peripheries, typical of most countries of the world. This is a predicament which recalls the centre-periphery model, conceived by Johan Galtung, and dependency theory, with the distinction that today the information divide is discussed almost as much as economic and political gulfs between North and South.[11]

The conditions in developing countries are however fundamentally different, and the 'digital divide' in these countries also requires a different kind of explanation. Far from ageing, the population here tends to be dominated by children, adolescents and young adults. The resulting low level of commitment to conventions and the structurally high degree of potential willingness to learn how to use information technology make developing countries 'Internet countries' *par excellence*. The computer training courses common in India at markets and bazaars show very clearly that people in developing countries are more willing to learn about information and communication technology (ICT) than in industrialized countries, especially if it holds out the promise of social advancement. Their future might be bright were it not for the old problems characteristic of the North–South conflict such as poor (telecommunications) infrastructure, extremely unequal income distribution and illiteracy, which will make Internet and ICT use in the developing countries the privilege of small elites for the foreseeable future. Ninety per cent of the global population still lacks Internet access, and the majority of human beings have never had a telephone conversation. The dearth of libraries, of access to information within the educational and health systems, often limited opportunities for the free exchange of information as a result of authoritarian conditions, and other shortcomings, make the Internet a genuine source of hope for the future of developing countries.

A number of international institutions have recently pointed to the dangers of the 'digital divide'. The Internet Society Task Force, an NGO with members in 170 countries, has warned that the number of Internet users in developing countries is often almost impossible to measure, while the 'digital divide' between the US or Canada and the other highly industrialized countries and the developing countries is constantly increasing. This group is urging politicians across the world to create the structural conditions necessary to counter this trend, for example by reducing the high customs duty on computer technology and liberalizing telecommunications markets. As things stand at present, according to the Task Force, it is entirely possible that the industrialized countries will extend their lead over the developing countries through the New Economy, rather than reducing it with the help of ICT and the Internet, as many participants in the globalization debate have hoped. At the Millennium Summit of the United Nations, General Secretary Kofi Annan also urged the developing countries to see the new information technologies as an incentive to 'leapfrog' stages of modernization such as industrialization and invest directly in the New Media.

The heads of government at the G8 summit in Okinawa (22–23 July 2000) also warned of the problems of a growing informational gulf. In their 'Okinawa Charter' they outlined the risk that the poorest countries will fall yet further behind as a result of the rapid progress in the field of information technology in the industrialized countries, advanced NICs and even some developing countries. This would apply mostly in cases where the shortcomings of the telecommunications infrastructure hamper the spread of the Internet. The G8 also called upon developing countries to create the best possible structural conditions, particularly in the political sphere, and resolved to found a working group, 'Dot Force', to clarify what contribution the industrialized countries can make to the development of the Internet in the developing countries.[12]

Finally, in its World Employment Report 2001, *Life at Work in the Information Economy*, the International Labour Organization (ILO) also starts from the assumption that the existing 'digital divide' between North and South constitutes a severe hindrance to reducing global unemployment.[13] The report argues that only around 5 per cent of the world population uses the Internet, around 88 per cent of this in the industrialized countries. There are currently 160 million (registered) unemployed worldwide. It is estimated that over the next ten years, not least because of population growth, 500 million new jobs will be needed to halve unemployment. The report makes it clear that the 'digital divide' between industrialized and developing countries – with a few exceptions – causes fewer jobs to 'trickle down' to developing countries. Most jobs are being created in those countries most committed to ICT (such as the Netherlands and parts of Scandinavia).

This does not however mean, first of all, that information technology has produced a net gain in jobs in the industrialized countries as a whole, as losses caused by rationalization and restructuring, which occurred before or in parallel, have to be factored in. Second, there are indications that, within the information society, the developing countries could fall yet further behind in terms of overall job creation and in comparison to the industrialized countries than they are already. The World Employment Report provides some grounds for hope for developing countries, especially in its description of the suitability profile of those countries which have achieved the status of NIC partly with the help of IT. Such different countries as Brazil, China, Costa Rica, Israel, Malaysia and Romania have managed to occupy niches in the ICT sector over the last decade.

The ILO report identifies two key features these countries have in common. They have managed (a) to establish IT training of reasonable scale and quality, including software programming; and (b) to overcome domestic infrastructural deficits with the help of new information technologies, particularly in the field of wireless telephony and telecommunications (so-called 'leapfrogging'). The World Employment Report concludes that IT could create jobs in the developing countries if its potential is fully exploited. However, it expresses fundamental doubts about whether most countries enjoy the prerequisites for optimal use. While the industrialized countries will apparently be in the position to turn the risks and opportunities of ICT to their own advantage in the near future, the report is sceptical about the prospects for most developing countries.

The report predicts that society will continue to be divided into two classes in terms of IT and Internet use for a long time to come. The vast majority of countries are barely networked at all and thus fail to fulfil, in the field of the Internet, even the basic condition and minimal theoretical criterion of communicative globalization: *connectivity* (see chapter 1, p. 9). Far from ameliorating the North–South divide, that is, the so-called 'knowledge gap' between industrialized countries and their developing counterparts, as the key thinkers writing on the Internet assumed, the industrialized countries are in fact increasing their stock of knowledge while the developing countries fall further behind. Inequalities are thus being reinforced in the information age.

Those states and societies which can claim to be part of the global Internet community because they can increase the quantity of international data exchange on the basis of large numbers of users are at the same time subject to the rules of a growing multilingualism on the Net. Multilingualism increases the proportion of those able to participate in Internet discourse worldwide, but also strengthens national and regional patterns of interaction and impedes cross-cultural global exchange. Apart from cosmopolitan or internationally oriented 'virtual communities', which are in any case only being created to any significant extent between industrialized countries, the Internet may, rather like satellite television (chapter 3, p. 69), mainly strengthen the formation of national and regional virtual communities in future. It is thus impossible to simply equate the Internet with global interconnections given the numerous technological, socioeconomic and linguistic-cultural barriers which bedevil it.

Virtual cosmopolitanism

One's line of reasoning is shaped significantly by the methodological level at which one is working. Comparative data on quantitative indicators such as the number of Internet connections and users in North and South are sobering. Despite the fact that developing countries are achieving massive rates of growth in Internet connections, they are starting from a very low level. The balance sheet might however look quite different should the focus shift to qualitative aspects, that is, away from the Net's limited spread to deployment of the Internet by individual actors, some of which is highly socially significant. A single scholar making use of the Internet, a single organization or party, which mobilizes the global public sphere and changes a political landscape with the help of the Internet, may be more meaningful than the communicative powerlessness of the unnet-worked global majority.

There are as yet no solid studies of the characteristics, structure or orientation of Internet-based global info-elites. Who goes online regularly to inform themselves or others across borders? Which social classes and occupational groups do users belong to, and which epistemological and informational processes are set in motion through this particular type of long-distance communication via the Internet? What are the likely social consequences?

It is not the global availability of websites but actual cross-border use, that is, the number of users rather than technological reach, which generates globality.[14] Existing groups of users show, however, even in industrialized countries with a nominally high number of users, that Internet use within societies is highly unequal. A 'digital divide' exists within the highly industrialized countries, that is, above all in the US and Europe, which may plunge the Internet into a crisis of adaptation in the medium term. According to a study by the Zukunftsinstitut (Future Institute) in Kelkheim in Germany, the number of users in Europe and the US will stagnate over the next few years. The euphoria about the Internet as a revolutionary technological utopia that will transform economy and society will die away.[15] The Internet may well fulfil its promise in the long term, but over the short term the stagnation of mass use cannot be ruled out, as it is still too complicated and slow in its present form. Even in the Western world, the Internet mainly serves the middle classes, the well educated and the self-employed, who make up the major portion of the info-elites. Women and older people, according to the Zukunftsinstitut, will have to be the new core groups targeted by innovative Internet strategies.

What has caused this 'digital divide' within the highly industrialized countries? Two reasons suggest themselves, the first technological, the second social. The personal computer (PC) continues to be the main point of entry and thus barrier to access for a section of the population which has no computing skills or which is unable to afford such a machine. Whether the PC might one day lose its role as main access route depends on which technology replaces it: the fusion of television and Internet still seems unlikely and the future of UMTS technology remains uncertain. Predictions of the number of households with an Internet connection in the near future have proven unrealistic given the extent of PC use.

Technological hurdles alone, however, hardly constitute a satisfactory explanation. We must instead start from the assumption that large numbers of Europeans and Americans, particularly adults and older people, fail to perceive or cannot imagine that they will get anything out of using the Internet. Studies such as those by Michael Margolis and David Resnick in the country most advanced in its Internet use, the United States, have shown that the Net is used mainly for entertainment or as a helpful tool for managing everyday affairs, and only by the info-elites as a source of political information too.[16] The authors explain these deficiencies with reference to the limits of human time budgets. For specialized info-elites, the switch from book to Internet may prove advantageous, in terms of quality and time, mainly at the level of straightforward checking of facts and obtaining information. For those media consumers focused chiefly on entertainment and everyday matters, television, radio and books are still easier to integrate into the daily schedule. They have little time or opportunity to devote themselves to the research-intensive Internet.

National borders rapidly disappear online only if one has cleared all the hurdles to Internet access – media use skills, language, finances. Interest groups may be reconfigured across national borders. New knowledge elites as well as 'fun groups' may develop, which exchange knowledge on international topics, express their views and provide sources of mutual cultural mobilization.[17] It is very difficult to estimate how large this global communication elite is. It is certain, however, that it makes up only a fragment of the general population, and in all probability only a few Internet users regularly engage in cross-border exchange, whether through e-mail contact or other types of Net use. The characteristics of this global info-elite are unclear and have not as yet been sufficiently covered in the research. In any event, members of this elite have severe problems making themselves understood, depending on how many languages are being actively used. It makes a difference whether one is primarily able to 'surf' the English-language Net or whether, like some educated Japanese for example, one has a mastery of the world languages of English and French, as well as, alongside Japanese, a certain passive understanding of Chinese and Korean. This would enable one to move around with substantially more flexibility within the multilingual World Wide Web and other networks.

However, despite the Tower of Babel syndrome, which separates even the global Net elites from one another, such users may have sociodemographic features in common. John Micklethwait and Adrian Wooldridge have coined the term 'cosmocrats' for a stratum comprising around 50 million people with a relatively high income. These are the real winners of globalization. They are not only au fait with modern communication technologies, but also benefit most financially from globalization:

> Even if its roots are commercial, globalization is already provoking profound social, political, and cultural questions. For instance, one social result is a broadening class of people – we dub them the cosmocrats – who have benefited from globalization. These people constitute perhaps the most meritocratic ruling class the world has seen, yet they are often as worryingly disconnected from local communities as the companies they work for are.[18]

Despite the differing definitions of global info-elites and 'cosmocrats', the very lack of ties to the local sphere is a problem common to the new elites of globalization which may be termed 'virtual cosmopolitanism'. Journalist Charlotte Wiedemann puts it in the following penetrating way:

> The Internet beats new paths for the interpretation of foreign cultures. If it is available online, a single English-language newspaper may mould this country's international image more than all the media in the national language put together. In case anyone should misunderstand me: the Internet has made it vastly more straightforward to find out about other countries. I lived in Malaysia for four years, with no decent newspaper and no major library close by. The Internet was like a lifeline. I first found out about the countries in the region online, then offline. I was astonished how splendidly you can prepare yourself with the help of the Internet – and how greatly the virtual reality differed from the actual reality every time. In the virtual Cambodia, an international tribunal prosecuting the remaining leaders of the Khmer Rouge is long overdue. The Internet does not convey the great, traumatised silence that prevails on this topic in the country, beyond a small circle of activists. You can familiarize yourself online with the views of highly interesting people – once you arrive in the country, you soon realise: almost no one knows who they are. They are virtually prominent. In many countries the digital divide marks an inner divide, a divide of the mind, of perception, a social one in any event. Only in its virtual, odourless aspects does the world appear to be moving closer together, to be getting smaller – not in its messy ones. In some places, the political opposition is strong only on the Internet. Many ethnic minorities demonstrate a cohesion online which they lost a long time ago offline. Separatists, fighting hopelessly in the jungle, appear triumphant on the virtual stage. Individuals, groups, whole peoples are able to create the identity of their dreams on the Internet. What is at stake here? What do we know? A middle class area in the Philippines may look to us like a slum. We are blind as soon as we leave our familiar cultural setting, the

zone of symbols familiar to us. A more simple and yet more difficult task than interpreting a Tibetan scroll painting is deciphering everyday life. Interpreting fences, size of field, width of roads. Reading roofs. What is poor? How many cooking pots indicate upward mobility? What does the good life smell like in dire circumstances? The yardsticks for such things enter our minds only offline, through observing and comparing.[19]

Not all global info-elites, to be sure, can be accused of lacking ties to the local sphere. Yet it must be acknowledged that the Internet represents various forms of media-based or, to some extent, interpersonal media-based communication. The perception of distance characteristic of the Internet certainly differs from the large media and its international reporting, as it is interactive, can be selected by the user herself and is based on a highly diversified range of options. Yet this itself is a new epistemological problem, for the concept of 'confidence in the source' is shaken to its roots on the Internet. How credible is the information obtained from far-off lands? There is no quality control on the Internet.

The Internet is capable not only of generating a global public sphere; it can also tear it down again. Of the various forces present on the Internet, many are almost unknown in their own country. NGOs which appear influential and deserving of support as a result of skilful media tactics are in reality quite often minor political players. Such uncertainties have become a serious problem whenever attempts are made to initiate and develop alliances via the Internet.

It would certainly be unfair to talk of an antinomy between globalization and experience – yet the notion resonates nonetheless. It is no accident that the Internet is closely bound up with concepts such as 'virtuality'. People who spend a lot of time romping around in the global spaces of the Internet can expand their knowledge of the world in all directions. But there is no guarantee of authenticity.

The 'Zapatista effect'

When Charlotte Wiedemann talks of the virtual political opposition, she is touching upon another key myth of the Internet: the notion of a 'global civil society' cooperating across national borders to promote human rights and democracy worldwide. Since it first spread on a massive scale, the Internet has been bound up with the idealized notion that it is a driving force and catalyst of global democracy. It was and is often thought to be realizing the Brechtian aspiration of a media transformed from an 'apparatus of distribution' into a 'public apparatus of communication'.[20] Bertolt Brecht, the communist, had assailed the media world, dominated by monopolistic tendencies of state and capital. Here press barons such as Alfred Hugenberg and state radio stations encouraged, as one would say nowadays, a 'one-way flow of communication', thus turning the citizens of the Weimar Republic into passive consumers of information. The Internet now appears to be disrupting this one-way informational street because of its interactive nature. Many of the key thinkers writing about the Internet can even envisage a society featuring constant plebiscitary votes online and virtual party conferences.[21]

At an international level, the Internet lends credence to the notion of an international alliance of social movements and democratic forces.[22] At the interface between globalization and democratization, the 'small medium' of the Internet obviously involves premises very different from the traditional mass media:

- the authoritarian state finds it more difficult to censor and control;
- as a low-budget medium, the Internet is accessible to the most varied range of political groups;
- even smaller political groupings have a public impact, rather than coming to grief on the news threshold of the large media;
- journalism no longer functions as the 'gatekeeper' for authoritarian states;
- the uniform platform of the World Wide Web makes it easier for social and political movements to pursue strategies of internationalization and to form alliances.

The Internet is a melting pot of information on the political situation in almost every country in the world. It de-monopolizes access to political information and gives rise to new discourses on issues of democratization. Innumerable shades of political discourse exist because the Net provides space to every political group and even to individual expressions of political opinion – an achievement with which traditional media cannot compete. Most people do not use the Internet to inform themselves about political matters (see p. 109). Nonetheless, the medium has developed into an information pool in which many information portals or open posting lists such as *Indymedia.org* engage in a political debate, which constitutes an alternative to established media, at least for interested informational elites.

Opposition forces, banned from the mass media in many countries, are successfully articulated on the Internet. It is thus an important informational hub linking political activists, the public sphere and the citizen. While the hope that authoritarian states will provide the opposition with access to press and broadcasting usually proves unfounded, the Internet is an important supplement to the system changer's usual arsenal of pamphlets and video tapes with political messages. Again and again, the hope has been expressed within the globalization debate that the Internet is changing the composition of social movements, the forms of their political activities and their power to mobilize.[23]

Recently, however, the same people have admitted that we as yet lack any robust scientific foundation for such a hope. Almost no case studies of Internet use among social movements have been produced, which, amorphous entities that they are, make difficult subjects of study.[24] The same authors who heralded the arrival of a new age of Internet-aided political activity in the 1990s now warn against viewing the Internet as an instrument that is replacing traditional forms of protest (demonstrations, collecting signatures, etc.).[25]

Further objections can be formulated from an international per- spective. The 'digital divide', which exists all over the world, clearly also restricts the value of the Internet for the opposition and other social groups. Active groups do manage to articulate their concerns in a constant struggle with the authoritarian state, which attempts to censor the Net. Yet the Internet's limited dissemination restricts its capacity for political mobilization largely to industrialized states, which have in any case usually had a very lively public sphere despite not having the Internet. Dana Ott and Melissa Rosser make a fair point when they state that there is no evidence that the Internet accel- erates processes of democratization. Democratization is certainly more likely to facilitate the development of the Internet than the other way round.[26]

Upon close inspection, it is clear that oppositional spheres world- wide have also adjusted to this state of affairs and are pursuing multi- media strategies. A study by the American RAND Corporation demonstrates that a large portion of the opposition in the Middle East has almost no Internet presence.[27] The fax machine and video tapes are often still more important than the Internet for political work.[28] The Internet has also failed, according to a study of Palestine, to improve coordination between NGOs and the opposition in any way.[29]

The claim that the Internet offers new opportunities for political movements to articulate their agenda worldwide and provides a democratic supplement to the existing media system can certainly not be dismissed. Its potential to transform the nation-state should not, however, be overestimated. Let us entertain the almost heretical thesis that in some countries even the old-fashioned tabloid press, with its tendency towards sensationalist reporting of politics, may contribute more effectively to the development of a culture of political criticism than the highly modern and seemingly global Internet.[30] The tabloid press in fact reaches many members of the *monolingual middle classes*, while the New Media often appeal only to narrow, elite sections of the population.

The mobilization of small, active informational elites is not a new feature of political transformation. The history of the pamphlet is after all several thousand years old. Yet there is an important difference between the conventional alternative and samizdat media on the one hand and the Internet on the other. The conventional small media tend not to cross the borders of the country involved, are almost impossible to access internationally and thus fail to open up genuine opportunities to link the opposition with sympathizers abroad. The Internet meanwhile offers unique opportunities for political self-presentation within global space. Content may be formulated in English or in various other languages and thus gain attention the world over, which in turn allows quite different oppositional strategies than without the Internet. This, at least, is a significant component of the myth-making involved in globalization.

What, though, is the nature of the small yet subtle distinction between the media? How significant is the Internet really, when it comes to forming international alliances and shaping politics? In theory at least, the medium gives political activists the chance to feed important information into political networks and to influence their domestic government like a global 'boomerang' (Sikkink and Keck) of political communication.[31] If communication between ruler and ruled is blocked by censorship, political messages can be sent beyond the national borders, to increase pressure on the domestic government via the indirect route of the global public sphere. There are plenty of examples of this procedure. When, for instance, the Tunisian journalist Tawfiq Ben Brik went on hunger strike in the summer of 2000 in protest against persecution by the Ben Ali regime, a campaign of solidarity quickly sprang to life on the Internet, helping ensure that this case, unlike many others of a similar kind, ended happily.

The so-called 'Zapatista effect' is surely the example of a boomerang mechanism mentioned most often.[32] Through its Internet presence, the rebellion by the Zapatista movement in the Chiapas region of Mexico captured the attention of the world. A detailed look at this case, however, points to special circumstances. The effect was anchored in an alliance between the national resistance movement and the anti-globalization movement. The Chiapas Rebellion was elevated by the latter to a central symbol of opposition to an unjust world order. Other Mexican provinces, suffering from the same problems, remained largely unnoticed. This is evidence of the significance of the Internet, but also underlines the special circumstances under which this alliance was formed. It was not the Zapatistas themselves who set the boomerang effect in motion: the initiative came from outside, from the ranks of a transnationally coordinated protest movement, which took shape around the WTO summit in Seattle in 1999. Other opposition movements have a much harder time gaining an international response and often go under amid the general cacophony produced by the torrent of information.

Along with the problem of excess information, which is directly linked with the limits of political mobilization, Dieter Rucht, a professor of sociology based in Berlin, mentions further criteria applicable to globalization in his critical assessment of the Net's political potential. It is being increasingly commercialized, and the opponents of social movements – terrorists and the authoritarian state – have also discovered the Internet for themselves.[33]

All the problems we have looked at, from linguistic ability, the 'digital divide', through the issue of global perception of distance and quality control to the Internet's negligible capacity to mobilize at the national and international level, cast lasting doubt on the vision of a global Net-based democracy. They reduce the Internet to an important but surely overestimated medium. The globalization debate has wrongly focused on the Internet, while other key forms of mass communication, such as international reporting and international broadcasting, have been neglected, despite being at least as significant to globalization.[34]

6

International Broadcasting – from National Propaganda to Global Dialogue and Back Again

For several decades, commentators have been suggesting that the days of international broadcasting may be numbered because of global satellite broadcasting. This debate is now going palpably into reverse. The consumption of national television programmes beyond national borders remains an exception because of linguistic barriers (see chapter 3, p. 57). Foreign-language programming such as that offered by international broadcasters thus has entirely new opportunities for expansion, particularly against the background of globalization. International broadcasters are playing an ever more important role because they broadcast in world languages such as English and can thus create global dialogues. Moreover, through their radio and television programmes in numerous national languages, they reach the monolingual but politically decisive middle classes across national borders, a group left untouched by regular satellite broadcasting.

International broadcasting is thus advancing globalization in the fields of migration, crisis intervention and the creation of transnational public spheres. Largely unnoticed by the public of the home countries of international broadcasting and in the slipstream of the globalization debate, one of the oldest forms of cross-border media is poised to develop functions that continue to elude many New Media.

This enormous potential is anchored in the fact that international broadcasting not only features *connectivity*, but is also *system interdependent*. It is dependent for its own survival not only on the financial support of the home government and society, but also on finding acceptance on foreign markets. In this sense, globalization via international broadcasting – radio as well as television – is not a by-product of national programmes, received via satellite more or less randomly by small elites in other countries and continents. It is the result of a far-reaching interdependence that has been systematically established.

The activities of international broadcasting are however generally dependent on state media policies. The future of the medium and, once again, the future of global communication, depends not least on the ability of the state to resolutely and single-mindedly shift international broadcasting away from Cold War propaganda towards dialogic global communication – but there are good reasons to be dubious.

In the Middle East, for example, following the attacks on the World Trade Center and the Pentagon on 11 September 2001, the radio and television airwaves were the site of a keenly contested race. The exclusive position of the Arab television network al-Jazeera was a shock to the system for the Western media. Despite superior Western news agencies and global media such as CNN, the West has practically no influence on opinion in the Islamic world. The administration of George W. Bush reacted with radio propaganda formulae long thought forgotten. Radio Free Europe and other international broadcasters are experiencing a new lease on life.

A flawed strategy, say European critics in particular, who call for new types of 'public diplomacy'. '9/11' is one of the key sources of pressure pushing German international broadcaster Deutsche Welle to reform its programming, which is to be modelled on the BBC. From a global comparative perspective, international broadcasting today is developing in diametrically opposed conceptual directions. European broadcasting concepts in particular are becoming trendsetters, because they obey the laws of globalization and create models for a utopian vision of global dialogue which still seems very far off in other fields of the media. Reforms are intended to win German international broadcasting, for example, new global recognition and hoist it to the top of international mass communication. A long road lies ahead, one on which the medium may easily come to grief.

After 11 September: the new war in the ether

The systems of international broadcasting reach the monolingual middle classes, which have shown themselves so important to the political and economic development of the countries and cultures of the world throughout history. When the BBC, Deutsche Welle, Voice of America and a whole host of radio and some television networks all over the world cross national borders, they consciously use the language of those groups of people to whom their media messages are addressed. Radio broadcasts by the BBC in the three national languages of Farsi, Dari and Pashtu, for example, were, alongside broadcasts from Iran, the last ones to which people still listened in Afghanistan during the war of 2001.

Despite the large number of cross-border broadcasts, the international broadcasting system as a whole is divided into two classes. The diversity of programmes and technological reach of the major Western providers exceed the potential of most countries in the Third World many times over. With regard to the VHF and MW frequency bands, which reach the largest audiences, Europe and the US are acting *globally* – most other countries in the world, meanwhile, have a merely *regional* orientation.

Following the terrorist attacks of 11 September and the Afghanistan and Iraq wars, a major reform of Western international broadcasting programmes was set in motion, which is likely to extend over several years. It is as yet unclear how this will impact on the responsibilities of programming. The BBC, Deutsche Welle and the second American international broadcaster Radio Free Europe/Radio Liberty (including 'Radio Free Afghanistan') have doubled the number of their broadcasts in Middle Eastern languages, and new cooperation agreements have been reached, with the Karzai government in Afghanistan for example. All Western networks are striving to increase the use of MW frequencies to extend their technological reach. American stations are for example broadcasting on a shared MW frequency.

An analysis of the programmes of Radio Free Europe/Radio Liberty, however, shows how American international broadcasting understands its mission. When US President George W. Bush visited Europe in May 2002 for example, his wife Laura Bush sent a message of greeting to the Afghans from the headquarters of Radio Free Afghanistan in Prague, in which she emphasized the role of the US in liberating the country.[1] The rest of the programming was and is also largely geared towards gaining acceptance for US foreign policy. The American broadcasters are pursuing a classic propagandistic programming concept in the Middle East, and making no attempt to achieve critical balance.

The success of Arab satellite channels such as al-Jazeera and their key role in Middle Eastern crisis-related communication has triggered new initiatives in the US and in many Western European countries aimed at making up lost ground in terms of Arab public opinion. Over the last decade, networks such as Voice of America and Deutsche Welle came to be regarded as remnants of the Cold War and had their funding cut. Their programming is now being expanded. The view has taken hold that neither diplomacy nor warfare can be successful if one fails to communicate to people in the Middle East why the West is doing what it is doing. In 2005 Deutsche Welle also launched an Arabic television programme.

'Attention Taliban! You are damned!' 'The alliance of nations is here to help you!' These are examples of the messages transmitted towards the end of 2001, during the Afghanistan campaign, by American military networks in the national languages of Dari and Pashtu. American broadcasting activities have intensified the fierce competition between the Western international broadcasters. The BBC criticized the American military networks as overly propagandistic and unprofessional. The Americans, for example, broadcast folk music, banned by the ruling Islamist Taliban, in the hope of reaching a larger audience. They overlooked the fact that some of this was wedding music, which must have seemed totally out of place to Afghans in time of war.

After the Iraq War of 2003, the US government launched a new initiative in the Arab world with the television channel al-Hurra ('The Free One'). It was clear soon after the channel got up and running that it was continuing the traditional concept of self-presentation characteristic of American international broadcasters. American media studies scholar William A. Rugh criticized, among other things, the fact that the network favoured American political opinion and actors in its news, revealing an astonishing weakness in coverage of American domestic politics.[2] Al-Hurra, whose name evokes its supposed determination to stand up for democracy and human rights, devotes too little attention to problems of domestic reform in the Arab world. It was finally discredited as the mouthpiece of the US government when President Bush made a speech in spring of 2004 justifying American use of torture in the Iraqi prison of Abu Ghraib. America's foreign policy is highly controversial in the Middle East, where only a few countries and individuals support its hard-line approach to Iraq. Yet such contested issues have no place in American international broadcasting. Chinese or Russian international broadcasters such as China Radio International[3] or Voice of Russia[4] have much the same propagandist approach.

Can this monolithic journalism really serve the ideal of democracy, democratic journalism and communication in a spirit of partnership in an age of globalization in which media wish to achieve cross-border acceptance? Rugh at any rate recommends withdrawing financial support from al-Hurra and investing it in more promising fields of American public diplomacy. Even the American Congress has been warning for several years of the inefficiency, backwardness and lack of competitiveness of US international broadcasting and US public diplomacy in the Middle East.[5]

In the influential journal *Foreign Policy*, the renaissance of old-style propaganda broadcasting, in which none other than the United States is playing such a leading role, has been described as a flawed strategy.[6] Mark Leonard, director of the Foreign Policy Institute in London, which is close to Prime Minister Tony Blair, criticized the American approach as outmoded. He suggests that public diplomacy, that is, the attempt to establish contact with other peoples in order, for example, to counter widespread anti-American sentiment, can succeed only if people enter into genuine dialogue. In endeavouring to familiarize Middle Eastern opinion leaders and publics with the motives of Western policy and make them more credible, Leonard also underlines the importance of facing up to disquieting criticism.

The BBC is more culturally attuned than American networks and is significantly more popular in the Middle East because of its dialogue-oriented approach to programmes.[7] Even when American and British units had begun to attack Afghanistan, the BBC interviewed the arch-enemy, Taliban leader Mullah Omar. The BBC, broadcasting in the national language of Farsi, is very popular in Iran, not least because it presents itself as a platform for various opposition forces. When, for example, the ultra-conservative religious leaders shut down yet another newspaper sympathetic to the reforms of ex-President Khatami, these forces were able to continue to express their concerns on the BBC. If Iranians want to know what is happening in Iran, they listen to the BBC.

Since 11 September at the latest, however, even the BBC has been engaged in international broadcasting's global struggle for public approval. Among other things, the British channel used new MW frequencies for Central and South Asia. From North Africa to the Middle East, a real battle for frequencies has broken out. Whoever dominates medium wave or even acquires local re-broadcasters for VHF can reach a far larger audience than the sometimes outdated short wave. Deutsche Welle has also tried in vain to acquire a MW relay station on Cyprus on several occasions, which would allow it to reach the entire Arab world.

Interdependence gaps and attempts at reform

Western dominance in the field of international broadcasting is not necessarily an expression of cultural imperialism. When Western international broadcasting allows national opposition forces to air their views, it helps promote democracy, a powerful fillip to dynamic cultural development worldwide. This role as cultural 'midwife' is however dependent on what form the programmes on offer take. Apart from *self-presentation functions* (conveying an image of one's own country), the following basic issues require discussion:

- To what extent does international broadcasting allow itself to be guided by the national interests of the home country, and does this include direct or indirect justification of alliances with and toleration of authoritarian regimes, both far from rare, in the network's target countries? Ideally, international broadcasting has a compensatory function in that it attempts to make up for the lack of pluralism in the media systems of many authoritarian countries by means of multi-perspectival news programmes on the target region (*compensatory function*).
- Are efforts to make programmes dialogic successful in the sense that the broadcasting countries' interest in presenting themselves in a particular way is balanced sensibly with the target countries' interest in information? One of the tasks of Western international broadcasting is to transmit news from the countries in which the broadcasting centres are based. It may however also be conceived as a platform for discussing international and regional issues, facilitating a 'dialogue of cultures' between North and South, or East and West (*dialogue function*).
- How successfully are international 'channels of communication' being kept open through international broadcasting, especially at times of war or other armed conflicts, helping get round the informational warfare practised by the combatants? It is one of the key tasks of modern international broadcasting to transmit independent information to regions in crisis or at war, to ameliorate attempts to manipulate the facts by the parties involved and take on the role of mediator and promoter of peace (*crisis intervention function*).

One of the most astonishing features of international communication rests on an apparent contradiction. On the one hand, international broadcasting systems are more system interdependent than almost any other form of media relevant within the context of the globalization debate. The home government of the particular network and the governments, publics and markets of the target countries respond largely to the range of programmes on offer. A programme that rubs people up the wrong way can easily lead to diplomatic interventions and complications. The major networks constantly carry out studies to determine how large an audience they are reaching to assess their success on foreign markets.

On the other hand, many observers of international broadcasting the world over have expressed the view that the medium is stagnating in terms of content. The professionalism of journalistic presentation often lags behind that of other television and radio programmes. Broadcasters fail to liberate themselves from national navel-gazing or else from a formalistic logic of objectivity. This is because of an interdependence gap, which some countries are only slowly beginning to close. International broadcasting is certainly linked with foreign markets *and* governments. Its counterpart in the home country, however, tends to be *solely* the government, while the home public usually knows nothing whatsoever about its own international broadcaster. There is no public debate on the form of programmes, such issues being considered, if at all, by experts and within a restricted academic sphere.

Programme reform may be slowed down for a number of reasons. In Germany, Deutsche Welle is formally part of the major public broadcasting corporation ARD but, because of its specific form of funding and unique programming responsibilities, it sits at the 'children's table' at executive meetings and is paid little attention. Even within most international broadcasters, Babel-like conditions prevail. There is very little opportunity to develop mutual understanding between the editorial departments, which broadcast in numerous languages, and quality assurance instruments often fail.

Draft legislation on Deutsche Welle, published by the Ministry of Culture in the summer of 2003, demands the introduction of new regulatory ideas. Fundamentally, these make the interdependent framework of international broadcasting more complete and may help bolster the organization of the medium along globalist lines.[8] The law includes a blanket clause allowing Deutsche Welle to determine the orientation of its programmes independently. This makes it possible to shift emphasis flexibly in line with the global situation, within the framework of the basic functions outlined above. Balancing out the increased programming freedom, Deutsche Welle is required to constantly review and discuss its work publicly. Debates in the Bundestag (the German parliament) and among experts, along with continuous evaluation of its own programmes, are meant to become par for the course. These are components of the regulation of modern broadcasting, which is flexible but also entails increased checks and balances.

One of the first steps towards achieving this new regulatory ideal was a study commissioned by Deutsche Welle on the quality of its own radio programmes broadcast in the Middle East.[9] Given that Western–Islamic relations are characterized by explosive political, cultural and religious issues, its radio programming required a strategic stock-taking after 11 September 2001. Which subjects and topics were dealt with? What were the geo-spatial foci (Germany, Europe, international affairs, target country, target region)? How are programmes aligned politically? How large an audience might be reached, given current broadcasting times and technological transmission capacity?

The study concluded that almost every area examined and most national and regional editorial departments were in need of substantial reform. Transmission times, editorial policies, forms of journalistic presentation, human resources policies: to make the most of its potential for globalization, Deutsche Welle's Middle Eastern radio programming requires comprehensive modernization. Despite promising beginnings and wider acceptance than American media, Deutsche Welle often fails to live up to its responsibility to function as a link between states and societies.

The study showed in exemplary form how vital it is to reconsider the 'Germany agenda'. The duty to provide the world with comprehensive information about Germany, still mentioned in the 1997 legislation (§ 4), was internalized by many employees of Deutsche Welle in such a way that some broadcasts have been of a decidedly Germanomaniac tenor, even in regions with no German minorities. Immediately after the end of the war in Afghanistan, for example, reports on the death of the footballer Fritz Walter and the 'Pisa Study' on the performance of German schools were broadcast to Afghanistan in the national languages of Dari and Pashtu. At a time when robust journalistic analysis of German perspectives on policies on the Middle East would have been highly desirable, programmes like this about a German footballing hero, who no one in Afghanistan is likely to have heard of, proved out of touch with global realities.

Another problem was the basic thematic orientation. On some days, German Middle East programming actually failed to include almost any reports on the target regions. Reports on Germany can make sense, but programming produced by an international broadcaster entirely lacking in reports from the transmitting region failed to do justice to the claim that the network was compensating for democratic deficits in the region and playing a moderating role in times of crisis. Such programming called into question the interdependency of relations with the target audience. It was therefore little wonder that studies produced internally often discovered very low listening rates in the Middle East.

Some programmes were unworthy of the name, consisting of fragments strewn throughout the day that failed to inspire listener loyalty. Short-wave frequencies were used despite the fact that radio receivers in the region are generally designed only for VHF and MW. There was a lack of business programmes. According to the Middle East study, Deutsche Welle was very far indeed from achieving its self-professed goal of providing a platform for the 'dialogue of cultures' by dealing with global and country- or region-specific problems from a range of perspectives, as well as German topics.

In one respect, however, Deutsche Welle is already better than many other international broadcasting institutions, particularly those based in superpowers and other major powers: it maintains a critical and balanced distance from German foreign policy and the local circumstances referred to in reports. Modern concepts of broadcasting are based on the principle of dialogue.[10] Providing a global forum for political and other types of dialogue is itself the best advertisement for the transmitting country. Programming tailored to the needs of propaganda is less likely than ever to meet with trust and acceptance and thus has no impact. The reputation of the United States in the Middle East has rapidly worsened in recent years, despite increased funding for international broadcasting. This is in sharp contrast to the case of the BBC, whose standing in the region certainly helped improve Britain's ruined reputation after its colonial rule came to an end amid bitter hostilities.

A report on European international broadcasting produced by Jo Groebel for the Friedrich-Ebert-Stiftung demonstrates how little this change of role has been grasped even by some media studies scholars. Referring specifically to globalization, it recommends focusing on portraying Germany abroad:

> As a result of the changed parameters (developments in media technology, new circumstances produced by regionalization and globalization, international politics) it is necessary to modify our duties (insufficiently debated in relation to the various amendments) and adapt our strategy. The priority must be the presentation of Germany abroad. It is the most extensive task in the global media scene.[11]

Erik Bettermann, director general of Deutsche Welle, sees things quite differently. Referring to the amendment to the Deutsche Welle legislation tabled in the Bundestag in 2004, Bettermann argued that prioritizing transmission of Germany's image abroad had been 'obsolete for a long time' and was incapable of maintaining the organization's competitiveness in the era of globalization. According to him, the priority should be to process information 'from the region for the region' and secure the acceptance of international broadcasting around the world with an 'intelligent mix of German, European and target area-related topics'.[12]

Only time will tell whether the reform efforts of Deutsche Welle and other European international broadcasters with similar plans such as Radio Netherlands will be successful. Great as international broadcasting's potential for interdependence under conditions of globalization may be, the prospects of governments providing funding and personnel for ambitious experiments in public broadcasting at a time of declining government expenditure may be meagre indeed. Without such support, it will surely be near impossible to achieve far-reaching changes in personnel structures, correspondents' networks and programme development. We shall have to wait and see which of the conceptual variants of international broadcasting – national propaganda or global dialogue – will become generally established globally in the long term.

7

Media and Immigration – Ethnicity and Transculturalism in the Media Age

The media contribute to the de-territorialization of information and ideas. Through them, the principles of the nation, the ethnic group and ultimately even those of state hegemony are amenable to globalization. Earlier conceptions of boundaries, such as that of the state as a territorial dominion, were based on the associated communicative possibilities: the state could only ever be as big as the fastest messenger service allowed. The medieval German empire collapsed not least because the emperor was unable to show up quickly enough in the various parts of his empire. The local rulers thus became independent.

The present, however, makes such communicative boundaries seem obsolete. The European Union, to take the same example again, is nothing other than the renaissance of the territorial dimensions of medieval rule, though it rests on an entirely new communicative foundation. Today information is widely available on every aspect of human life; it can be transferred from one end of Europe to the other in seconds. Similar may be said of communication processes on a global scale.

Despite these developments, there is something naive about the notion of media and communication overcoming borders. Modern media technology also generates new means of reconstructing ideas of borders. While, for example, Turkish immigrants in Germany as late as the 1980s were largely dependent on German television, they now have dozens of Turkish programmes at their disposal through direct broadcasting by satellite. Some observers believe that this is bolstering immigrants' media-based ties with their countries of origin, thus reinforcing national cultures. The potential impact of media globalization is in principle ambivalent. The de-territorialization of local cultures intensifies the dynamics of cultural change worldwide. At the same time, however, precisely the opposite is happening. Even among migrants, close contact may be maintained with the local culture of origin, and it seems less necessary than ever to adapt to the new cultural milieu. Is the globalization of the media a catalyst for the aggravation of ethnic conflicts in the wake of immigration?

Fears of this kind seem all the more plausible given that the racism and xenophobia of majority societies within the nation-states of the world show no signs of lessening. Despite all the talk of 'glocalization', of cultural mixing and progress, xenophobia is proving an immutable cultural deficit. Neither the Internet nor satellite television seem capable of changing the social fact that many people reject the 'Other' and identify with their 'own' group.

It was clearly vital to correct the naive globalism of the 1990s, which stressed the notion of a 'transculture' unifying everything under the sun. We must strive to replace it with a more subtle approach. The dominant cultural trend is clearly not the rise of a global transculture. Nonetheless, the mutual interaction of immigration and those old and new media that can be used all over the world is giving rise to a new complexity. It is by no means *inevitable* that the consumption of media in the language of one's native country blocks social and political integration, even among the first generation of immigrants. As one generation replaces another, differing styles of media use and production tend to develop, which may bolster both ethnicity and multi- or transculturalism.

Cultural exiles and biculturals: immigrant media use

It is a paradox. Since the early 1990s at the latest, scholars and experts have been preoccupied with the issue of how the transmission of distant, at times very distant, events, live in the living room, impacts on social contexts. The end of ethnocentrism appeared within reach, the 'global village' in which humanity's dream of international understanding and a meeting of cultures could be realized via the great 'Information Highway'. No sooner had these fond notions and visions been internalized than they were rent asunder by bad news. The media, it seems, have very different effects on immigrant communities, some of which are entirely out of synch with the notion of cultural globalization cherished hitherto.

The majority of media users tend to consume, via satellite and cable, an endless accumulation of programmes of the same or similar type from their own cultural and language area. No German is interested in Turkish television, unless he is of Turkish origin, except, perhaps, for a few media studies scholars or amateur Turkish studies enthusiasts. Of all the new programmes available, Indians and Pakistanis in Great Britain or Turks in Germany select the very programmes they have seen throughout their lives – those from their country of origin. We are thus faced with a predicament which no one, it seems, could have imagined. While Turks in Germany fifteen or twenty years ago were still more or less forced to consume German television programmes and thus absorb information on Germany, for there was as yet no other option, in the age of globalization they can make themselves at home more effectively than ever before in the old world of their own culture, ethnicity and religion. Dozens of Turkish television channels broadcast to Germany, while German offshoots of Turkish print media are widely available. This is media from dawn to dusk.

Is the media encouraging an 'ethnicization' of the multicultural immigrant community?[1] Are 'parallel societies' and 'ghettos' arising in our midst, with satellite dishes on roofs and balconies pointing in different directions a palpable manifestation of difference? Is this trend hampering the integration of minorities and encouraging ethnic tensions and conflicts? The answer to these questions cannot simply be reduced to an either/or, either 'globalization' *or* 'ethnicization'. The future of the multicultural society will be anchored in a complex interplay of old and new cultural orientations and lifestyles, and in 'identities' constructed *in* and *through* media. We can already make out the contours of these identities to some extent, but they are still very much under construction.

The relationship between multicultural societies and media has a special character. Migration is one aspect of globalization. It involves not only the migration of economic subjects – a labour force – to another country, but of people with cultural habits and values. These first migrate along with the people, establish themselves in a new location, influence the culture of the new milieu and are themselves subject to synthesis and change. Because every group and society needs media, which enable its members to communicate with one another well enough to ensure that the polity functions, the media used by immigrants and their habits of reception are also an element of globalization.

There are a number of basic assumptions about the nature of media-based communication in immigrant communities. Media, according to some, can contribute to integration in the new surroundings and thus to global cultural change, bringing nations closer together. Others claim that they may hamper integration, reinforcing the fragmentation and 'ethnicization' of society.

British researcher Marie Gillespie, taking the media behaviour of Indian immigrants in Southall in England as an example, has shown that none of these basic frameworks fully captures the processes at work.[2] Gillespie discovered that the different generations of immigrants – parents, their children and grandchildren – sometimes perceive the range of programmes offered by Indian and British media in quite different ways. While older people favour Indian film and video productions and maintain a distance from British television programmes for moral and political reasons, younger people, who often know India only from holidays, frequently lack background knowledge of Indian productions or any sense of connection to them. Their preferences are directed at the programmes on offer within the British–Western milieu in which they live. Generational conflict is pre-programmed. It is sparked off by the media and develops as people engage with them. This does not exclude the possibility that younger people retain a certain loyalty to the culture of their forebears. Throughout their lives, they may well watch Indian films now and again with their relatives, criticize the media in their new home for their prejudicial views of other countries and look for ways to change the media culture of the new setting to bring it into line with their way of thinking.

If, however, one and the same – either Indian or Western – range of programmes is 'read', received and interpreted by different immigrants in quite different ways, then it will become ever more difficult, as one immigrant generation is replaced by another, to speak of a uniform ethnic (for example 'Indian') standpoint or ethnicization by the media. The example of British Indians' mode of dealing with the media points to different, in part contradictory, tendencies in the development of the media internationally:

- the construction of virtual communities based on national cultures
- the promotion of multi- and transcultural developments.

'Virtual communities' are being formed, among other things, by a more intensive exchange of information between emigrants and their home countries than in the past. National publics form within the diaspora. Emigrants acquire, through the New Media, the cultural milieu with which they are familiar and which they find most appealing. They remain in close contact with political and social life in the home country. There is however no reason to focus only on the negative aspect of this development as a hindrance to integration and ethnicization. Even regular consumption of these media is not necessarily best understood as a sign of resistance to the new society and culture of the immigrant country, as we shall see.

Transculturalism means that wherever cultures coexist at close quarters, they always undergo synthesis, at least to some extent, forming something of a 'third culture'. The concept of the 'multicultural' society, generally considered progressive, is in fact also a little backward. It is based on the notion of cultures as little worlds in themselves, thought to be fundamentally different and alien and whose inherent tensions one would ultimately like to replace with peaceful coexistence – the 'multicultural society'. In the field of the media, multiculturalism finds expression in immigrants' use of the media of their culture of origin, but also, increasingly, those of the immigrant country. Transculturalism is connected with the production and consumption of autonomous cultural forms in and through media – the Franco-Arabic 'Cinéma Beur', featuring films such as *Le Thé Au Harem D'Archimède*, is a prime example.

It is vitally important to grasp that cross-border communication – Internet, satellite television, etc. – supports *both* basic tendencies of cultural development and the media's potential both to promote and hinder integration in the age of globalization.

To explain this we need to bear in mind that, in terms of integration, there exist quite different spheres of media activity. The media may impact on:

- civic integration (system integration)
- social integration
- cultural integration/identity formation

Media *may* influence people's attitudes in all these areas, but they do not necessarily do so. Mutual interactions may be developed to very different degrees in specific social segments and involve numerous types of linkage. In principle, there is a strong connection between media effects or uses and *cultural integration*. If an individual does not use the media of the country of immigration, she will find it hard to get her bearings in the prevailing cultural discourse. In principle, however, to the extent that social and political integration are based on values and norms, they are almost media-resistant because they are learned in the course of primary and secondary socialization. The media's potential to mould attitudes must be considered meagre.

A study on Turkish media use in Germany by Hans-Jürgen Weiß and Joachim Trebbe, commissioned by the Federal Press and Information Office of the German Government, has shown that, at the very least, the use of Turkish media does not exclude the possibility that users have a positive relationship to social and cultural integration.[3] Many immigrants are deeply engaged in both spheres – Germany and Turkey. They are well integrated into German society, but are simultaneously interested in Turkish media: a 'high degree of integration does not necessarily entail a diminished interest in the politics of the home context'.[4] The study's findings can be interpreted to mean that social integration can occur even if an individual continues to use Turkish-language media (at the same time as other media, as an addition or complement to them, in bicultural fashion), and that this does not necessarily undermine integration.

These findings update and add subtlety to a study by Jörg Becker, Elmer Lenzen and Klaus Merten commissioned by the German Ministry of Work and Social Affairs, Qualifications and Technology of the *Land* of North Rhine-Westphalia in 2001 for the Herne area. This states that the use of Turkish media 'has no negative effects whatsoever on integration and political behaviour'.[5] Similar studies in the Netherlands, such as those produced by Staring and Zorlu or Millikowski, also come to the conclusion that the use of Turkish satellite television by no means hampers the process of integration. People use it chiefly to obtain information about politics and society in Turkey.[6]

Another study on Turkish media use completed in 2002 by the present author, again commissioned by the Federal Press Office, drew up the following typology of media use. It is anchored in a nuanced concept of integration:[7]

- The *cultural exile user* uses Turkish media only. He tries to maintain cultural contact with his homeland in this way, feels ill at ease culturally in Germany, does not attempt to integrate culturally into Germany and remains largely unintegrated socially outside of the Turkish community. His faith in the German political and economic system is however greater than in the Turkish system. This phenomenon has been confirmed by several studies and runs counter to the assumption that the use of foreign language media gives rise to 'parallel societies' which make a society more prone to ethnic conflict.[8]
- The *political exile user*, in contrast, consumes Turkish media while consciously identifying with the Turkish state and system and

against the background of a negative image of Germany of a nationalist tenor. While this type of user is often inclined towards the
classic Turkish newspapers and the public broadcaster TRT, he is
quite often critical of the numerous new entertainment channels on
Turkish television. The television programmes available at present
thus make it easier for people to withdraw into a Turkish 'media
exile' – but this exile is largely apolitical and does not necessarily
strengthen the trend towards an ethnicizing-nationalist 'parallel
society' of Turks living in Germany.

- *Diaspora users* refers to consumers who also use Turkish media
  only, but are far more integrated socially and adopt no 'exile' perspectives. They use Turkish media for pragmatic reasons, because
  they lack the linguistic skills to access German media and because
  Turkish habits of use have become firmly entrenched. The
  advanced level of social integration (marriage and friendship with
  Germans, etc.) and the similarly high degree of trust in the German
  political system make diaspora use, and even more cultural exile
  use, seem a socially tolerable expression of cultural preferences in
  synch with the globalization of culture.

- *Bicultural users* are consumers who use both German and Turkish
  media. They are often highly skilled both at getting 'the best' out
  of both media realms, in line with their interests, and analysing the
  shortcomings of German and Turkish media. Biculturalism provides a comparative perspective and has an important cultural
  bridging function, helping overcome national and state informational boundaries. Bicultural users often criticize both the Turkish
  media's excessive focus on the Turkish nation-state and the limited
  and thus distorted view of Turkey found in German media.

- *Transcultural users* refers to those consumers who mainly use specific
  German-Turkish media offerings. This section of the media is
  growing, but is still struggling with market entry problems, as
  demonstrated by newspaper and magazine projects such as *Persembe*
  and *Etap*, which have now folded. The main reason is surely that
  transcultural interests are increasingly covered by German and
  Turkish media which, for example, provide space for Turkish actors
  (as on German television) or a globalized youth culture (as increasingly applies to Turkish media).[9]

- The counter-type to the exile user is the *assimilation user*, who uses
  only the media of the immigrant country – in this case, German
  media. This type feels a sense of strangeness when he comes into
  contact, not with German, but with Turkish culture and society, as
  conveyed by Turkish media. This mostly young type of user knows

Turkish culture only indirectly through parents and friends or through holidays in Turkey. Among the younger generations, which consist almost exclusively of bicultural, transcultural and assimilation users, a cultural change is clearly apparent, which is closely bound up with language ability. While most young people seem to speak fluent Turkish, this is often limited to a conversational level. Turkish youths who have grown up in Germany are often hardly able to follow Turkish news reports, as they lack the vocabulary and contextual understanding.

Bicultural, transcultural and assimilation users are culturally integrated and differ very little from other youngsters in their media use behaviour. Yet even members of these groups, integrated into culture, society and system, may still have reservations about integration (ruling out marriage with Germans for example). The consciousness of belonging to another nationality may persist among assimilation users. Those who have reservations about integration despite their cultural competence in the immigration country, a competence bolstered by the media, demonstrate that basic social and political attitudes are not a matter of the range of media on offer. This confirms the theoretical assumption that core values are often resistant to mass communication. The simple slogan 'the more someone uses domestic media, the better integrated she is' and the better is her relationship to the immigration country, seems too sweeping.

This also applies to the inverted interpretative model: 'the more foreign and foreign-language media someone uses, the less integrated he is.' Diaspora and to some extent also cultural exile use can be regarded as an obstacle to integration only to a very limited degree. Many immigrants are interested in information about both their country of origin and the immigrant country. Moreover, as strange as it may sound, the anti-integration effect of virtual national communities and of a focus on the home country context is often more apparent than real; acceptance of the immigrant country's culture may be enhanced through the back door. This ultimately makes it possible for the immigrant to keep his own horizon of experience alive, at least virtually, in the new everyday context. He can thus find a sense of intellectual and emotional direction within the otherwise uprooting diasporic predicament.

In a well-regarded work on Iranian television in Los Angeles, US-based Iranian media studies scholar Hamid Naficy – drawing on Stuart Hall among others – speaks of a 'strategic' ethnicization characteristic of many immigrants. Rather than watching native-language programmes in order to demarcate their own culture from that of the immigrant country, many Iranians do so to maintain their own capacity for social articulation. Among the first generations of immigrants in particular, this is linked with experiences abroad and the language they have brought along with them.[10]

All these developments and implications of migrants' media use show very clearly that the core phenomenon of globalization, the communicative linkage of countries and societies by means of cross-border media (see chapter 1), can have very different consequences for the worldwide evolution of immigrant communities and cultures. Cross-border media may both contribute to linking two or more cultural systems in the sense of multi- and transculturalism as well as doing the exact opposite. They may contribute to the survival and spread of national cultures and separatist ethnic and religious identities, intensify conflicts in the immigrant society and encourage the formation of 'parallel societies'. The media thus not only promote the dissolution of national cultures and 'glocalization' (see Robertson 1994a) through increased cultural contact, but also reinforce existing cultures.

Cross-border media use appears to have no one-dimensional integrating effect at all. When media cross borders, this does strengthen the globalization of culture by de-territorializing its production and use to a previously unimaginable extent. Yet phenomena such as the exile of minorities or their unwillingness to integrate, certainly as old as humanity itself, will not die away even under conditions of globalization. They may even be stimulated by the seemingly global media.

An immutable cultural deficit: xenophobia in the age of global media

David Morley and Kevin Robins have pointed to the paradox that in the middle of the era of globalization a counter-tendency has arisen: people are increasingly eager to assert their national identity; xenophobia and racism are undergoing a revival:[11] '[The] desire for clarity, this need to know precisely where Europe ends, is about the construction of a symbolic geography that will separate the insiders from the outsiders (the "Others"). Implicit in these words is the suggestion that the next Iron Curtain should divide Europe from, and insulate it against, the Islamic Other.'[12]

The European Monitoring Centre on Racism and Xenophobia (EUMC) in Vienna has carried out comparative research on media and racism for the period 1995–2000. The result is a comprehensive report, including both country studies and a systematic general report.[13] As an example of problems involving immigration, frequently evident in the mass media, the EUMC report mentions that media regularly create public panic by 'zooming in' on problems involving small numbers of immigrants (violence, false and forced marriage). These, it is suggested, then determine the image of immigrants in a kind of *pars pro toto* effect.[14]

Furthermore, according to the report, once established, discourses on immigrants (such as the asylum issue) remain on the public agenda long term and may thus imbue the image of immigrants as a whole. The tendency identified in the EUMC report is remarkable, since media often tend to shift from one set of topics to another relatively quickly to increase their appeal. The definition of 'news' is bound up with the occurrence of new events. Even serious crises at home and abroad may be forgotten as soon as the media debate has passed its peak. The fact that the media approach to immigrants often revolves around 'fixed repertoires' points to the tremendous impact of stereotypes and negative concepts of the 'Other', which obviously favour fixed thematic foci.

The EUMC report mentions another influencing factor, namely the dominant position of politics.[15] Popular prejudices are often transformed into a media agenda only through political initiatives, which pick up on people's latent attitudes. From a systems theory perspective, it would be interesting to examine how the media in Europe would respond if there was broad consensus among politicians (as there is to some extent in the UK and has been in the Netherlands for many years) that it is unacceptable to cast fundamental doubt on immigrants' membership of the state and to refrain from making them the subject of election campaigns, as happens in other countries time after time. The media would then find themselves in a situation in which they would have to cope with the lack of thematic stimuli from politics by coming up with their own topics and working out a determined and responsible editorial policy.

From a comparative European perspective it is evident that xenophobia is characteristic not only of the popular media but also of their serious counterparts.[16] Cultural differentialism, that is, the notion that certain cultures or religions are incapable of integration, is a widely held view which has found expression in most European media in one form or another.[17] When, for example, conservative political circles claim that Turkey is not suited to EU membership because of its Islamic character, this is a deeply cultural differentialist thesis. It rests upon the assumption of the inevitable separation and incompatibility of the Christian and Islamic hemispheres, although this fails entirely to stand up to close analysis.[18] The metropolitan culture of the western and southern coast of Turkey in particular is in many respects more Western-oriented than many regions and social groups in those Eastern European states which have joined the EU as it has expanded eastwards. It is crucial to grasp that the potentially violent racism typical of some individuals is flanked by currently 'socially acceptable' views. Those who hold them reject violence, but largely agree with violent racists in defining the problem of what constitutes the 'Other' or the 'foreigner'; they do not shrink from allowing the state to increase its *structural* potential for violence (by making it easier to deport people, for instance).

EUMC points to the fact that ethnic references in the media are often made in connection with criminality, without the presence of any obvious functional connection.[19] A headline such as 'Turk murders old woman' would thus be illegitimate if the fact that the murderer is Turkish has nothing to do with the fact that he has committed a crime. At the same time, however, while the term 'Russians' mafia' would be disparaging in a certain sense, the term 'Russian mafia' would be justified in that Russian language and origin is the self-selected definitional criterion of this mafia type. The German Press Council, the country's highest authority with responsibility for the ethical self-regulation of journalism, has included in its press code (§ 12.1) offences against the precept of ethnic neutrality when reporting crimes and deals regularly with such cases. Yet the fact that the EUMC report holds that this problem persists shows that professional self-regulation is failing to a considerable extent.

The frequent failure of reports on foreigners and immigrants to include sufficient information on social context has emerged as another key problem area. It is for example entirely possible that the rate of criminality among foreigners at certain times and in certain regions is higher than average. We must however take into account that immigrants to Europe from Southern countries often belong to the least privileged third of society, mainly representing the lower and lower-middle classes. Comparisons should therefore be with the corresponding social and income group within the domestic population, rather than the population as a whole, if one is to avoid producing a distorted picture.

While foreigners are often linked with negative things such as criminality to an unusually high degree, they are under-represented in the media when it comes to other topics. The educational elites, which exist in every immigrant community – there are lawyers, doctors and intellectuals among the Turks in Germany – and other immigrants to Europe are rarely consulted by journalists on matters of general interest, unless they touch upon typical 'foreigner issues'. Immigrants often appear, as an inevitable consequence, as a de-individualized and anonymous mass. There is a lack of everyday perspectives which might correct the negative image. Because media discourse is a discussion about rather than with immigrants, it becomes a discourse of domination whose terminology, from the 'flood of asylum seekers' through 'economic refugees' to 'leading culture', transports prejudices and aids their social reproduction.[20]

A final, marked tendency typical of how European media deal with 'others' and foreigners is the special position – usually interpreted negatively – of specific ethnic-religious minorities within perceptions of the 'Other' as a whole. The EUMC report mentions Roma and Sinti as well as Muslims as examples. Longitudinal studies of the German press have in fact shown that Islam is one of the topics of reports on immigrants most heavily loaded with negative event valences – the links made in media reports with events considered negative (such as terrorism, etc.).[21] There have as yet been no attacks by Islamist extremists in Germany either before or after the events of 11 September 2001. Despite this, there is a danger that an image of violence, of external origin and linked with extreme Islamic fundamentalism in North Africa and the Middle East, may be transposed on Muslims living in Germany.[22] Opinion polls show that a substantial portion of Germans fears and is discomforted by Islam (see chapter 2, p. 41).

Within the context of the globalization debate, the most compelling interpretation of these at times shocking findings is that neither the old nor the new routes of cross-border communication, neither Internet nor satellite television nor the international reporting produced by national media, have contributed to a clear improvement in coverage of immigrants and foreigners. Quite the opposite: international reporting continues to have a negative effect on the immigrant community. The image of a minority may be influenced via the indirect route of international reporting, without the active involvement of the minority, through the depiction of events abroad and the formation of associated intrasocietal discourses.

Andrea Böhm, for example, observed a shift in the perception of Kosovars in Germany during the Kosovo war of 1999. Often seen as asylum seekers and criminals before the war, after it broke out they underwent a public re-evaluation as victims of 'ethnic cleansing'.[23]

This change of image cannot be interpreted as a response to the actions of Kosovars in Germany, to demonstrations during the war for example, but was the knock-on effect of a dominant interpretation of an event abroad (the Kosovo war) on the image of an ethnic minority in Germany.

No one has as yet studied the connection between the prevailing image of *foreign countries* and that of *foreigners*, for example between the image of a nation and that of the corresponding ethnic-religious minority. We must however assume that the image of foreigners in the media is an amalgam of images of foreigners living in a certain country and the image of foreign countries, a mixture of image constructions of the familiar world and of a distant world. These components are fused, at the latest, at the level of media use by consumers. Future research might probe whether the notion of 'mafia-ridden Russia' is linked with the image of 'Russians' mafia' in Germany, whether terrorism in the Middle East influences the image of Arabs or whether Muslim or Jewish minorities undergo a kind of 'orientalization' in their media images and among consumers of media.

Public opinion research has shown, for example, that the contemporary image of Israel among the German public and the image of Jews correspond closely,[24] and that almost half of all Germans assume that Jews identify more with Israel than Germany.[25] This not only implies the existence of structural similarities between the image of Israel and that of Jews, but that cognitive connections are being formed. Every international report which can be linked with a corresponding minority gives rise to an intrasocietal 'second image'. Media communication is thus not only capable of encouraging cultural contacts and conflicts at a global level. International reporting, the multicultural society and ethnic-religious conflicts may also be linked within a given society.

When Indian-born Muslim writer Salman Rushdie was condemned to death in 1989 by the then Iranian revolutionary leader Ayatollah Khomeini for the alleged blasphemy in his novel *The Satanic Verses*, British and German media took this as an opportunity to raise doubts about the 'multicultural society'[26] – despite the fact that Germany was free of book burning and other expressions of disapproval.[27] The German newspaper *Die Zeit* asked whether the core liberal ideal of cultural relativism, in the sense of the coexistence of different cultures, was still in keeping with the times. In the right-wing *Welt*, the supposed cultural difference between the Islamic world and the West was considered confirmation of its long-cultivated opposition to multiculturalism and cultural relativism; the Rushdie affair was regarded as a reason to renew calls for the cultural assimilation of immigrants. The Berlin *tageszeitung* rightly concluded that the Rushdie case had stoked fears of Muslims in Germany and impaired German society's ability to deal with its minorities.[28]

Cross-border communication thus clearly has an intrasocietal dimension. The theoretical separation of the spheres of cultural communication 'within the cultural area' and 'between cultural areas' is difficult to maintain in practice. How the media convey events in distant cultures influences the discourse on social change within the state and social system in which media exist. The media image of distant cultures impacts on the 'multicultural society'. Even in the age of globalization, the national and stereotypical lenses through which the media perceives the world often mars the image of immigrants.

It is high time that scholars and commentators paid due attention to the interaction between images of familiar and distant worlds, between projections of the world and the image of immigrants reflected in the media. International reporting in its current state, with its strong fixation on a chaotic and crisis-ridden world, produces distorted, illusory images of the 'Other', which shift between genuine attempts at tolerance and a xenophobia that often results from fear and a sense of being unable to cope. As with the connection between media and integration, we need to question whether the impact of the media is as extensive as often assumed. Opinion differs on whether media function as 'psychological arsonists' igniting xenophobia or whether racism represents a deeper, media-resistant attitude. What is certain is that neither the quality of media content nor attitudes towards foreigners have noticeably changed or become more sophisticated in the era of globalization. The norms of a cosmopolitan superculture will certainly not take root solely as a consequence of the growing quantities of information provided by cross-border communication media. They require structural intervention in the media system of economic and political interdependence. The way people are dealing with social change culturally, for example, as 'the Danes' become 'Europeans' and 'citizens of the world', is however currently characterized by nationalistic regression and a clinging to models of identity bound up with the nation. In part this is because the true state of global news reporting and the contemporary culture of international reporting (see chapter 2), with its focus on crisis-ridden political news, increase the desire for a return to national harmony and stability.

8

Media Policy – why the State Continues to Play a Role

One of the key and most persistent arguments about the media within the globalization debate holds that in an era of increasing cross-border communication via the Internet, satellite television and other media, national media policy must submit to the primacy of global policy and global legal realities. According to this line of reasoning, whenever the state is no longer in a position to protect its territorial borders from uninvited communication, it loses some of its sovereignty. Here, the networking of media and societies turns the nation-state into a networked state, and may even lead to its downfall as the leading hegemonic entity. The image evoked is of a world dominated by 'linked' governments – *global governance* – under the aegis of strengthened supranational bureaucracies, strong civil societies and a global media policy that embodies the free flow of information as a practised human right. The reality is very different.

In many respects, international media policy reflects a mode of media production and use still highly adapted to national needs and interests (see chapters 2 and 3). What is more, while at least certain formats and topics are evident in global space (for example within entertainment culture) that might underpin a global discourse, and the interdependence of societies and markets is increasing in specific fields, so far the nation-state has dominated media policy almost completely. Even vigorous confederations such as the European Union are no exception. The transnational networking of media and markets is too weak to strengthen the global political level. Without a pioneering political change of course, even in the age of globalization, most of the media systems in the world risk becoming trapped in a condition of repressive 'semi-slavery' under authoritarian rule. The utopian vision of globalization sees it as a cultural movement enforcing key human rights. In reality, it at least enables people to make 'brief forays' beyond national borders to consume media. The political and legal orders constraining national media systems, meanwhile, are proving resistant to globalization.

The 'New World Information Order' in the age of globalization: the rudiments of a pan-capitalist vision

The political and scholarly discussion on a New World Information Order was provoked in the 1970s by developing countries' criticisms of their industrialized counterparts' global informational and media dominance (see chapter 2, p. 26). The debate ran more or less in parallel to that on a New World Economic Order. As with their global hegemony over raw materials, argued the non-aligned countries in particular, the Western industrialized countries' power of disposal over information and communication was a form of resource control and colonialism in a new guise. Military imperialism, on this view, was being replaced or complemented by cultural and informational imperialism; the domination of the physical human subject was now flanked by intellectual domination.

UNESCO had organized the debate on the New World Information Order. In 1978, in its declaration on the mass media, it adopted the principle of the 'free and balanced flow of information' and initiated an international comparative study of the flow of information, the 'MacBride Report', named after the Nobel Prize winner and former Irish foreign minister responsible for it, Sean MacBride. This entered the modern history of North–South relations in 1984 at the latest, when the United States and Great Britain left UNESCO, blaming its media policy.[1] Since the basic problems of global information flow have changed very little since then and the developing countries' informational and media inferiority persists, the debate on the New World Information Order goes on. Having abated over the course of the 1980s, it was revived at the turn of the twenty-first century.[2]

One of the problems acknowledged in the debate was that the international information and communications flow was not and is not uniform. It features various zones and currents of greater and lesser intensity (figure 8.1). Despite a range of obstacles to the international information flow, one of the main problems consists of the asymmetrical relations of exchange between the Western industrialized countries and their developing counterparts. Here, it is important to

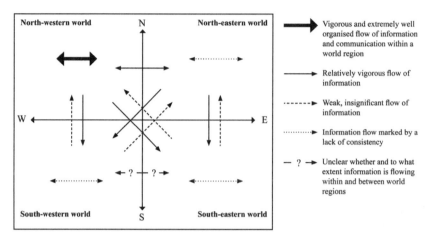

Figure 8.1 International flow of information
Source: Based on Florian Fleck, *Einige Bemerkungen zum Post-MacBride Bericht*,
Publizistik 29, 1984

distinguish between problems affecting the flow of information from the developing to the industrialized countries and vice versa.

In the debate on the New World Information Order during the 1970s and early 1980s, the oligopoly enjoyed by the four big news agencies – Agence France-Press (AFP), Associated Press (AP), Reuters and United Press International (UPI) – was blamed for the thin and often distorted stream of news from the developing countries. As described already in relation to international reporting, the MacBride Report criticized a range of basic problems typical of the views of foreign countries conveyed by the media: *overemphasizing events* of little importance; fitting together disparate facts to make an artificial whole (*making news*); suggesting flawed conclusions (*misinterpretation by implication*) and failing to report significant developments and problems.

The problems afflicting the flow of information from the Western industrialized countries to the developing ones in the field of the mass media tend to arise not as a result of under-supply but over-supply. The development of satellite technology in particular aroused hopes in the socialist states and in developing countries that Western informational dominance could be countered more effectively. After the Second World War, the United Nations adopted the principle of the 'free flow of information', which embodied the freedom to gather and disseminate information across borders. This was derived from the basic principles of liberal democratic laws on freedom of speech and of the press, but had a dual character. It was both an international law supported by the UN and a political doctrine dear to the US and Western Europe. During the Second World War, this doctrine initially helped the US news agencies to win through against the established British, French and German services in the former colonial states and later became an instrument in the ideological struggle with the Soviet Union.[3]

The developing countries were concerned about the possible export of Western values and conceptions of society, but also took steps to counter the over-saturation of their media markets with Western entertainment goods.[4] The principle of the 'free and balanced flow of information', forged in the debate on the New World Information Order, expressed the desire to improve the exchange of information by representing the developing countries more strongly in the media of the industrialized countries (the flow of information *from* the developing countries *to* the industrialized countries). It also reflected, however, the developing countries' intention to control political content of Western origin disseminated by the media. The US in particular criticized the fact that the discussion on the New World Information Order shifted away from an emphasis on the aspect of exchange towards that of control at the instigation of many autocratically governed states. This shift also saw the newly formulated principles of communication policy functionalized as political doctrines by the developing countries. The United States left UNESCO as a consequence.[5]

The political development of the concepts of the New World Information Order laid the foundations for an international controversy among the Western industrialized countries, mainly emanating from the US, but also apparent in public responses in Western Europe. The activities of UNESCO were paid far less attention in the Western European media than in the developing countries, and were frequently portrayed as a campaign launched by the socialist states.[6]

Yet it is no wonder that what was surely the most significant challenge to and relativization of the North–South information divide to date was once again closely linked with American politics. During the war in Afghanistan of 2001 and the Iraq War of 2003, the Arab satellite television network al-Jazeera succeeded in breaking the oligopolistic position of the big global agencies Associated Press, Reuters and Agence France-Presse and major networks such as CNN or the BBC, which had dominated the flow of international news (see chapter 3, p. 75). The US and Great Britain protested repeatedly about the network, pressuring its owner, Emir al-Thani of Qatar, to censor it, arguing that it was putting the United States and Western citizens at risk by showing video messages from the terrorist Osama bin Laden. This, however, had little to do with al-Jazeera's controversial programming policies and straddling of pro-democracy and pan-Arabist agendas. The network was merely providing an alternative to its American counterparts with their striking patriotism.

The American protests against al-Jazeera were in fact part of a struggle over informational dominance on the front line. The situation in 2001 (the war in Afghanistan) and 2003 (the war in Iraq) had changed fundamentally in comparison with the second Gulf War of 1991. Then, the first boom in satellite dishes had begun in the Middle East. Arabs in particular felt insufficiently informed about events in Kuwait and Iraq by the existing Arab networks – al-Jazeera was founded only in 1996 – and watched the American network CNN on a large scale. At the very least, they gained access to footage live from the theatre of war, though it soon emerged that the American armed forces were carrying out almost perfect censorship. There were probably more than 100,000 victims of the war in Iraq. Thanks to the information pool established by the US in Dhahran in Saudi Arabia, they failed to make it onto a single television screen.

Today, the Arab public and the world public, the latter linked with al-Jazeera through numerous cooperation agreements, is no longer dependent on CNN, Western media and news agencies. The flow of information from North to South has in some respects been reversed – one more reason for the US to step up its efforts in the sphere of international broadcasting (see chapter 6). For a network like al-Jazeera appears entirely capable of mobilizing the 'average Arab citizen'. Whenever a government attempts to mollify criticism of US Middle East policy widespread among its own citizenry, al-Jazeera exposes policies of every type to sometimes sharp critique.

Southern countries have made some progress. For the first time, certain countries in Asia, Africa and Latin America have managed to inform the global public sphere of their concerns in unfiltered fashion and evade the 'communication imperialism' of the industrialized countries by means of the new instrument of direct broadcasting by satellite. Yet we should avoid overstating their achievements. Given the attention paid to a network such as al-Jazeera in the West, we are clearly dealing with an exceptional phenomenon that occurs during times of crisis. Neither Western media nor Western consumers as yet typically obtain news directly from the media of a developing country, that is, without it first being filtered by news agencies and journalists within the national media system.

The world information system still exhibits fundamental structural asymmetries. There is still a need for the kind of political regulation addressed in the debate on the New World Information Order. The globalization of international journalism, which has relied on technological innovations in satellite communication (or in journalism on the Internet), has changed this situation very little. Linguistic and other barriers are simply still too high for the peoples of the world to understand one another directly (see chapter 3). Most Western journalists have access, at best, to a small selection of media viewpoints from non-European media discourses. The global journalistic opinion leaders still tend to privilege Western media such as the *New York Times* and CNN. The big agencies continue to supply the world with news. This means, for example, that an African country quite often has to report on a neighbouring country via the indirect route of London (Reuters) or Paris (AFP) – a detour during which media reports are often refocused through a specifically Western lens.

There is thus still a major need for media regulation, particularly in the international context of the major mass media. When the UN World Information Summit was held in Geneva in 2003, however, it was clearly apparent that the international community has never recovered from the departure of the US and UK from UNESCO in 1984. While both countries had long since rejoined the cultural organization, there was simply no debate on the flow of information and sources characteristic of the big media and the need to reorder it. At the end of the day, despite computers and the Internet, it is still these media that imbue the consciousness of most consumers.

Instead, the documents produced by the World Information Summit – the 'Declaration of Principles'[7] and 'Plan of Action'[8] – bear witness to a total withdrawal from the debate on the realities of international news provision in television, radio and the press. The individual and group medium of the Internet, which functions as a new information policy paradigm for the international community, is now very much to the fore. In the ten-page Declaration of Principles, the classic media are mentioned in just one paragraph. The key sentence referring to the international order states: 'We reaffirm the necessity of reducing international imbalances affecting the media, particularly as regards infrastructure, technical resources and the development of human skills' (§ 9). Hidden in the latter pages of the Plan of Action we find some cryptic demands, which will surely never form the basis for international action on media policy, such as: '(We) encourage the media – print and broadcast as well as new media – to continue to play an important role in the Information Society' (§ C9).

Clearly, such programmatic statements are a mere caricature of the debate on the New World Information Order in the 1970s and 1980s. It is tacitly accepted that the mass media are a matter for nation-states, which remain largely unsupervised competitors tussling over the raw material known as 'information'. Within this nation-based liberal globalism, the imbalance of forces between the United States and Europe on the one hand and the developing countries on the other remains unchanged. There is no reference to promoting global media, by establishing independent news agencies for example. We find no declaration of political intent to promote cooperative agreements on the exchange of footage or news. There is merely a very feeble call for international cooperation on the education of journalists (§ C9d).

In the era of globalization, media policy and media law remain firmly in the hands of nation-states – with a few striking exceptions, namely whenever the nation-state threatens global capitalist interests. One example of this is the agreement on the protection of intellectual property rights within the global trading system (TRIPS), one of the few multinational agreements in the field of the media. This agreement, which prohibits the developing countries from making pirate copies of Western intellectual property, from computer software to simple television programmes, is certainly enhancing the protection of such property. Industrialized countries and a few advanced developing countries may benefit from the improved safeguards on intellectual authorship and the resulting stimulus for further research and development provided by the TRIPS agreement. Yet in many developing countries, welfare is suffering on the path to modernization. The stimuli for the creation of knowledge fail to outweigh the disadvantages – increased prices and reduced dissemination of information goods.[9] Particularly in developing countries, pirating does a great deal to help develop technological competence. So far, however, there is a dearth of solid evidence that tightening up property rights has boosted the investment climate for research and development. We also lack sufficient evidence that property rights increase the import of technology to developing countries.

A further example of the power of Western capital to assert its interests within certain limited fields of international media policy is the World Trade Organization (WTO). In the view of many experts, the WTO agreements with China entail many opportunities for the development of the Chinese telecommunications sector, but also uncertainties and risks.[10] China has proved willing, as a new member of the WTO Basic Telecommunications Agreement, to undertake extensive deregulation of telecommunications (facilitating pricing in line with market conditions; guaranteeing networking rights, lowering import duty, etc.). Geographical restrictions on mobile telephony are to be abolished in the next five to six years. The current ban on foreign direct investment will be modified: in future a foreign stake of up to 49 per cent is to be allowed. This also applies to the audio-visual sector, where it has been agreed that foreign investors may own up to 49 per cent of *joint ventures* distributing videos, sound recordings and film rights.

For China, the WTO agreements mean a reduction in import duties of around 13 per cent to 3 per cent and less by 2005, which will boost the import of foreign products in the field of telecommunications and ICT. China can also export its own products more easily, as import restrictions on goods from China will be lifted in certain countries. While China will thus gain certain advantages in the import–export trade, its own production industries will face significant competition on the domestic market, having lost their price advantage.

While trade in telecommunications products has been made easier by WTO agreements, concerned commentators in the US are asking what would happen if China failed to comply with its contractual obligations. What kind of sanctions could the WTO apply to a major power like China, should it fail to liberalize as agreed? How would China respond to external pressure to liberalize, and would it submit to WTO jurisdiction? China's membership of the WTO may, according to American experts such as Bruce Stokes of the Council of Foreign Relations, lead to an existential dilemma for the organization. On the one hand, it is vital to ensure that the WTO functions properly. On the other hand, for political reasons, expelling China as *ultima ratio* seems almost unthinkable. The logic of the WTO, based on economic calculation rather than the premises of development policy, is being subjected to scrutiny; according to Stokes, it is vital to formulate a pre-emptive risk strategy.

Freedom of the media: the regressive paradox of globalization

Some experts, such as Canadian media studies scholar Marc Raboy, believe that a global media policy is taking shape and is poised to marginalize national media law. The main evidence alluded to is the agreements mentioned above in the field of copyright protection, WTO measures or the EU television guidelines of 1997 (see p. 153).[11] Raboy contradicts himself by conceding that the nation-state continues to be 'the main site of communications and cultural policy-making'.[12] To be considered epoch-making, global media policy would have to cover more than a few international agreements in the future market for information technology. Many key theorists of globalization have placed much emphasis on its democratizing impact. The constructs of a 'global public sphere' and 'global civil society' have received much attention. They have, however, usually been conceived without taking into account necessary media policy parameters, in the silent hope, perhaps, that in the emerging era media policy will soon be as superfluous as economic policy, as the actors of civil society wrest regulatory authority from the state, even against its will.

At least in the field of international communication, this thoroughly appealing vision has proved extremely naive. Unless media policy is refashioned globally, globalization leaves plenty of scope for national regulation, reinforcing the political and legal stagnation of media systems across the world. Transnational NGOs such as Freedom House, Reporters Sans Frontières or the Committee for the Protection of Journalists provide clear evidence that while media freedom has improved over the last quarter century, the great era of improvements was the 1980s and early 1990s, as a result of the political upheavals in Latin America and Eastern Europe. The following decade, up to the present, has meanwhile been characterized by preservation of the status quo and even regressive tendencies, as a glance at the data of the American NGO Freedom House illustrates:

Table 8.1 Trends in media freedom identified by Freedom House*

	1983/4	%	1994	%	2004	%
Free	36	19.5	67	34.9	73	37.8
Partly free	58	31.5	69	35.9	49	25.4
Not free	81**	43.8	51	26.6	71	36.8
Information unavailable	10	5.4	5	2.6	0	0
Total number of countries	**185**	**100**	**192**	**100**	**193**	**100**

[*] Survey years always refer to the past year. The figures for the 2004 Index thus pertain to the situation in 2003. Countries whose press and broadcasting sectors for the period 1983/1984 were ranked separately and in a non-uniform manner (e.g. press = free, broadcasting = partly free or press = partly free, broadcasting = not free), are categorized here as 'partly free'. [**] In this table, to avoid distorting the real trends within media systems, the former Soviet and Yugoslav republics, which were clearly subject to authoritarian rule, are included in the 'not free' category although these states are classified under 'information unavailable' in the Freedom House list.

Source: compiled by the author, drawing on <www.freedomhouse.org> (rounded percentage figures)

The situation of the media improved markedly as a result of the increase in free media systems between 1983–84 and 1994, matched by an equally sharp drop in the number of unfree media systems over this period. In 1994 only 26.6 per cent of all countries were still categorized as 'not free'. This means that within ten years the number of restrictive media systems had been reduced by half – a dramatic development associated with the abating, then end, of the East–West conflict. The decade of intensifying globalization on the other hand – 1994 to 2004 – saw only a very small increase in free media systems and a notable parallel increase in their unfree counterparts. From a global comparative perspective, the last decade proved a regressive period for media freedom. As the major new transnational media, direct satellite broadcasting and the Internet, spread only from the early 1990s on, there can be only one conclusion. The very communicative technologies which have stimulated the globalization debate so much, which indeed first triggered this debate, have failed thus far to contribute to media freedom. This provides quantitative substantiation that the 'Third Wave of Democratization' remained untouched by the information revolution.[13]

Regardless of all the technological progress that has been made and the introduction of new techniques of communicative *connectivity*, it is wrong to claim that globalization has brought about *political system change* by increasing global press and media freedom in a linear fashion.

The communication studies scholar Verena Metze-Mangold has correctly pointed out that the information society of the future is not necessarily a more free society. It features numerous new paradoxes,[14] including, among other things, new restrictions related to the struggle against terrorism and the changed international political equilibrium after 11 September 2001. Transnational media fusions have the potential to weaken the authoritarian nation-state. This potential is, however, quite often rendered null and void by transnational enterprises' tendency to reach agreements with authoritarian leaders that amount to pledges of loyalty (see chapter 9). The spread of the Internet in China entails the potential for an alternative, democratic public sphere. However, in 2003–04, the Chinese state responded very successfully by deploying perhaps 30,000 censors.

The new media of satellite broadcasting and the Internet have produced a diversity that has increasingly marginalized the official media in authoritarian regimes. Yet fifteen years of the information revolution, which spread across the world following the political transformation of 1989, were also a period of democratic stagnation worldwide. The new media in particular often offer 'old wine in new bottles'. The aesthetic and journalistic professionalization on offer since the last decade on all continents, above all in Asia, Africa and Latin America, has rarely entailed increasing pluralism of content (see chapter 3).

How, though, could anyone expect democracies to arise through the development of media technology and cross-border communication? Is this not to overestimate totally the power of the media and to rashly discount the power of politics? After all, when political upheavals occurred in Eastern Europe and Latin America, freedom of speech and of the media instantly improved – not the other way round. And here, of course, lies the failure of global media policy on the path to a New World Information Order in the middle of the age of globalization, an age evoked so eagerly by politicians to justify their actions. The onus is on the major Western powers and superpowers to get the development of media freedoms onto the agenda by reformulating international media policy. Multilateral agreements and goal-setting in this field would have to become a fixed feature of development policy.

One might at least have expected that prohibitions on receiving foreign satellite programmes and Internet services, imposed in states such as Iran, Saudi Arabia and Cuba, or rigid laws imposing prison sentences for unlawful use as in Tunisia would have been subject to the same kind of vigorous liberalization by the world community as economic legislation, which is at the centre of the activities of the WTO, World Bank and International Monetary Fund (IMF). The notion that the new media, which can be received and used worldwide, would solve such problems on their own was at best far too optimistic. At worst, however, the argument that globalization has a democratizing effect must be understood as a smokescreen, which directly concealed the fact that the mass media and freedom of expression could scarcely be less important within current international politics, and in any case less so than in the early 1980s, when the debate on the New World Information Order was in full swing.

One example of the failure of media policy is the largely abortive attempt to extend the field of influence of the representatives for media freedom at the Organization for Security and Cooperation in Europe (OSCE) beyond the European signatory states.[15] The office of media freedom representative, occupied until 2003 by the former German Bundestag deputy Freimut Duve, still lacks any power of sanction. In associated states in Central Asia or in the Islamic world, where the OSCE has been highly active, there has been very little response. The extension of the OSCE mechanism to other states would however be worth striving for, as it would involve the creation of a forum for discussion and strategic planning legitimized by the powerful.

Even authors such as Seán Ó Siochrú, Bruce Girard and Amy Mahan, who are of the view that authority for media policy will slowly shift from the national to the global level, concede that at present the economy clearly dominates. At the moment, in their opinion, Global Media Governance is least developed where it is most needed – in the field of political freedoms and in the bodies and international documents of the United Nations.[16]

European media policy: reactive subsidiarity

Europe is perhaps the most dynamic region in the world, featuring numerous existing and emerging relations of interdependence between the member states of the European Union in economics, politics and society. If in no other, one might at least expect to find a process of media policy integration in this region of the 'globalized' world. Yet this is the case only to a limited extent. Europe-wide institutions, laws and authorities, intended to regulate cross-border issues of media communication or national developments related to media freedom, exist only wherever economic interests encourage this.

As globally, so in the European Union: with a small number of exceptions, national media policy and laws set the tone. The EU guidelines on television, modified in 1997, regulate the European circulation of advertisements and the harmonization of national regulations on advertising, sponsoring and teleshopping. The member states are also urged to take steps to ensure that events important to the Community are broadcast on television (such as sport). Beyond this, however, the attempt to introduce a quota for European television productions – to protect film and television productions from European countries against the supremacy of American films for example – which does exist in the cinematic field (see chapter 4), was toned down to such an extent that the relevant regulations remain de facto at the discretion of member states.

Policies of this kind seem to fit neatly with the idea of a falling away of borders worldwide and of a regionalization that is open to globalization. Europe is not to shut out non-European products, even if countries like the US still do, when, for example, it grants broadcasting licences to Americans only. The way in which the guidelines on television have been formulated, however, makes it clear that the European Union – with the exception of certain major European events and the field of advertising – has basically declared itself not responsible *in any way* for regulating issues of broadcasting, even in matters other than quotas. The Amsterdam Protocol – part of the Revision of the EC treaty by the 1997 Treaty of Amsterdam – mentions public broadcasting for the first time[17] and confirms that it is the task of the member states to organize and define broadcasting. There have at least been attempts in recent years, if not with legal means then at least through increased funding, to improve the weak position of European films.

This, however, does not plausibly explain why regulatory authority should remain largely in the hands of the nation-state despite the fact that programmes systematically cross national borders through satellite broadcasting. Those responsible for media policy in the European Union, as at the global level, cooperate only very sporadically. The concentration of private televisual power in the hands of Italian prime minister Silvio Berlusconi is, for example, repeatedly criticized by the European Union. Within the framework of its own regulations, however, the EU has to sit idly by and do nothing. The clause on cultural compatibility in the Maastricht Treaty (art. 128, paragraph 4), according to which one might argue that the situation in Italy is no longer compatible with the basic value of media pluralism held by the EU, and that Brussels must therefore take action, is being ignored.

The Maastricht Treaty includes in art. 3b, paragraph 2 the principle of subsidiarity, according to which the Community takes action only when the member state is incapable of solving problems alone. If one recalls the actual extent of media use, it is clear that European politicians, with their undemanding media policy, are very much in synch with the habits of European consumers. The same applies in Europe as globally: regular cross-border media use, by means of satellite television for example, is the exception rather than the rule (see chapter 3, p. 57).

However, while no political system exists within the global context apart from the feeble United Nations, which exercises an influence only in situations of extreme crisis via the Security Council, the European Union has a supranational government with considerable powers in the shape of the European Commission. It can and does intervene effectively in the governance of member states. A common constitution, a common market featuring the free movement of labour: many indicators bear witness to a high degree of integration, which offers plenty of space for influencing media policy as well. A passive approach prevails, however, not only in the sphere of media law, but also as regards political action at the institutional level.

National subsidiarity is emphasized, while the mass media are conceived as market-based service providers. There is little sign of initiatives aimed at establishing public television for Europe, which might play an important role in creating a European public sphere beyond feeble and uncompetitive networks such as EuroNews. Such moves might encourage the formation of a European identity and combat Europeans' rampant disinterest in European issues.[18]

At both the European and global levels, media policy and laws should thus be understood not only as reactive instruments aimed at the behaviour of media and consumers in individual states. They have an (as yet) untapped potential to shape the process of globalization.

The refashioning of authoritarian national media policy

One of the arguments heard most frequently within the globalization debate states that it should be near impossible for authoritarian systems to stop people from receiving foreign radio and television programmes directly. The national and regional media systems of Asia, Africa and Latin America have often responded to the globalization of the media by increasing the political control of information. This behaviour can be interpreted from various standpoints. It can be seen as evidence that the globalization of the media – contrary to the expectations of many – can be brought into line with the prevailing national system relatively easily. The fact that the authoritarian state is having to take action on media policy in the first place can however be regarded as an indication of the power of global media to open up and democratize. The state, though, has thus far always managed to reinvent itself, to respond effectively for the most part and hamper any liberal opening of the media as a response to globalization (see above, p. 149).

There are numerous examples of anti-globalist counter-regulation in authoritarian states, such as prohibitions on satellite dishes in Saudi Arabia and Iran and restrictive legislation on the Internet in countries such as Cuba, Turkey, Tunisia and China. In Malaysia, access to the opposition forum created by supporters of Anwar Ibrahim, *Malaysianini.com.my*, has been blocked by the Mahathir regime several times since 2001, the dictator arguing that it damages Malaysia's international standing.

Developments in the institutional structure of the media system are emerging as a new trend in the arsenal of authoritarian media policy. These are aimed only peripherally at global media influences, but are bound up with them nonetheless. While on the one hand there is evidence of a tentative shift towards the development of independent associations of journalists in a number of states (such as Algeria and Indonesia), in other states institutions are being created whose civil society status is more apparent than real. They are in reality pseudo-NGOs launched by the state. The umbrella organization for many national journalists' associations, the International Federation of Journalists (IFJ), for example, protested when the Botswanan government introduced a draft law to establish a new 'media council'. As well as monitoring the media to ensure adherence to journalistic ethics, it is also to have the authority to impose fines of up to $1,000 and prison sentences of up to three years if 'media ethics' are breached. The IFJ called upon the government to leave the affairs of the journalistic trade and ethics to journalists. It also urged the government to take steps to ensure greater freedom, rather than further restricting freedom of speech and of the media.

An analogous development has been apparent since 2001 in Jordan, where the government has dissolved the ministry of information and established a Higher Media Council in its place.[19] The council is not a self-regulatory body. Its tasks largely match those of the former ministry in controlling information and carrying out censorship. Examples of pseudo-institutionalization can also be found in media law, in the normative-programmatic sphere of institutions. In 2000, Pakistan's military regime produced a draft law creating a new information order (*Freedom of Information Ordinance*). The document states that the public right to information is to be improved and government actions made more transparent. It looks at first sight like an attempt to extend the government's duty to provide its citizens with information.[20] Careful analysis, however, reveals that the government retains extensive room for manoeuvre to this day. It can classify government documents as secret, rendering the duty to provide information practically meaningless.

In the Middle East, as in many parts of Asia and Africa, the pressure of globalization has clearly produced counter-regulation within the media system. This adopts the guise of modern media policy but is unable to conceal its authoritarianism. International norms demand the democratization of the media, and the states of the Third World appear to be organizing their media systems on the model of Western democracies. On closer inspection, however, many institutions are only apparently modern. At the same time, there is in some societies a trend towards institutionalization 'from below', with independent journalists' associations developing in Algeria and Indonesia for example.[21] Moreover, by no means all state attempts at regulation succeed. Satellite television has taken hold in Iran, for example, despite being banned. The globalized media world forces actors to adapt to 'professional' working standards, modern legislation and regulation, an adaptation necessary for technological reasons if for no other. Whether this form of globalization of the media merely involves imitating 'techniques' of democratization or whether democratic 'values' are being internalized as well can be judged only on a case-by-case basis.

9

Media Capital – the Limits of Transnationalization

One of the gravest malformations of the globalization debate is the view, held by numerous observers, that globe-spanning Western media capital is the key motor driving the globalization of the media.[1] This has come about because the debate has been unduly restricted to a small number of well-known transnational broadcasters, above all CNN, MTV and Star TV. Their market share, given the many hundreds of satellite channels broadcasting in numerous national languages (see chapter 3), which reach by far the largest portion of the worldwide public, is in fact negligible, not to mention radio and most print media, which are in any case mostly a product of local ownership. Furthermore, too much significance is attached to processes of media concentration in the Euro-American-Australian context, for the global development of media capital is a dynamic process occurring at all levels, nationally, regionally and globally. Neither the presence of the global broadcast networks nor the existing direct investment by Western companies in national and regional media point to a general shift in power towards large Western companies such as, for example, AOL Warner, News Corporation (Rupert Murdoch) or Bertelsmann.

Western media companies are globally influential in the selling of music, film and software rights (the TRIPS Agreement being a prime example, see chapter 8). They are active exporters of entertainment culture, partners or majority shareholders in many enterprises, and have mechanisms at their disposal that shape the global news system, above all through the major news agencies and international radio broadcasts. The present situation of media around the world is however a far cry from the economic domination of global journalism by transnational (Western) firms, in whose wake – one might logically conclude – the homogenization of media content would follow.

Quite the opposite. Media capital's lack of global reach is, along-side the political persistence of the nation-state and the major differences that mark the media discourses of the world's nation-states or cultural areas, the key reason why the globalization of the media today is taking place to a far more modest degree and at a far slower pace than is generally assumed.

Imponderables of the international flow of capital

Otfried Jarren and Werner A. Meier have rightly pointed to the limits of the internationalization of the media. The tendency for European publishers such as Bertelsmann to merge with American and Australian media firms is frequently regarded as an index of economic globalization. The globalization of media capital is however merely *one* facet of the economic shifts under way at the present time and does not affect all countries and continents to the same degree. Even in the USA and in many European countries, the media sector features a large number of protectionist obstacles to investment. In the USA, for example, foreign media companies have been impeded in their attempts to acquire broadcasting licences.[2]

In Germany too, the bankruptcy of the media firm owned by Leo Kirch in 2002 triggered a discussion strongly anti-globalist in complexion. To make it more difficult for Rupert Murdoch to gain a permanent foothold in the German market – and many of those responsible for media policy were keen advocates of this – it was argued that protectionist buffers ought to be put in place. Such demands, however, not only touch upon the fundamentals of media policy within the framework of the EU. They also challenge the underlying pro-globalization tenor that dominated the media debate in the 1990s. This entails falsely redefining critical questions about the quality of the media landscape, particularly the relationship between information, entertainment and sensationalism, as issues of 'protection from globalization'. Rupert Murdoch clearly does *not* represent quality journalism – but do private television networks like RTL or media trusts such as the Axel-Springer-Verlag, the owner of Europe's largest tabloid *BILD*? Did Leo Kirch, who achieved success by selling American B-movies?

European and American media markets feature substantial anti-globalist reflexes, while at the same time Western media policy, via WTO and GATT agreements, suggests or even prescribes free trade for the countries of Asia, Africa and Latin America. The existing imbalance in terms of media policy is however smaller than one might imagine, because the weakest developing countries, the so-called 'Least Developed Countries' (LDCs), are anything but lucrative markets for Western makers of media. As a rule, therefore, the mechanisms of the IMF and World Bank fail to effectively force these countries to liberalize. The attractive markets of the 'Third World', led by Asia and above all China, are managing to 'protect' themselves by keeping the power of capital on a tight leash within their own territories.

The story of Rupert Murdoch's network, Star TV, is a prime example of the imponderables and limits of the international flow of capital in the media industry, particularly because it has a presence in continents such as Asia. From an economic point of view, Star TV is less successful than those running it had initially hoped. It has in fact gone into the red. Several years ago, Murdoch complied with the wishes of the Chinese government by taking the BBC news out of his programming. He even offered to develop encryption software for the Chinese television market if Star TV received access to the Chinese cable network in return. This initially promising initiative, however, failed to produce results.

Despite Asian markets' enormous potential for growth, this continues to be a high-risk area. Success has even eluded Murdoch's News Corporation, one of the largest Western media companies. A 1994 study by UNESCO confirmed that Asian countries (with the exception of the Philippines) are less transnational than their European counterparts in that they have significantly fewer imported television programmes.[3] Even in the contemporary era, a small portion only of the sales and revenue of the large media companies such as AOL Warner, Disney, Viacom, News Corporation, Bertelsmann and Seagram is generated in Asia, Africa and Latin America.

On the whole, the same situation applies today. In 2002, in the journal *Foreign Policy*, Benjamin Compaine, a leading scholar at the Massachusetts Institute of Technology (MIT), exposed the myth of the 'global player' in the media industry:

> The notion of the rise of a handful of all-powerful transnational media giants is [. . .] vastly overstated. Some media companies own properties internationally [. . .], but no large media conglomerate owns newspapers, book publishers, radio stations, cable companies, or television licenses in all the major world markets. News Corp. comes closest to being a global media enterprise in both content and distribution, but on a global scale it is still a minor presence.[4]

The notion of transnational media companies ruling the world, which has formed part of the globalization debate from the outset, is so far away from the reality that one wonders how it arose in the first place.

The triumph of regional princes over global players

The Eurocentrism of what is perhaps the best-known text on the economic globalization of the media, Edward S. Herman and Robert W. McChesney's *The Global Media*,[5] is characteristic of how the globalization debate has been distorted. The authors warn of the dangers of the global dominance of Western media enterprises. In the empirical section, it will come as no surprise, they provide evidence drawn almost exclusively from companies and linkages in North America, Europe, Australia/New Zealand and occasionally Latin America and India.[6] The empirical base of their argument clearly lies in Europe and North America, and they present an entirely justified critique of the increasing influence of monopoly capital *within* Western countries and Latin America, the 'backyard' of US imperialism, and economically liberal India.

Yet even in the case of Latin America and India, the assumption that Western media capital dominates the market is foreshortened and exaggerated. The authors are entirely wrong to argue that Anglo-American media capital is having the same impact in every region of the world.[7] This is to assert a market dominance which Western media companies do not in fact enjoy in Asia, Africa, the Middle East or Latin America. Even in Europe, on the German market for example, apart from film imports and despite American majority shares of networks such as Pro 7 and Sat 1, American media play a very limited role; they are by no means dominant.

What does Herman and McChesney's reference to Western domination of the 'global media system', as they call it, mean, given that they also, generally in passing and apparently contradicting the main message of their work, note that:

> Although the global media continue their growth and consolidation, and the tide of commercialization and centralization remains strong, this process has met local and national resistance, which has sometimes slowed it down and helped to preserve indigenous cultural-political media space. Within any specific nation, domestic media, traditions, language, and regulation still play key, often predominant, roles in determining the media culture. The development of a global commercial media system is not a linear process but, rather, a complex one characterized by fits and starts; and while the trendline seems clear its future remains uncertain.[8]

The 'global players', the major Western media giants, are in reality regional concerns with a strong presence in North America, Europe and Australia and more or less active off-shoots in other world markets. However, they do not as yet reign supreme in the latter. Indigenous media capital is far more widely dispersed. Meanwhile, the other major regional players of the world, national and regional media companies, ignored almost entirely in the globalization literature, have used the age of globalization to extend their influence on a grand scale. They are in no way inferior to the global companies and in most cases are in fact superior to them.

The large Arab media players, such as Prince al-Walid (Alwaleed) bin Talal bin Abdulaziz al-Saud, member of the Saudi royal family, master of a large Arab media empire and major international investor, are the main reason why US capital today is involved only to a very limited extent in the more than 150 Arab television channels broadcast via satellite. In the 2004 *Forbes* List of the world's richest people, the prince is at number 4, only three places behind software billionaire Bill Gates, while a Western media mogul like Silvio Berlusconi only makes it to number 30, and the Australo-American Rupert Murdoch trails in at number 43.[9]

Rupert Murdoch's limited investments in Middle Eastern television markets are due to his good relations with Prince al-Walid, who has acquired a stake in Murdoch's News Corporation in return.[10] Over the last decade, the television industry has seen regional capital interests develop with particular vigour, emanating from the Arabian Peninsula to the entire Arab world.[11] These are bound up so closely with the national leadership in Saudi Arabia and the Gulf states, via family ties and a wide range of personal channels, that competing capital from Europe and the US can always be kept at arm's length via state patronage. Saudi activities have also unleashed regional competition. Some other Arab states have been compelled to deregulate their television markets to prevent a Saudi monopoly of opinion.[12] It will be interesting to see how CNN's plans for an Arab programme unfold against the background of the high degree of regionalization which typifies this particular television market.

Murdoch's and other Western media companies tend to play a rather thankless role in the Middle East. In effect, they fill in the gaps in the supply chain of film and entertainment goods. The presence of capital in this form, as Naomi Sakr correctly puts it, reflects a type of globalization lacking in social and economic depth. Western capital is not strongly represented in Arab media markets, and is allowed into them in the first place only through personal relations with Arab media

empires. Indeed, it does so in an economically, politically and culturally blunted form which demonstrates clearly that media capital in the
Middle East functions in almost every respect like a globalization filter:

> [The globalisation process] stretches far but does not run very deep. [. . .]
> [It] is not clear that these far-flung interconnections involve more than a
> super-rich elite of individuals whose personal importance to their busi-
> nesses relies heavily on their own one-to-one connections with each other
> and to the centres of power in world capitals. [. . .] [T]he concentration
> of ownership in Arab satellite television helped to minimize the number
> of separate links with foreign suppliers. Choices about content, especially
> for digital channels, were based on the need to fill space and protect infra-
> structural investment without breaking editorial taboos.[13]

It could be argued that the resistance to global media capital found
in the Arab world and the Middle East is a speciality of the region,
which makes more effort to seal itself off from external influences than
the rest of the world. It is true that the authoritarian state is even more
entrenched in the region than for example in Latin America, where
comprehensive democratization has been in progress for twenty years.
The re-Islamization which began with the Iranian Revolution of 1979
is another factor bolstering an anti-globalist climate, despite being
significant only in certain countries and among specific strata of the
population.

The tendency for the New Media and direct television broadcasts
by satellite to strengthen national and regional media capital is
however international, and is evident elsewhere. Why Herman and
McChesney regard Brazil and Mexico, for instance, as parts of a television empire run by the major Western transnational companies, is
best known to themselves.[14] In these two countries, native media concerns such as Globo and Televisa dominate around two thirds of the
television advertising markets. Indigenous productions, and not only
in the shape of the famous 'soap operas', are very much to the fore.
Western investors are far from having a dominant market position.[15]

India is also mentioned by Herman and McChesney as an example
of the power of Western companies. Rupert Murdoch is in fact a major
investor in the largest private television conglomerate, Zee TV. The
public broadcasting group Doordashan, however, continues to hold a
monopoly on terrestrial television broadcasts, which still enjoy the largest audience among the poor of India. In the satellite television market,
Subhash Chandra, founder of Zee TV, managed to stave off Rupert
Murdoch's efforts to acquire a majority share in the company in the late
1990s. Today, Zee TV is the first Indian media company to combine

production and distribution.[16] Murdoch's network, Star TV, has a merely subordinate position on the Indian market. Zee TV, not Star TV, has proved the most important competitor of Doordashan within the South Asian national and regional context over the last decades.[17]

Jarren and Meier are right to point out that, alongside strong national and regional competitors, lack of know-how also hinders global media players' success in international markets. National and regional programmes can respond much faster to cultural trends. The splintering of MTV into a number of regional sub-networks is an attempt to keep pace with this. The strategy of 'recycling' media products, the majority of them in the English language, in Asia, Africa and Latin America, products which have already paid for themselves on the American and European markets, has reached its limits. The dynamics of know-how encourage the particularization of programme content, push global actors to adapt to local programme preferences and favour local media capital.

While the tendency towards globalization in the television industry is at least clearly recognizable, though far less extensive than is often assumed, the degree of interdependence in the radio industry is even more limited. American and British pop music has certainly spread around the world. In the early 1990s, more than 70 per cent of pop music was being produced by big firms such as EMI, Warner and Sony.[18] Yet, in comparison to television, the conditions are very favourable for the production of radio programmes in terms of both entertainment and information. This guarantees that radio tends to be structurally decentralized, and focused on nation-states or even sub-regions. The compulsion to expand across national borders, to access larger markets for expensive products such as American films, is replaced in the case of radio by the ability to reach even very small groups of listeners and make a profit.

From a comparative global perspective, the structure of radio markets themselves is even more decentralized than that of television markets. While they may indeed offer American and British pop music, the 'image', a 'language' which can be understood across national boundaries, is absent. While television programmes in linguistically homogenous areas find a cross-border audience, radio programmes are not usually listened to even in neighbouring countries. Worldwide, the editorial portions of the radio programme are thus in the hands of national producers. David Hendy:

> [Even poorer countries] can establish their own radio production base without too much burden. Similarly, the international trade in

completed radio programmes is also negligible compared with that for the television industry. Radio programmes cannot of course be dubbed or subtitled, so the essentially language-based character of the radio medium sets its own very firm limits to imports and exports. German talk programmes may be happily consumed in Austria, but the market there for French or Italian radio programmes will be virtually non-existent. The worldwide English-language market is potentially huge, but again the low costs in radio production remove any economic motive for significant levels of imports and exports between, say, the UK and the USA. This makes any discussion of Americanization, or cultural imperialism more generally, much less appropriate for the global radio industry than it may be for television, in strictly economic terms at least.[19]

All in all, it is evident that the transnationalization of media capital is a national or regional rather than global phenomenon. The ill-considered catchphrase 'global commercial media system', dominated by 'some ten mostly U.S.-based transnational media conglomerates' (Herman and McChesney),[20] conceals the fact that media markets are by no means characterized by complex interdependence (see chapter 1, p. 21), even if specific transnational linkages – such as those between the geo-cultural area Europe/US – are far advanced. Even here, however, local and regional capital continues to set the tone and is shielded, when push comes to shove, by a protectionist media policy.

The debate on the connection between media and globalization has failed to privilege rational market analysis. It tends to be fixated on a small number of 'global players'. Even in fundamental areas such as media economy, and despite the high degree of business integration, these could easily be investigated to establish the facts. As long as the current fixation persists, the concept of 'globalization', rather than reflecting an objective reality, will remain a self-fulfilling prophecy which acknowledges only that which serves to sustain it.

While we may be in a position to draw some convincing conclusions at this point, further questions as to the social meaning of media capital in the process of globalization remain unanswered. Rupert Murdoch's impact in China, his political agreements with the communist leadership, which induced him, for example, to remove the critical BBC news from the Cantonese Star TV, show that Western capital is willing to come to commercially driven political arrangements to stabilize the authoritarian state. It may thus affirm the prevailing cultural conditions. Global media companies feature the same inconsistencies as their regional counterparts, which tend to promote the politics of the status quo, though they do sometimes contribute to political modernization. By no means do global media enterprises strengthen a global democratic culture.

From a systems theory point of view, once again the key seems to lie in the nation-state's still leading role in media policy. Global inter-dependencies in the media system exist, if at all, exclusively between elites, that is, within the political-economic complex (Murdoch and al-Walid being an example) which subjects global capital to political domestication and tends to prevent the deepening of relations between global media and their audience.

Conclusion: Globalization – a Necessary Myth

Casting light on the myth of 'globalization' as it affects cross-border communication does not mean exposing it as pure fiction. Nor does it mean denying the significance of myths generally. The ceaseless alternation between the formation and transformation of myths is one of the key dynamics in the creation of culture. In his examination of the history of myths from early modern book culture to the modern information society, Michael Giesecke suggests that myth functions to bring order to cultures, reduce the complexity of the social environment and guide behaviour:

> As acts of reflexive self-simplification, myths are indispensable. The expression 'demystification' may thus be misleading. Since the creation of myths is an unavoidable element in the formation of individual and cultural identity, all demystification leads to new myths. All we can aspire to is to find myths in keeping with the times while suppressing those which prove obstacles to progress.[1]

If we view the globalization of media and communication as a myth, it is without doubt one which has encouraged a reorientation of scholarship and innovative ways of looking at a range of processes. 'Globalization' has proven one aspect of the trans-disciplinary preoccupation with international processes, to an even greater extent than the intellectual paradigm of 'modernization', which is immanent in the epochal term 'modernity' itself and which shaped many subjects after the Second World War. 'Globalization' facilitates an examination, appropriate to the contemporary era, of the modern nation-state and the national culture associated with it, a historical formation which is by no means entitled to expect to be around for ever. Its relativization is already clearly evident in the supranational transferral of sovereignty, especially in the case of the European Union.

Yet the myth of globalization entails hegemonic elements. It adheres to the laws of public discourse and is riddled with perceptual errors, ideological projections and political interests and is thus in constant need of correction. Just as every major intellectual problem goes through periods of revision when its premises shift and taken-for-granted elements are subjected to critical examination, the globalization debate has also featured fundamentally critical strands from the very beginning. These have never gone away. They have often found a home in media studies and communication science, though these disciplines have never been able to assert themselves against their big counterparts in the social and economic sciences, which set the tone in discussions of globalization.

The mainstream globalization debate ascribes major importance to the media and cross-border communication as the communicative interlinking of states, groups and individuals increases rapidly. On this view, these processes have a massive influence on the transformation of national political and cultural systems and are fundamentally regarded as irreversible, progressive and interdependent. Yet at present, none of the theoretical fields concerned can claim to rest on a firm empirical foundation. Many of the supposedly core elements of globalization cannot be interpreted as evidence of globalization or, astonishingly, have been researched to such a meagre extent that profound empirical uncertainty prevails. All of this is suppressed in the euphoria. The globalization of cross-border communication is proceeding, in many fields, significantly more slowly and opaquely than has often been assumed. Global communicative integration, often understood as an increase in knowledge of the world, does not even encompass all its functional elites. It has in no way significantly transformed important media sectors such as international journalism. Meanwhile, in this modern information and media age, major population groups have often been reinforced in their local, national or at best regional communicative habits, rather than encouraged to obtain information via the media, or even exchange views, across borders. When scrutinized without preconceptions, all the phenomena derived from cross-border mass communication – system change, the growing together, hybridization or 'glocalization' of national cultures, up to and including a decrease in negative concepts of the 'Other' and inter-state friction – turn out to be blurred projections of the future rather than adequate descriptions of the present.

In the first theoretical field, that of international and transnational *connectivity*, a number of counter-tendencies characteristic of global communication are having such disastrous effects that the necessity for cross-border communication is more apparent than ever, particularly after the events of 11 September. When all is said and done, transnational media, which might in theory constitute supranational global institutions and the key media within a 'global public sphere' liberated from specific national and cultural influences, are as yet non-existent. This applies even to the American television network which claims to be the global opinion leader, CNN. Even today, national media agendas are in synch with the world only in a very superficial way. A small number of major international events are reported all over the world. Such reports should not, however, be mistaken for a profound knowledge of developments across the world. Moreover, even in the modern 'media age', such events can be 'domesticated' by national interest groups almost at will.

The worldwide coverage of the attacks of 11 September 2001 and the Iraq War of 2003 have revealed the paucity of evidence of a communicative integration which supposedly helps alleviate conflicts and liberates the media from the traditionally strong influence of belligerent governments and patriotic cultural influences. Through one-sided coverage in wartime and highly fragmentary discourses, it is still possible to literally seal peoples and entire world regions off from one another and mobilize them for war. We have little reason to assume that a global media network has significantly reduced the susceptibility of societies, even democratic ones, to war propaganda.

Quite the opposite. The technology of direct broadcasting by satellite became widely established at around the same time as the techniques of war propaganda reached the peak of perfection – during the Second Gulf War of 1991. Since then, as the unremittingly critical literature produced by the time of the third Gulf War of 2003 lays bare, while changes have taken place, there has been only minor progress in making wartime communication truly global. Despite increasing the global exchange of images, even the televisual revolutions in the 'South' – in the Arab world for example – were unable to prevent 11 September from becoming the defining event for highly insulated and conflictual media discourses on Middle Eastern and world politics. Only in cases where, as in the case of British war coverage in 2003, the state is already in retreat as a result of multinational integration (the European Union in this case), is there any sign of a slow turning away from particularistic national war coverage. In general, however, at a time when the nation-state is poised to set the tone for generations to come, the notion that the wholesome influence of the media is ridding us of wartime deception as it opens up to the world is a truly out-of-touch aspect of the myth of globalization. We should have nothing more to do with it.

Cross-border media use by large numbers of people is largely limited to specific linguistic regions. Foreign-language media use, meanwhile, remains the privilege of small knowledge elites or special groups such as immigrants. Alongside the still dominant production and use of media within national media areas, contemporary developments in the media are marked by a regionalism of a geo-linguistic hue. At present, it is impossible to state with confidence whether this is open to globalization or not. Major language areas such as the Spanish, Chinese, Indian and Arab are currently experiencing a boom in native-language media. When national borders get in the way, satellites and other types of small-scale border traffic ensure that there is no escape. Under such circumstances, there is a danger that major cultural regions may act as a kind of 'insulation' against global influences. This is the media policy substance of the 'clash of civilizations'. Samuel Huntington, who came up with the slogan, failed to ponder this issue, although it is at least as significant as the essentialist differences which he claims typify the major cultures and religions of the world.

The Internet has introduced a new subtlety to the global array of information, but cross-border linkage is obviously growing more slowly than local and national interactions in many areas. The new uncertainties of the information flow are generating an often 'virtual' knowledge of the world, which is almost impossible to harmonize with verifiable reality. This is 'virtual cosmopolitanism', which has little in common with the attitude of the 'true' cosmopolitan, who has got to know the world and knows the global ropes. The increasing linguistic diversity of the Internet is creating new Babelesque dividing lines. The potential of some political campaigns to mobilize people on a global scale may be impressive, but this occurs only when very specific conditions and alliances are in place. The 'digital divide' between industrialized and developing countries raises doubts about whether the comparative political advantages of a global civil society are making themselves felt to any real extent and are managing to change policies when faced with the power of governments.

In light of this sobering appraisal of connectivity, we clearly have to assess the influence of cross-border mass communication on *system change* with much care. Today, every political and social change, from the fall of the Berlin Wall through the political upheavals in Ukraine,

Lebanon and Kyrgyzstan to the Pope's funeral is thought to be moulded by the global media. Yet we are clearly getting ahead of ourselves. Mass gatherings following the death of a pope have been common throughout history, long before the modern mass media, and political revolutions and uprisings are nothing new either. Quite the opposite. During the era of the information revolution, all appearances to the contrary, the number of free social and media systems has by no means increased. It has in fact decreased or at least stagnated. The information revolution has been left untouched by the 'Third Wave of Democratization', which basically finished with the upheavals in Eastern Europe before the New Media of the Internet and direct broadcasting by satellite had become established. So-called 'demonstration effects' are claimed to promote social change, cross borders by means of the mass media, serve as models of political action for people in other countries and help democracy, supposedly the best political order, to break through across the globe. Yet they have a latent influence and are in any case difficult to measure. The political impact of the media can be proven to exist, if at all, only during phases of political transition, that is, when long-term processes of transformation enter brief periods of radical change.

Ultimately, as far as cultural change is concerned, the globalization debate has produced an internally inconsistent dual myth. This is the notion that culturally imperialist 'Americanization' or 'Westernization' may be accompanied by the 'glocalization' or 'hybridization' of cultures. The European film market as well as much of the pop music listened to worldwide are surely examples of Americanization. These individual pieces of evidence, alluded to again and again, do not, however, allow us to generalize. They permit no overall conclusions about cultural globalization. In many countries and in most world regions, American film imports are in the minority, not to mention television films, produced in the vast majority of countries by national or regional industries. Even in Europe, a cultural stock-taking of film, music, the arts and science would by no means necessarily endorse the thesis of Americanization, which retains coherence only against the background of an inadmissibly narrow analytical focus on popular culture.

The second variant of the myth of globalization asserts not only that American and Western cultural hegemony is expanding, but takes possible counter-arguments into account by conceding that non-European cultures are capable of making local adaptations in response to globalization. Indian rap, for example, is claimed to be a typical hybrid culture. How very true. Many of these cultural fusions could not, however, be re-exported to Western markets. This points to the way the globalization debate confuses globalization and modernization. External stimuli may serve to spark off cultural change. What follows, however, is autonomous development on the basis of a universal logic of rationalization and renovation characteristic of all great literate cultures. Even today, without borrowing constantly from other countries, the most modern cultural productions in the non-Western world may trigger a sense of 'strangeness'. The world evolves – as it always has done – through cultural developments with a momentum of their own within language areas and nation-states. Neither 'Westernization' nor the simple notion of an all-embracing process of fusion can do anything to change this.

In light of globalization, the challenge for scholars is to describe the cultural fusions which are in fact its main sphere of action, to analyse their extent and growth and to adequately grasp their role in a super-culture taking in all of humanity. They ought, however, to refrain from exaggerating the nature of the alleged 'transculture'. In this regard, it would be highly valuable to work out the very different global logics and rates of linkage typical of music, images and text. It is music and images that characterize entertainment culture as the core area of globalization – and it is text, news and interpretations of the world which are proving to be the basis of local resistance and independence.

Are we seeing resistance 'in our midst' as well? In the 1990s, for a brief period, the notion of 'virtual communities' of immigrants, linking up with each other and with their country of origin across the world on the basis of a common language, was identified as a characteristic feature of communicative globalization. This interpretative trend then quickly abated. It was recognized that while they are indeed equipped with the instruments of technological globalization, such communities may ultimately encourage conservative, nation-based, even chauvinistic cultures. The Islamic fundamentalist Net-based International is but the tip of the iceberg. Yet the debate's rapid change of direction, away from multiculturalism to the negative features of a parallel society, is also rash and poorly thought out. There is no causal relationship between integration and media use. The recent assumption that the local is simply relocated through migration and globalization is just as misleading as the old one that crossing borders works to open up cultures. A refined typology and enhanced theoretical work are urgent necessities.

In striving to understand why cross-border processes of communication have palpably failed to generate connectivity and system change, it is essential to look at the fundamental relations between the transmitters and receivers of mass communication. When all is said and done, how *interdependent* are states or regional and national cultures when viewed from the perspective of communication? What would a theory of international relations spawned by communication science look like? The world media system undeniably features structural shortcomings which it will be no easy task to remedy. There is as yet no global communication system. Despite the extensive exchange of information and news, media systems are firmly in the grip of nation-states. National owners, investors and publics dominate; transnational media (such as the German-French television network Arte) are hardly used; the transnationalization of media capital mostly ends at sub-regional borders. Entertainment may have a global hue in many respects. News and information, however, can be domesticated almost at will, because they are created for a very limited, usually national group of consumers typified by national interests, reservations, stereotypes and cultural expectations. The media have to respond to these. While doing so, they are constantly reproducing them. Who could expect global media diplomacy from such provincial systems?

Nonetheless, there are signs of increasing structural interconnection. Large networks such as CNN are developing foreign-language spin-offs in other parts of the world or, like the Arab television channel al-Jazeera, an English homepage. Such measures may gradually free relations of interdependence from a one-sided attachment to the home base, though the implications for media content are unclear. It remains to be seen whether one and the same product – such as news – can catch on universally in the foreseeable future. American consumers, confronted with unrelenting criticism of US policy on the Middle East? Japanese putting up with Chinese reproaches regarding the Second World War? Ultimately, even supposedly transnational projects risk the fate which befell the music channel MTV years ago. Its programming has broken down into a decentralized form and remains linked with the parent company solely in an economic sense. In terms of content, it has long consisted of a patchwork of different audience interests. The transnationalization of the press, which found expression, for instance, in a growing interest among American consumers in European online newspapers during the Iraq War of 2003, is also at a very early stage. Will the commercial and capitalist form of globalization which currently dominates the media system show the way here? Given how the big Western media companies such as News Corporation (owned by Rupert Murdoch), whose global influence is in any case vastly overrated, have conformed to political realities in the past, this seems very doubtful.

What, though, are the alternatives? Do we need a new privileging of politics within global media communication, a new drive for *global media governance*? Why not? British coverage of the Iraq War of 2003 proves that the logic of closed mass communication, geared towards national borders and cultural boundaries, can be relativized when states move towards one another or grow closer together. At present, however, global media policy remains largely restricted to areas in which commercial interests demand regulation (such as copyright protection), leaving little prospect of a new approach.

It is no accident that many commentators have evoked civil society as a third force alongside companies and governments. Many hoped that a 'global civil society' would spring into life – but here too there is no question of there being mature interdependence. Perceptual distortions and informational uncertainties typify global exchanges via the Internet as much as they do classical journalism. Societies' enhanced ability to present themselves to the world has helped generate a flood of information, making the Internet surfer an isolated 'laptop anthropologist' and facilitating manipulation of every kind (up to and including *cyber war*). Here too there is a dearth of binding and stable processes of informational feedback. Moreover, Net-based political alliances, typically casual in nature and characterized by arbitrary selection and random events, lag far behind 'offline politics', in other words the quotidian actions of national governments, which tend to feature binding and structured elements. It says something about the structure of the globalization of the mass media that one of the few media which is interdependent to some extent, international broadcasting produced for other countries, features a lack of interdependence in relation to civil society in the home country. No one there knows about or uses international broadcasting, leaving it at the mercy of the national government and making it susceptible to propaganda.

Globalization – a necessary myth? The present writer would certainly answer the question posed by economists Paul Hirst and Grahame Thompson in the affirmative.[2] The task now at hand is to fortify a magnificent utopia through sober and unprejudiced analysis.

Notes

Introduction

1 Stefan Münker and Alexander Roesler (eds), *Mythos Internet*, Frankfurt: Suhrkamp 1997, p. 8.
2 Walter Truett Anderson, *All Connected Now: Life in the First Global Civilization*, Boulder: Westview 2004, p. 89.
3 Münker and Roesler 1997; Rudolf Maresch and Florian Roetzer, *Cyberhypes: Möglichkeiten und Grenzen des Internet*, Frankfurt: Suhrkamp 2001; Daniel Egloff, *Digitale Demokratie: Mythos oder Realität? Auf den Spuren der demokratischen Aspekte des Internets und der Computerkultur*, Wiesbaden: Westdeutscher Verlag 2002.
4 Paul Hirst and Grahame Thompson, *Globalization in Question*, Cambridge: Polity 1999 (2nd edn), p. 95 f.
5 Ibid., pp. 1–18.
6 Günter Joetze, Politische Grenzen der Globalisierung, in: *Internationale Politik* 54 (1999) 6, p. 56 ff.
7 Marjorie Ferguson, The Myth of Globalization, in: *European Journal of Communication* 7 (1992) 1, pp. 69–93.
8 Joseph D. Straubhaar, Distinguishing the Global, Regional and National Levels of World Television, in: Annabelle Sreberny-Mohammadi, Dwayne Winseck, Jim McKenna and Oliver Boyd-Barrett (eds), *Media in Global Context: A Reader*, New York: Arnold 1997.
9 Georgette Wang, Anura Goonasekera and Jan Servaes, *The New Communications Landscape: Demystifying Media Globalization*, London: Routledge 2000.
10 John Sinclair, Elizabeth Jacka and Stuart Cunningham (eds), *New Patterns in Global Television: Peripheral Vision*, Oxford: Oxford University Press 1996a.
11 Claude Moisy, Myths about the Global Information Village, in: *Foreign Policy* 107/1997, pp. 78–87.
12 Silvio Waisbord and Nancy Morris (eds), *Media and Globalization: Why the State Matters*, Lanham: Rowman & Littlefield 2001.

13 Daya K. Thussu, *Electronic Empires: Global Media and Local Resistance*, London: Arnold 1998.
14 Colin Sparks, Is There a Global Public Sphere? in: Daya K. Thussu, *Electronic Empires: Global Media and Local Resistance*, London: Arnold 1998, pp. 108–24; Colin Sparks, The Global, the Local and the Public Sphere, in: Georgette Wang, Jan Servaes and Anura Goonasekera (eds), *The New Communications Landscape: Demystifying Media Globalization*, London and New York: Routledge 2000, pp. 74–95.
15 James Curran and Myung-Jin Park, Beyond Globalization Theory, in: James Curran and Myung-Jin Park (eds), *De-Westernizing Media Studies*, London and New York: Routledge 2000, p. 11.
16 Andreas Hepp, Friedrich Krotz and Carsten Winter (eds), Introduction in: *Globalisierung der Medienkommunikation. Eine Einführung*, Wiesbaden: Verlag für Sozialwissenschaften 2005, p. 5, 8 f.
17 Cees Hamelink, quoted in John Tomlinson, Cultural Imperialism, in: Frank J. Lechner and John Boli (eds), *The Globalization Reader*, Oxford: Blackwell 2000, p. 312.
18 Annabelle Sreberny-Mohammadi, Dwayne Winseck, Jim McKenna and Oliver Boyd-Barrett (eds), *Media in Global Context: A Reader*, London: Arnold 1997, pp. xiii–xiv, xv.
19 Marianne Beisheim and Gregor Walter, 'Globalisierung' – Kinderkrankheiten eines Konzepts, in: *Zeitschrift für internationale Beziehungen* 4 (1997) 1, p. 175 f.; Joyce S. Osland, Broadening the Debate: the Pros and Cons of Globalization, in: *Journal of Management Inquiry* 12 (2003) 2, pp. 137–54.
20 Frank J. Lechner and John Boli (eds), *The Globalization Reader*, Oxford: Blackwell 2000, p. 1.

Chapter 1 Theory – Structural Transformation of the Global Public Sphere?

1 Manuel Castells, *The Information Age*, 3 vols, Cambridge, MA, and Oxford: Blackwell 1996–7.
2 Cf. among other contributions Sreberny-Mohammadi, Dwayne Winseck, Jim McKenna and Oliver Boyd-Barrett 1997; David Held and Anthony McGrew (eds), *The Global Transformation Reader: An Introduction to the Globalization Debate*, Cambridge: Polity 2003; Andreas Hepp and Martin Löffelholz (eds), *Grundlagentexte zur transkulturellen Kommunikation*, Constance: UTB 2002.
3 Cf. Kai Hafez, *Die politische Dimension der Auslandsberichterstattung*, vol. 1, Baden-Baden: Nomos 2002a, p. 35 ff.
4 See ibid., p. 72 ff. and 88 ff.
5 Roland Robertson, Globalization or Glocalization? in: *Journal of International Communication* 1 (1994a) 1, pp. 33–52; Roland Robertson, Mapping the Global Condition: Globalization as the Central Concept, in: Mike Featherstone (ed.), *Global Culture: Nationalism, Globalization and*

Modernity, London and Newbury Park: Sage 1994b, pp. 15–30; see also Marwan M. Kraidy, Glocalisation. An International Communication Framework? in: *Journal of International Communication* 9 (2003) 2, pp. 29–49.

6 David Held, Anthony McGrew, David Goldblatt and Jonathan Perraton, Rethinking Globalization, in: David Held and Anthony McGrew (eds), *The Global Transformations Reader: An Introduction to the Globalization Debate*, Cambridge: Polity 2000, p. 68.

7 James Lull, Superkultur, in: Andreas Hepp and Martin Löffelholz (eds), *Grundlagentexte zur transkulturellen Kommunikation*, Constance: UTB 2002, pp. 750–73.

8 *Global Trends 2015: a dialogue about the future with non-government experts*, http://www.cia.gov/cia/reports/globaltrends 2015 (1 March 2006).

9 Kathryn Sikkink and Margaret E. Keck, *Activists beyond Borders: Advocacy Networks in International Politics*, Ithaca, NY: Cornell University Press 1998.

10 Jürgen Habermas, *Strukturwandel der Öffentlichkeit*, Frankfurt: Suhrkamp 1990 (orig. 1962).

11 Ingrid Volkmer, *News in the Global Sphere: A Study of CNN and its Impact on Global Communication*, Luton: University of Luton Press 1999.

12 Jo Groebel, *Die Rolle des Auslandsrundfunks: Eine vergleichende Analyse der Erfahrungen und Trends in fünf Ländern*, Bonn: Friedrich-Ebert-Stiftung 2000.

13 Marshall McLuhan, *Understanding Media*, London: Sphere 1967.

14 Ithiel de Sola Pool, *Technologies without Boundaries: On Telecommunications in a Global Age*, Cambridge, MA: Harvard University Press 1990, pp. 132–7.

15 On the link between international reporting and globalization, see also Kai Hafez, International News Coverage and the Problems of Media Globalization: In Search of a 'New Global–Local Nexus', in: *Innovation. The European Journal of Social Sciences* 12 (1999b) 1, pp. 47–62.

16 Michael Gurevitch, Mark R. Levy and Itzhak Roeh, The Global Newsroom: Convergences and Diversities in the Globalization of Television News, in: Peter Dahlgren and Colin Sparks (eds), *Communication and Citizenship: Journalism and the Public Sphere*, London and New York: Routledge 1993, pp. 195–216.

17 Kai Hafez, 2002a, vol. 1, p. 123 ff.

18 Emanuel Richter, *Der Zerfall der Welteinheit. Vernunft und Globalisierung in der Moderne*, Frankfurt and New York: Campus 1992, p. 163 ff., esp. p. 165.

19 See for example Robert O. Keohane and Joseph S. Nye, *Power and Interdependence: World Politics in Transition*, Boston and Toronto: Little, Brown 1977.

Chapter 2   International Reporting – 'No Further than Columbus . . .'

1 For an introduction to the basic issues and theory of international report-ing, see Hafez, *Die politische Dimension der Auslandsberichterstattung*, 2 vols, Baden-Baden: Nomos 2002a.

2 *Washington Post*, 21 March 1979, quoted in: Kai Hafez, Islam und Modernität in der *Washington Post* zur Zeit der Iranischen Revolution 1978/79, in: *Asien, Afrika, Lateinamerika* 21 (1993) 4, p. 377.

3 Anthony Giddens, *The Constitution of Society: Outline of the Theory of Structuration*, Cambridge: Polity 1984; Anthony Giddens, *The Nation-State and Violence*, Berkeley: University of California Press 1987.

4 Sonia Mikich, Geistige Provinzialisierung: Eine Zustandsbeschreibung, in: Claudia Cippitelli and Axel Schwanenbeck (eds), *Nur Krisen, Kriege, Katastrophen? Auslandsberichterstattung im deutschen Fernsehen. Dokumentation der 21. Tutzinger Medientage*, Munich: Reinhard Fischer 2003, p. 119.

5 Marc Raboy, Television and Deregulated Global Markets, in: John Sinclair (ed.), *Contemporary World Television*, London: BFI 2004, p. 21.

6 Markus Kriener and Miriam Meckel, Internationale Kommunikation: Begriffe, Probleme, Referenzen, in: Markus Kriener and Miriam Meckel (eds), *Internationale Kommunikation: Eine Einführung*, Opladen: Westdeutscher Verlag 1996, p. 15 f.

7 Thomas Schuster, *Staat und Medien: Über die elektronische Konditionierung der Wirklichkeit*, Frankfurt: Fischer Taschenbuch 1995, p. 39.

8 On the debate on the New World Information Order, see also Jörg Becker, *Massenmedien im Nord–Süd-Konflikt*, Frankfurt: Campus 1985.

9 *Many Voices – One World. Communication and Society Today and Tomorrow*, London: UNESCO 1980.

10 See George Gerbner, Hamid Mowlana and Kaarle Nordenstreng (eds), *The Global Media Debate: its Rise, Fall, and Renewal*, Norwood, NJ: Ablex 1993.

11 *Many Voices – One World*, p. 145.

12 Ibid., p. 38.

13 Ibid., p. 156 ff.

14 Ibid., p. 158.

15 Ibid., p. 159.

16 Annabelle Sreberny-Mohammadi, Kaarle Nordenstreng, Robert Stevenson and Frank Ugboajah (eds), *Foreign News in the Media: International Reporting in 29 Countries. Final Report Undertaken for UNESCO by the International Association for Mass Communication Research*, Paris: UNESCO 1985.

17 Lutz M. Hagen, Ausländische Berichterstattung über Deutschland: Erste Ergebnisse der *Foreign News Studie* über Umfang und Themen von Nachrichten über Deutschland in verschiedenen Ländern, in: Siegfried Quandt and Wolfgang Gast (eds), *Deutschland im Dialog der Kulturen: Medien – Images – Verständigung*, Constance: UVK 1998, pp. 203–11.

18 Birgit Schenk, Die Struktur des internationalen Nachrichtenflusses: Analyse der empirischen Studien, in: *Rundfunk und Fernsehen* 35 (1987) 1, pp. 36–54; Jörg Becker, Internationaler Nachrichtenfluß: Eine Stellungnahme zum Aufsatz von Birgit Schenk, in: *Rundfunk und Fernsehen* 36 (1988) 1, pp. 45–55; Birgit Schenk, Internationaler Nachrichtenfluß: Einige Anmerkungen zur Stellungnahme von Jörg Becker, in: *Rundfunk und Fernsehen* 36 (1988) 2, pp. 247–9.

19 Annabelle Sreberny-Mohammadi, Kaarle Nordenstreng, Robert Stevenson and Frank Ugboajah 1985, pp. 39–43.

20 See for example Manfred Wöhlcke, *Lateinamerika in der Presse: Inhaltsanalytische Untersuchung der Lateinamerika-Berichterstattung in folgenden Presseorganen: Die Welt, FAZ, NZZ, Handelsblatt, Le Monde, Neues Deutschland, Der Spiegel*, Stuttgart: Klett 1973, p. 30; *Dritte Welt und Medienwelt: Entwicklungspolitik und das Bild der Dritten Welt in Presse, Hörfunk, Fernsehen, Eigenerhebungen und Sekundäranalysen des Zentrums für Kulturforschung and Bonn*, Bonn: Zentrums für Kulturforschung, Bonn, und Bundesministeriums für wirtschaftliche Zusammenarbeit 1983, p. 49; Winfried Schulz, *Die Konstruktion von Realität in den Nachrichtenmedien: Analyse der aktuellen Berichterstattung*, Freiburg and Munich: Alber 1990 (2nd edn), p. 84; Wolfgang Pütz, *Das Italienbild in der deutschen Presse: Eine Untersuchung ausgewählter Tageszeitungen*, Munich: Ölschläger 1993, p. 44.

21 Cf. Günther Rager, *Publizistische Vielfalt im Lokalen*, Tübingen: Tübinger Vereinigung für Volkskunde 1982.

22 Sreberny-Mohammadi et al. 1985, p. 52.

23 Ibid., p. 46.

24 Josef Eckhardt, Berichterstattung über die Dritte Welt im ARD-Programm und im Westdeutschen Fernsehen, in: *Media Perspektiven* 12/1982, p. 768.

25 Kurt Luger, Zwischen Katastrophen und Shangri La: Bilder von der Dritten Welt, in: *Dialog* 16 (1989) 3, p. 22 f.; Daniel Glass, *Die Dritte Welt in der Presse der Bundesrepublik Deutschland: Eine ideologiekritische Fallstudie*, Frankfurt: Haag und Herchen 1979, p. 207 ff.; Kurt Luger, Dritte-Welt-Berichterstattung: eine einzige Katastrophe? Die Konstruktion von Wirklichkeit in Theorie und Praxis, in: *Die Dritte Welt in den Massenmedien*, Salzburg: Institut für Publizistik- und Kommunikationswissenschaft der Universität Salzburg 1985, p. 8.

26 Helmut Asche (eds), *Dritte Welt für Journalisten: Zwischenbilanz eines Weiterbildungsangebotes, im Auftrag des Modellversuchs Journalisten-Weiterbildung an der Freien Universität Berlin*, Saarbrücken and Fort Lauderdale: Breitenbach 1984, p. 17.

27 Glass 1979, pp. 162–206; Luger 1989, p. 23.

28 Sreberny-Mohammadi et al. 1985, p. 29.

29 Glass 1979, pp. 254–78; Luger 1989, p. 23; Luger 1985, p. 7.

30 Glass 1979, pp. 279–317; Asche 1984, p. 25 f.

31 Verena Klemm and Karin Hörner (eds), *Das Schwert des 'Experten': Peter*

Scholl-Latours verzerrtes Araber- und Islambild, Heidelberg: Palmyra 1993.

32 Hafez 2002a, vol. 1, p. 72 ff.

33 On news agencies' political tendencies see Jeremy Tunstall, Worldwide News Agencies – Private Wholesalers of Public Information, in: Jim Richstad and Michael H. Anderson (eds), *Crisis in International News: Policies and Prospects,* New York: Columbia University Press 1981, pp. 258–67; Lutz M. Hagen, *Informationsqualität von Nachrichten. Meßmethoden und ihre Anwendung auf die Dienste von Nachrichtenagenturen,* Opladen: Westdeutscher Verlag 1995, pp. 252–64.

34 Gadi Wolfsfeld, *Media and Political Conflict: News from the Middle East,* Cambridge: Cambridge University Press 1997.

35 W. Lance Bennett and David L. Paletz (eds), *Taken by Storm: The Media, Public Opinion, and U.S. Foreign Policy in the Gulf War,* Chicago and London: University of Chicago Press 1991; Hafez 2002a, vol. 1, p. 151 ff. and vol. 2, pp. 194–207; Martin Löffelholz, Krisen- und Kriegskommunikation als Forschungsfeld, in: Martin Löffelholz (ed.), *Krieg als Medienereignis II. Krisenkommunikation im 21. Jahrhundert,* Wiesbaden: Verlag für Sozialwissenschaften 2004, p. 34 f.

36 Hafez 2002a, vol. 1, p. 137 ff.

37 Hans J. Kleinsteuber, Bausteine für einen dialogischen Journalismus: Zur Umsetzung des Prinzips 'Dialog der Kulturen', in: Jörgen Klussmann (ed.), *Interkulturelle Kompetenz und Medienpraxis. Ein Handbuch,* Frankfurt: Brandes and Aspel 2004, p. 52 f.

38 *Far Eastern Economic Review,* 8 November 2001, p. 20 f.

39 Amy Reynolds and Brooke Barnett, 'America under Attack': CNN's Verbal and Visual Framing of September 11, in: Steven Chermak, Frankie Y. Bailey and Michelle Brown, *Media Representations of September 11,* Westport, CT and London: Praeger 2003, pp. 85–101.

40 Ibid., p. 94 ff.

41 In the same vein, see David Domke, *God Willing? Political Fundamentalism in the White House, the 'War on Terror' and the Echoing Press,* London and Ann Arbor: Pluto 2004.

42 Hafez 2002a, vol. 2; Jochen Hippler and Andrea Lueg (eds), *Feindbild Islam,* Hamburg: Konkret 1993.

43 Kai Hafez, Salman Rushdie im Kulturkonflikt. Zum Problem der transkulturellen Kommunikation in der deutschen Presseberichterstattung, in: *Orient* 37 (1996a) 1, pp. 137–61.

44 Kai Hafez, The Algerian Crisis as Portrayed in the German Press: Media Coverage of Political Islam, in: *Communications. The European Journal of Communication Research* 21 (1996b) 2, pp. 155–82.

45 Christina Ohde, *Der Irre von Bagdad: Zur Konstruktion von Feindbildern in überregionalen deutschen Tageszeitungen während der Golfkrise 1990 and 91,* Frankfurt: Peter Lang 1994.

46 Cover article on 21 September 2001.

47 The following cover articles are examples: *Die Woche,* 21 September 2001;

Focus, 1 October 2001; *Stern*, 4 October 2001; *Der Spiegel*, 8 October 2001; *Stern*, 25 October 2001.

48 *Focus*, 40/2004, p. 62 ff.

49 John Strawson, Holy War in the Media: Images of Jihad, in: Steven Chermak, Frankie Y. Bailey and Michelle Brown, *Media Representations of September 11*, Westport, CT and London: Praeger 2003, pp. 17–28.

50 Examples include *Stern*, 15 November 2001; *Die Woche*, 7 December 2001.

51 'Frames' refer to the core rationales which demarcate the 'framework' of a debate.

52 *Al-Ahram Weekly* (Egypt), 20–26 September 2001, p. 13.

53 For examples, see *Al-Hayat* (Saudi Arabia), 15 September 2001, p. 5; *Al-Ahram Weekly* (Egypt), 13–19 September 2001, p. 3; *Al-Ahram Weekly* (Egypt), 20–26 September 2001, pp. 5, 13.

54 *El Watan* (Algeria), 16 September 2001, p. 4 f.; *El Watan* (Algeria), 14–15 September 2001, p. 3.

55 *El Watan* (Algeria), 16 September 2001, p. 4.

56 *Realités* (Tunisia), 27 December 2001, p. 16.

57 Ibid., p. 17.

58 Nach dem 11. September ist Attac nötiger denn je, <www.attac.de/kongress/2010v.html> (1 March 2006).

59 Howard Tumber and Jerry Palmer, *Media at War. The Iraq Crisis*, London: Sage 2004; Stephen Hess and Marvin Kalb (eds), *The Media and the War on Terrorism*, Washington, D.C.: Brookings Institution Press 2003; Daya Kishan Thussu and Des Freedman (eds), *War and the Media*, London: Sage 2003; David Miller (ed.), *Tell Me Lies. Propaganda and Media Distortion in the Attack on Iraq*, London and Stirling: Pluto 2004.

60 Jim Naureckas, When 'doves' lie. The *New York Times* plays down anti-war opinion:<www.fair.org/extra/0304/nyt-doves.html> (1 March 2006).

61 Merissa Marr, BBC chief attacks U.S. media war coverage, <www.veteransforpeace.org/BBC_chief_attacks_042403.htm> (1 March 2006).

62 Steve Rendall and Tara Broughel, Amplifying Officials, Squelching Dissent, <www.fair.org/extra/0305/warstudy.html> (1 March 2006).

63 TV patriotism helped swing British opinion on Iraq War, Agence France-Presse, <http://quickstart.clari.net/qs_se/webnews/wed/az/Qiraq-war-britain> (10 May 2003).

64 Ibid.

65 Doing the dissent thing? <http://news.bbc.co.uk/1/hi/uk/2907599.stm> (1 March 2006).

66 *The Independent*, 22 March 2003.

67 *The Independent*, 2 April 2003.

68 We are liberating a country that is enslaved by a lunatic, *The Times*, 20 March 2003.

69 The blitzing of Baghdad, *The Times*, 22 March 2003.

70 Ruthless despot who can't resist a gamble, *The Times*, 20 March 2003.

71 Ted Turner calls Murdoch warmonger, <www.thetruthseeker.co.uk/article.asp?ID=727> (7 May 2003).

72 *Frankfurter Rundschau*, 13 February 2003, p. 2.

73 Ingrid A. Lehmann, Transatlantic Media Divide over Iraq, in: *Medien Tenor Forschungsbericht* 147, September 2004, pp. 66–9.

74 On the 'rallying round the flag' phenomenon, see John E. Mueller, *War, Presidents, and Public Opinion*, New York: Wiley 1973.

75 'The myth of mediatization' was the guiding theme of the annual conference of the German Society for Journalism and Communication Science in May 2004 at the University of Erfurt.

76 Thomas Meyer, *Mediokratie: Die Kolonisierung der Politik durch die Medien*, Frankfurt: Suhrkamp 2004.

77 Volkmer, *News in the Global Sphere: A Study of CNN and its Impact on Global Communication*, Luton: University of Luton Press 1999.

78 Piers Robinson, *The CNN Effect: The Myth of News, Foreign Policy and Intervention*, London and New York: Routledge 2002; Royce J. Ammon, *Global Television and the Shaping of World Politics: CNN, Telediplomacy, and Foreign Policy*, Jefferson and London: McFarland 2001; Eytan Gilboa, The CNN Effect: the Search for a Communication Theory of International Relations, in: *Political Communication* 22 (2005) 1, pp. 27–44.

79 Kai Hafez, Dialog mit dem Islam: Die Debatte über Medien und Außenpolitik, in: *Die Brücke* 93/1997c, pp. 56–9.

80 Robinson 2002, pp. 126, 129.

81 Miriam Meckel, Internationales als Restgröße? Struktur der Auslandsberichterstattung im Fernsehen, in: Klaus Kamps and Miriam Meckel (eds), *Fernsehnachrichten: Prozesse, Strukturen, Funktionen*, Opladen: Westdeutscher Verlag 1998, pp. 257–74.

82 Robinson elucidates this through examples such as the Kosovo war: Robinson 2002, p. 108 f.

83 Claude Moisy, Myths about the Global Information Village, in: *Foreign Policy* 107/1997.

84 Hafez 2002a, vol. 1, pp. 175–7 and vol. 2, pp. 261–5.

Chapter 3   Satellite Television – the Renaissance of World Regions

1 The term 'spiral of silence' was originally borrowed from the German context: Elisabeth Noelle-Neumann, Die öffentliche Meinung und die Wirkung der Massenmedien, in: Jürgen Wilke (ed.), *Fortschritte der Publizistikwissenschaft*, Freiburg: Alber 1990, pp. 11–23.

2 Forum Barcelona 2004, UNESCO <www.barcelona2004.org/eng/banco_del_conocimiento/documentos/ficha.cfm?IdDoc=230> (1 March 2006).

3 Anthony Giddens, Lecture 1 – Globalization, <www.news.bbc.co.uk/hi/english/static/events/reith_99/week1/week1.htm> (22 February 2006).

4 John Tomlinson, Globalisation and National Identity, in: John Sinclair (ed.), *Contemporary World Television*, London: BFI 2004, p. 27.

5 Stephen Dahl, Communications and Culture Transformation: Cultural Diversity, Globalization and Cultural Convergence, <www.stephweb.com/capstone/capstone.shtml> (1 March 2006).

6 David Held, Anthony McGrew, David Goldblatt and Jonathan Perraton, Global Transformations, <www.polity.co.uk/global/executiv.htm#whatis> (1 March 2006).

7 Rem Evelyn S. Lieberman, Challenges of Globalization, Remarks at Al-Akhawayn University, April 5, 2000, <usembassy.ma/Themes/ EconomicIssues/lieberman.htm> (23 December 2004).

8 Quoted in: Colin M. Wilding, 151 Million Listeners – but What Does it Mean? Uses and Misuses of Global Audience Estimates, in: Oliver Zöllner (ed.), *An Essential Link with Audiences Worldwide. Research for International Broadcasting*, Berlin: Vistas 2002, p. 62. In the same vein, see also: Graham Mytton, A Billion Viewers Can't Be Right, in: *Intermedia* 19 (1991) 3, pp. 10–12; Graham Mytton, Global TV Audiences: How Many are Actually Reached? Let's be Honest. Nobody Yet Knows, in: *ESOMAR News Brief* 7 (1999) 7, p. 18 f.

9 Richard Collins, *From Satellite to Single Market: New Communication Technology and European Public Service Television*, London and New York: Routledge 1998, p. 199.

10 Ibid., p. 11.

11 Uwe Hasebrink and Anja Herzog, Mediennutzung im internationalen Vergleich, in: *Internationales Handbuch Medien 2004/5*, Hans-Bredow-Institut, Baden-Baden: Nomos 2004, p. 157.

12 Anandam P. Kavoori, Trends in global media reception, in: Daya Kishan Thussu (ed.), *Electronic Empires. Global Media and Local Resistance*, London: Arnold 1998, pp. 193–207.

13 Cf. the figures in: Hasebrink and Herzog 2004, p. 151; Karsten Renckstorf and Paul Hendriks Vettehen, Watching Foreign TV Channels, in: Karsten Renckstorf, Denis McQuail and Nicholas Jankowski (eds), *Media Use as Social Action: A European Approach to Audience Studies*, London: John Libbey 1996, pp. 103–12.

14 It is impossible to be more precise here, because the figure mentioned of 4.8 per cent includes local channels. Cf. Hasebrink and Herzog 2004, p. 151.

15 See for instance the table showing the proportion of foreign television watched in Hasebrink and Herzog 2004, p. 151. Countries like Germany, Finland and Greece are certainly more typical and representative here than Switzerland, as they feature almost no regional effects.

16 *Europe 2004: A Survey of Decision Makers and Leading Consumers*, Harrow: IPSOS Media 2004.

17 See for example Annabelle Sreberny-Mohammadi, The Global and the Local in International Communications, in: James Curran and Michael Gurevitch (eds), *Mass Media and Society*, London: Arnold 1994a, pp. 177–203; Joana Breidenbach and Ina Zukrigl, *Tanz der Kulturen: Kulturelle Identität in einer globalisierten Welt*, Munich: Kunstmann 1998, pp. 61–7.

18 Belkacem Mostefaoui, Ausländisches Fernsehen im Maghreb – ein Medium mit kulturellen und politischen Auswirkungen, in: *Wuquf* 10–11/ 1995–96, Hamburg 1997, pp. 425–55.

19 Larbi Chouikha, Etatisation et pratique journalistique, in: *Revue tunisienne de communication* 22, 1992, pp. 37–46.
20 Hasebrink and Herzog 2004, p. 152.
21 Mark Rhodes and Carole Chapelier, 'Balance-seekers' and New Information Sources: Media Usage Patterns in the Middle East, in: Oliver Zöllner (ed.), *Beyond Borders: Research and International Broadcasting* 2003, Bonn: CIBAR 2004, p. 83.
22 John Sinclair, Elizabeth Jacka and Stuart Cunningham, Peripheral Vision, in: John Sinclair, Elizabeth Jacka and Stuart Cunningham (eds), *New Patterns in Global Television: Peripheral Vision*, Oxford: Oxford University Press 1996b, pp. 6–8.
23 In the same vein see: Bella Thomas, Was die Armen im Fernsehen anschauen: Die Auswirkungen westlichen Fernsehens auf Entwicklungsländer sind geringer als weithin angenommen, in: *Überblick* 39 (2003) 4, pp. 14–24.
24 Patrick H. O'Neil, Democratization and Mass Communication: What is the Link? in: Patrick H. O'Neil (ed.), *Communicating Democracy: The Media and Political Transitions*, Boulder and London: Lynne Rienner 1998, p. 12.
25 Anthony R. DeLuca, *Politics, Diplomacy, and the Media: Gorbachev's Legacy in the West*, Westport and London: Praeger 1998.
26 Annabelle Sreberny-Mohammadi and Ali Mohammadi, *Small Media, Big Revolution: Communication, Culture, and the Iranian Revolution*, Minneapolis: University of Minnesota Press 1994b.
27 On the theoretical foundations, see: Kai Hafez, Globalization, Regionalization and Democratization: the Interaction of Three Paradigms in the Field of Mass Communication, in: Bob Hackett (ed.), *Democratizing Global Media: One World, Many Struggles*, New York: Rowman & Littlefield 2005b, pp. 145–63.
28 Kathryn Sikkink and Margaret E. Keck, *Activists beyond Borders: Advocacy Networks in International Politics*, Ithaca, NY: Cornell University Press 1998 p. 12 ff.
29 Samera Zagala, *'Kampf der Kulturen' – 'Krieg der Zivilisationen': Theorien zum Konflikt zwischen dem Westen und dem Islam in deutschen Nachrichtensendungen: Eine inhaltsanalytische Untersuchung*, MA thesis at the Institute for Journalism, University of Dortmund, Dortmund 2004, p. 91.
30 Ibid.
31 Ibid., p. 92.
32 Hafez 2002a, vol. 2, p. 73 ff.
33 Ibid., pp. 134–43.
34 Hafez 2005b.
35 See, for example, Saloumeh Peyman, Iranian exiles use satellite TV to promote change, <www.antiwar.com/ips/peyman.php?articleid=3811> (1 March 2006).
36 Sreberny-Mohammadi and Mohammadi 1994b.

37 Straubhaar 1997, p. 285; in the same vein, see: Joseph Straubhaar, Brazil: the Role of the State in World Television, in: Nancy Morris and Silvio Waisbord (eds), *Media and Globalization:Why the State Matters*, Lanham: Rowman & Littlefield 2001, pp. 133–53.

38 Sinclair, Jacka and Cunningham 1996b, p. 2; Kai Hafez, Mass Media in the Middle East: Patterns of Societal Change, in: Kai Hafez (ed.), *Mass Media, Politics, and Society in the Middle East*, Cresskill, NJ: Hampton 2001a, pp. 1–20.

39 Shaun Breslin, Christopher W. Hughes, Nicola Phillips and Ben Rosamund (eds), *New Regionalisms in the Global Political Economy*, London and New York: Routledge 2002; Stefan A. Schirm, *Globalization and the New Regionalism: Global Markets, Domestic Politics and Regional Cooperation*, Cambridge: Polity 2002.

40 Sinclair, Jacka and Cunningham 1996b, p. 12 f.

41 David Page and William Crawley, *Satellite over South Asia: Broadcasting Culture and the Public Interest*, New Delhi: Oxford University Press 2001.

42 Norbert Wildermuth, Satellite Television in India, in: Stefan Brüne (ed.), *Neue Medien und Öffentlichkeiten*, vol. 2, Hamburg: Deutsches Übersee-Institut 2000, p. 225.

43 Manas Ray and Elizabeth Jacka, Indian Television: an Emerging Regional Force, in: John Sinclair, Elizabeth Jacka and Stuart Cunningham (ed.), *New Patterns in Global Television: Peripheral Vision*, Oxford: Oxford University Press 1996, p. 96.

44 Aggrey Brown, In the Caribbean, a Complex Situation, in: *Media and Democracy in Latin America and Caribbean*, Paris: UNESCO 1996, p. 43 ff.

45 Luis Suárez, Mass Communications and the Major Challenges, in: *Media and Democracy in Latin America and Caribbean*, Paris: UNESCO 1996, p. 51.

46 On the situation in the Middle East, see Rhodes and Chapelier 2003, p. 84.

47 Samuel P. Huntington, The Clash of Civilizations? in: *Foreign Affairs* 72 (1993) 3, pp. 22–49; Samuel P. Huntington, *The Clash of Civilizations and the Remaking of World Order*, New York: Simon & Schuster 1996.

48 Representative examples include: Christoph Butterwegge, Kampf oder Dialog der Kulturen? Samuel P. Huntingtons These vom 'Zusammenprall der Zivilisationen', in: *Zeitschrift für Migration und soziale Arbeit* 17 (1996) 2, pp. 44–7; Kai Hafez, Islam and the West – the Clash of Politicized Perceptions, in: Kai Hafez (ed.), *The Islamic World and the West: An Introduction to Political Cultures and International Relations*, Leiden: Brill 2000, S. 3–18.

49 On the concept of political and cultural hegemony in the work of Gramsci and others, see Robert Bocock, *Hegemony*, London and New York: Tavistock 1986.

50 Stuart Hall, Who Needs 'Identity'?, in: Stuart Hall and Paul du Gay (eds), *Questions of Cultural Identity*, London: Sage 1996, pp. 1–17 (esp. p. 5).

51 The classic example, mentioned earlier, is the use of videos by Ayatollah Khomeini to lay the ground for the Iranian Revolution of 1978–79.

52 Shir Mohammed Rawan, Traditionelle Kommunikation und moderne Massenmedien in Afghanistan, in: *Orient* 36 (1996) 3, pp. 495–509.

53 Kai Hafez, Editor's Preface, in: Kai Hafez (ed.), *Media Ethics in the Dialogue of Cultures: Journalistic Self-Regulation in Europe, the Arab World and Muslim Asia*, Hamburg: Deutsches Orient-Institut 2003a, p. 14.

54 Sinclair, Jacka and Cunningham 1996b, p. 3.

55 Douglas A. Boyd, Saudi Arabia's International Media Strategy: Influence through Multinational Ownership, in: Kai Hafez (ed.), *Mass Media, Politics, and Society in the Middle East*, Cresskill, NJ: Hampton 2001, pp. 43–60.

56 Naomi Sakr, *Satellite Realms: Transnational Television, Globalization and the Middle East*, London and New York: I. B. Tauris 2001; Mohammed El-Nawawy and Adel Iskandar, *Al-Jazeera: The Story of the Network that is Rattling Governments and Redefining Modern Journalism*, Cambridge, MA: Westview 2003; Muhammad I. Ayish, *Arab World Television in the Age of Globalization: An Analysis of Emerging Political, Economic, Cultural and Technological Patterns*, Hamburg: Deutsches Orient-Institut 2003; Hugh Miles, *Al-Jazeera: How Arab TV News Challenged the World*, London: Abacus 2005.

57 Kai Hafez, Arabisches Satellitenfernsehen – Demokratisierung ohne politische Parteien?, in: *Aus Politik und Zeitgeschichte* B 48/2004, pp. 17–23; see also the edited and extended version of the paper: Kai Hafez, Arab Satellite Broadcasting – Democracy without Political Parties?, in: *Transnational Broadcasting Studies* 1 (2005) 2, pp. 275–97.

58 Contrasting war coverage, in: *Middle East Economic Survey* 46 (2003) 14, <www.mees.com>(11 September 2004). See also: Lawrence Pintak, *Reflections in a Bloodshot Lens: America, Islam and the War of Ideas*, London: Pluto 2006.

59 *One Year After: Media Comments on the First Anniversary of September 11*, Paris: Panos Institute 2002, p. 17.

60 Mamoun Fandy, Information Technology, Trust, and Social Change in the Arab World, in: *The Middle East Journal* 54 (2000) 3, p. 388.

61 Cf. Rudolph Chimelli, Im Garten des Meinungsmonopols, in: *Süddeutsche Zeitung*, 10 May 2004.

62 Muhammad I. Ayish, Political Communication on Arab World Television: Evolving Patterns, in: *Political Communication* 19 (2002) 2, p. 150.

63 Nawawy and Iskandar 2003, p. 54.

64 See Krystian Woznicki, *Die vierte Macht*, 28 June 2004, <www.heise.de> (20 September 2004).

65 *One Year After* (Panos 2002), p. 24.

66 See: *Deutsch-arabischer Mediendialog*, Institut für Auslandsbeziehungen, Beirut, May 2004, <www.ifa.de/dialoge/dbeirut_protokoll.html> (17 September 2004).

Chapter 4   Film and Programme Imports – Entertainment Culture as the Core of Media Globalization

1 Uwe Hasebrink and Anja Herzog, Mediennutzung im internationalen Vergleich, in: *Internationales Handbuch Medien 2004/5*, Hans-Bredow-Institut, Baden-Baden: Nomos 2004, p. 152.

2 Charles Krauthammer, Who needs gold medals?, *Washington Post*, 20 February 2002, quoted in Robert J. Lieber and Ruth E. Weisberg, Globalization, Culture, and Identities in Crisis, in: *International Journal of Politics, Culture and Society* 16 (2002) 2, pp. 273–96.

3 Marshall McLuhan, *Understanding Media*, London: Sphere 1967.

4 Tamar Liebes and Elihu Katz, *The Export of Meaning: Cross-Cultural Readings of Dallas*, New York and Oxford: Oxford University Press 1990, p. 13.

5 Ibid., p. 6.

6 Ibid., p. 4.

7 Ien Ang, *Watching Dallas*, New York and London: Routledge 1985.

8 Herta Herzog-Massing, Decoding *Dallas*, in: *Society* 24 (1986) 1, pp. 74–7.

9 Joelle Stolz, *Les Algériens regardent* Dallas. Les Nouvelles Chaînes, Paris : Presse Universitaire de France and Institut d'Études du Développment 1983.

10 Michael Thiermeyer, *Internationalisierung von Film und Filmwirtschaft*, Cologne: Böhlau 1994, p. 276 f.

11 See the conference report: Kai Hafez, The Ethics of Journalism: Comparison and Transformations in the Islamic–Western context, Schloss Bellevue, Berlin, 29–30 March 2001, in: *Orient* 42 (2001b) 3, pp. 403–15.

12 Thiermeyer 1994, pp. 270–8.

13 Lieber and Weisberg 2002, p. 281.

14 See, for example, Joseph S. Nye, *The Paradox of American Power: Why the World's only Superpower Can't Go It Alone*, New York and Oxford: Oxford University Press 2002.

15 Lieber and Weisberg 2002, p. 279.

16 World Culture Report 2000: Cultural Diversity, Conflict and Pluralism, UNESCO, New York: UNESCO 2000.

17 *Television 2004, International Key Facts*, Cologne: IP and RTL Group 2004.

18 Ibid.

19 Joseph Straubhaar, Brazil: the Role of the State in World Television, in: Nancy Morris and Silvio Waisbord (eds), *Media and Globalization. Why the State Matters*, Lanham: Rowman & Littlefield 2001, p. 148.

20 Ibid., p. 136.

21 Wang Ning, *Chinese Cinema Challenged by Globalization: A Cultural and Intellectual Strategy*, <www.culstudies.com/rendanews/displaynews.asp?id=1403> (1 March 2006); slightly edited quotation.

22 Sinclair, Jacka and Cunningham 1996b, p. 51 ff.

23 Vijay Mishra, *Bollywood Cinema: Temples of Desire*, New York and London: Routledge 2002.

24 Straubhaar 2001, p. 148.

25 Hyangjin Lee, *Contemporary Korean Cinema: Identity, Culture, Politics*, Manchester and New York: Manchester University Press 2000, p. 56.

26 *Der Spiegel*, No. 31, 2004. In the 'belles-lettres' category, five of the 20 most-read works were by American authors or publishers (Dan Brown, Patricia Cornwell, Stephen King, Richard Powers, John Grisham), as also in the 'non-fiction' category (Bill Clinton, Michael Moore (twice), Richard A. Clarke and Bill Bryson).

27 For example, 45 Nobel Prizes for physics between 1901 and 2002, first place among all countries: *Pocket World in Figures 2005*, London: *The Economist* 2004, p. 96.

28 Twelve Nobel Prizes for literature between 1901 and 2002, second place behind France. Ibid.

29 For a critique of Robertson, see Fredric Jameson, Preface, in: Fredric Jameson and Masao Miyoshi (eds), *The Cultures of Globalization*, Durham: Duke University Press 1998, pp. xi–xii.

30 The Honolulu Statement, the MacBride Round Table, Honolulu, Hawaii, 20–23 January 1994, in: Richard C. Vincent, Kaarle Nordenstreng and Michael Traber (eds), *Towards Equity in Global Communication. MacBride Update*, Cresskill, NJ: Hampton 1999, pp. 331–34.

31 Jan Assmann, Kollektives Gedächtnis und kulturelle Identität, in: Jan Assmann and Tonio Hölscher (eds), *Culture und Gedächtnis*, Frankfurt: Suhrkamp 1988, pp. 9–19.

32 See, for example, Friedemann Büttner, Islamischer Fundamentalismus: Politisierter Traditionalismus oder revolutionärer Messianismus? in: Heiner Bielefeldt and Wilhelm Heitmeyer (eds), *Politisierte Religion. Ursachen und Erscheinungsformen des modernen Fundamentalismus*, Frankfurt: Suhrkamp 1998, pp. 188–210.

33 Barbara Pusch, Neue Muslimische Frauen in der Türkei: Einblicke in ihre Lebenswelt, in: Mechthild Rumpf, Ute Gerhard and Mechthild M. Jansen (eds), *Facetten islamischer Welten. Geschlechterordnungen, Frauen und Menschenrechte in der Diskussion*, Bielefeld: Transcript 2003, pp. 242–55.

34 See Gary Bunt, *Virtually Islamic: Computer-Mediated Communication and Cyber-Islamic Environments*, Cardiff: University of Wales Press 2000; Rüdiger Lohlker, *Islam im Internet: Neue Formen der Religion im Cyberspace*, Hamburg: Deutsches Orient-Institut 2001 (2nd edn).

35 Frederic Lagrange, *Al-Tarab: Die Musik Ägyptens*, with a preface by Rabih Abou-Khalil, Heidelberg: Palmyra 2000.

36 Nye 2002, pp. 95, 98, 99.

37 Mbye Cham, *Afrika globalisieren? Der afrikanische Film zwischen Négritude und Globalisierung*, <www.vsp.vernetzt.de/soz/000516.htm> (1 August 2004).

38 Reinhard Schulze, Is there an Islamic Modernity? in: Kai Hafez (ed.), *The Islamic World and the West: An Introduction to Political Cultures and International Relations*, Leiden: Brill 2000, pp. 21–32.

Chapter 5   The Internet – the Information Revolution Which Came Too Late for the 'Third Wave of Democratization'

1 David Potter, David Goldblatt, Margaret Kiloh and Paul Lewis (eds), *Democratization*, Cambridge: Polity 1997, p. 9.
2 *Global Internet Geography Database and Report. The Definitive Guide to Global Internet Backbones and Traffic*, <www.telegeography.com> (30 July 2004).
3 Alexander Halavais, National Borders on the World Wide Web, in: *New Media and Society* 2 (2000) 1, pp. 7–28.
4 This is, for example, the view of Marie Lebert, *Multilingualism on the Web*, <www.etudes-francaises.net/entretiens/multieng1.htm> (1 March 2006).
5 *Der Spiegel*, No. 44, 2000, pp. 240–4.
6 See, for example, Taik-Sup Auh, *Promoting Multilingualism on the Internet: Korean Experience*, <www.unesco.org/webworld/infoethics_2/eng/papers/paper_8.htm> (1 March 2006).
7 The methodology used in the study is not entirely transparent. Recent studies have however substantiated a figure of around 50 per cent of English as opposed to 70 to 80 per cent in older works. For an overview, see <www.netz-tipp.de/sprachen.html> (2 August 2004).
8 For an introduction to the UNL-System, see <http://encyclopedia.thefreedIKTionary.com/Universal%20Networking%20Language> (26 August 2004).
9 *Nord–Süd aktuell* 15 (2001) 2, p. 235.
10 Michael Schmiedel, Das Internet in der VR China – Ein Netz, zwei Systeme? in: *Nord–Süd aktuell* 15 (2000) 3, pp. 501–12.
11 Johan Galtung, Eine strukturelle Theorie des Imperialismus, in: Dieter Senghaas (ed.), *Imperialismus und strukturelle Gewalt: Analysen über abhängige Reproduktion*, Frankfurt: Suhrkamp 1972, pp. 29–104.
12 See Kai Hafez, Über den 'digitalen Graben'? Das Medien- und Kommunikationswesen in Asien, Afrika und Lateinamerika, in: *Asien Afrika Lateinamerika* 29 (2001c) 6, pp. 545–53.
13 See ibid.
14 Susanne Offenbartl, *Globalisierung durch Vermittlungsmedien? Vortrag auf der Jahrestagung des Arbeitskreises universitäre Erwachsenenbildung* (AUE), 23–24 September 1999, Deutsches Institut für Erwachsenenbildung (DIE), Bonn, <www.die-frankfurt.de/esprid/dokumente/doc-1999/offenbartl99_11.htm > (1 March 2006).
15 *Die Zukunft des Internets. Auf dem Weg zum 'Digitalen Realismus'*, <www.zukunftsinstitut.de> (1 March 2006).
16 Michael Margolis and David Resnick, *Politics as Usual. The Cyberspace 'Revolution'*, Thousand Oaks: Sage 2000.

17 Offenbartl 1999.
18 John Micklethwait and Adrian Wooldridge, *A Future Perfect: The Challenge and Hidden Promise of Globalization*, New York: Crown Business 2000, p. xxii.
19 Charlotte Wiedemann, Die gerahmte Welt, in: *Freitag*, 12 March 2004, p. 12.
20 Bertolt Brecht, Der Rundfunk als Kommunikationsapparat. Rede über die Funktion des Rundfunks; Vorschläge für den Intendanten des Rundfunks; Radio – eine vorsintflutliche Erfindung?, all in: *Werke*, vol. 21, Schriften I, Berlin 1989– Der Flug der Lindberghs. Ein Radiolehrstück für Knaben und Mädchen, in: *Werke*, vol. 3, Stücke III, Berlin 1989.
21 Claus Leggewie and Christian Maar (eds), *Internet und Politik: Von der Zuschauer- zur Beteiligungsdemokratie?*, Cologne: Bollmann 1998.
22 See, for example, Roza Tsagarousianou, Damian Tambini and Cathy Brian (eds), *Cyberdemocracy. Technology, Cities and Civic Networks*, London and New York: Routledge 1998; Wim van de Donk, Brian D. Loader, Paul G. Nixon and Dieter Rucht (eds), *Cyberprotest: New Media, Citizens and Social Movements*, London and New York: Routledge 2004.
23 Van de Donk et al. 2004, p. 5.
24 Ibid., p. 2.
25 Ibid., p. 18.
26 Dana Ott and Melissa Rosser, The Electronic Republic? The Role of the Internet in Promoting Democracy in Africa, in: Peter Ferdinand (ed.), *The Internet, Democracy and Democratization*, London: Frank Cass 2000, p. 152.
27 Grey E. Burkhart and Susan Older, *The Information Revolution in the Middle East*, St Monica: RAND Corp. 2003.
28 Mamoun Fandy, CyberResistance: Saudi Opposition between Globalization and Localization, in: *Society for Comparative Study of Society and History* 41 (1999) 1, p. 144.
29 Peter Schäfer, *Internet als politisches Kommunikationsmittel in Palästina*, Hamburg: Deutsches Orient-Institut 2004, pp. 62, 89.
30 Adam Jones, From Vanguard to Vanquished: the Tabloid Press in Jordan, in: *Political Communication* 19 (2002) 2, pp. 171–87.
31 Kathryn Sikkink and Margaret E. Keck, *Activists beyond Borders: Advocacy Networks in International Politics*, Ithaca, NY: Cornell University Press 1998.
32 Harry M. Cleaver, The Zapatista Effect: the Internet and the Rise of an Alternative Political Fabric, in: *Journal of International Affairs* 51 (1998) 2, pp. 621–40; David Rondfeldt, *The Zapatista Social Netwar in Mexico*, prepared for the United States' Army, Santa Monica, Cal.: RAND Arroyo Center 1998.
33 Dieter Rucht, *NGOs, Internet und Globalisierung*, presentation at the DGB-Bildungszentrum Hattingen, 23 January 2003, <www.hattingen.dgb-bildungswerk.de/doku/2003INK/20123_6Rucht_Internet_NGOs 6.html> (1 March 2006).

34 Hans-Jürgen Bucher's Critical Contribution is a Welcome Exception: Hans-Jürgen Bucher, Internet und globale Kommunikation. Ansätze eines Strukturwandels der Öffentlichkeit? in: Andreas Hepp and Martin Löffelholz (eds), *Grundlagentexte zur transkulturellen Kommunikation*, Constance: UTB 2002, pp. 500–30.

Chapter 6   International Broadcasting – from National Propaganda to Global Dialogue and Back Again

1 <www.rferl.org and specials/lbush/> (13 June 2002).
2 William A. Rugh, *Comments on Radio Sawa and al Hurra Television*, <www.foreign.senate.gov/testimony/2004/RughTestimony040429.pdf> (28 August 2004).
3 <www.chinabroadcast.cn> (12 July 2004).
4 <www.vor.ru and world.html> (12 July 2004).
5 *U.S. Public Diplomacy: State Department and the Broadcasting Board of Governors Expand Efforts in the Middle East but Face Significant Challenges*, United States General Accounting Office, Washington 2004; *U.S. International Broadcasting. New Strategic Approach Focuses on Reaching Large Audiences but Lacks Measurable Program Objectives*, United States General Accounting Office, Washington 2003.
6 Mark Leonard, Diplomacy by Other Means, in: *Foreign Policy* 132/2002, pp. 48–56.
7 Muhammad Ayish, Foreign Voices as People's Choices: BBC Popularity in the Arab world, in: *Middle Eastern Studies* 3/1991, pp. 374–89.
8 *Epd-Medien*, No. 51, 2 July 2003.
9 Kai Hafez, *Auslandsrundfunk im 'Dialog der Kulturen'. Konzeptionelle Überlegungen Zur Gestaltung der Programme der Deutschen Welle in der islamischen Welt*, final report on the evaluation and advisory project, Erfurt: University of Erfurt 2003b (unpublished).
10 Hans J. Kleinsteuber, Auslandsrundfunk in der Kommunikationspolitik. Zwischen globaler Kommunikation und Dialog der Kulturen, in: Andreas Hepp and Martin Löffelholz (eds), *Grundlagentexte zur transkulturellen Kommunikation*, Constance: UTB 2002, pp. 345–72.
11 Jo Groebel, *Die Rolle des Auslandsrundfunks: Eine vergleichende Analyse der Erfahrungen und Trends in fünf Ländern*, Bonn: Friedrich-Ebert-Stiftung 2000, p. 74.
12 DW-Intendant Bettermann: Gesetzentwurf stärkt Unabhängigkeit des deutschen Auslandsrundfunks, <www.dw-world.de> (28 August 2004).

Chapter 7   Media and Immigration – Ethnicity and Transculturalism in the Media Age

1 Jörg Becker, Die Ethnisierung der deutschen Medienlandschaft – türkische Medienkultur zwischen Assoziation und Dissoziation, in: Christine

Lieberknecht (ed.), *Der Staat in der Informationsgesellschaft*, 9, Ettersburger Gespräche, Erfurt: Ministry for Federal Affairs 1998, pp. 71–5.

2 Marie Gillespie, Local Uses of the Media: Negotiating Culture and Identity, in: Annabelle Sreberny-Mohammadi, Dwayne Winseck, Jim McKenna and Oliver Boyd-Barrett (eds), *Media in Global Context. A Reader*, London: Arnold 1997, pp. 323–37.

3 Hans-Jürgen Weiß and Joachim Trebbe, *Mediennutzung und Integration der türkischen Bevölkerung in Deutschland.* Findings of a survey by the German Press and Information Office, Berlin: Federal Information Office of the German Government 2001.

4 Ibid., p. 49.

5 *Fernsehnutzung der türkischen Bevölkerung in Herne.* Research project commissioned by KOMTECH, Solingen: KOMTECH 2001, p. 18.

6 R. Staring and S. Zorlu, Thuis voor de buis: Turkse migranten en satellitteevee, in: *Migrantenstudies* 12 (1996) 4, pp. 211–21; M. Millikowski, Zapping between Dutch and Turkish: Satellite Television and Amsterdam Turkish Migrants, in: *Migration and Identity*, London 1998.

7 Kai Hafez, *Türkische Mediennutzung in Deutschland: Hemmnis oder Chance der gesellschaftlichen Integration.* Eine qualitative Studie, Berlin: Federal Press and Information Office of the German Government 2002b.

8 Ulrich von Wilamowitz-Moellendorff, *Türken in Deutschland: Einstellungen zu Staat und Gesellschaft*, Konrad-Adenauer-Stiftung, Sankt Augustin: Konrad Adenauer Stiftung 2001.

9 See also Asu Aksoy and Kevin Robins, Thinking across Spaces: Transnational Television from Turkey, in: *European Journal of Cultural Studies* 3 (2000) 3, pp. 343–65.

10 Hamid Naficy, *The Making of Exile Cultures: Iranian Television in Los Angeles*, Minneapolis and London: University of Minnesota Press 1993, p. 197.

11 David Morley and Kevin Robins, *Spaces of Identity: Global Media, Electronic Landscapes and Cultural Boundaries*, London and New York: Routledge 1995.

12 Ibid., p. 22.

13 Jessika Ter Wal (ed.), *Racism and Cultural Diversity in the Mass Media: An Overview of Research and Examples of Good Practice in the EU Member States, 1995–2000*, Vienna: European Monitoring Centre on Racism and Xenophobia 2002. Methodologically, the report features many problems related to the comparability of international research findings, these being based on very different standards of quantitative and qualitative content analyses and user surveys.

14 Ibid., p. 36 f.

15 Ibid., p. 37 ff.

16 Ibid., p. 39.

17 Kai Hafez, Öffentlichkeitsbilder des Islam. Kultur- und rassismustheoretische Grundlagen ihrer politikwissenschaftlichen Erforschung, in: Siegfried Jäger, Helmut Kellerhohn, Andreas Disselnkötter and Susanne

Slobodzian (eds), *Evidenzen im Fluß: Demokratieverluste in Deutschland*, Duisburg: Duisburger Institut für Sprach- und Sozialforschung 1997a, p. 196 ff.

18 Hafez 1997a.

19 Ter Wal 2002, p. 43 f.

20 Matthias Jung, Thomas Niehr and Karin Böke, *Ausländer und Migranten im Spiegel der Presse: Ein diskurshistorisches Wörterbuch zur Einwanderung seit 1945*, Wiesbaden: Vandenhoek and Ruprecht 2000.

21 Hafez 2002a, vol. 2, p. 92 ff.

22 Kai Hafez, Antisemitismus, Philosemitismus und Islamfeindlichkeit: ein Vergleich ethnisch-religiöser Medienbilder, in: Christoph Butterwegge, Gudrun Hentges and Fatma Sarigöz (eds), *Medien und multikulturelle Gesellschaft*, Opladen: Leske and Budrich 1999, pp. 122–35.

23 Andrea Böhm, Die mediale Täter-Opfer-Falle: Ausländer als Objekte journalistischer Begierde, in: Christoph Butterwegge, Gudrun Hentges and Fatma Sarigöz (eds), *Medien und multikulturelle Gesellschaft*, Opladen: Leske and Budrich 1999, p. 95.

24 *Allensbacher Jahrbuch der Demoskopie 1984–1992*, ed. by Elisabeth Noelle-Neumann and Renate Köcher, Munich: Verlag für Demoskopie 1993, p. 998.

25 Ibid., p. 1000.

26 Bhikhu Parekh, The Rushdie affair and the British Press, in: Dan Cohn-Sherbok (ed.), *The Salman Rushdie Controversy in Interreligious Perspective*, Lewiston: E. Mellen Press 1990, p. 79; see also Simon Cottle, Reporting the Rushdie affair: a Case Study in the Orchestration of Public Opinion, in: *Race & Class* 32 (1991) 4, pp. 45–64.

27 Cf. the empirical study in Hafez 1996a.

28 Islamische Strömungen in Berlin, *die tageszeitung*, 17 February 1990; Sonia Seddighi, Feindbild Muselmann, jetzt auch im Kino, *die tageszeitung*, 11 April 1991.

Chapter 8   Media Policy – Why the State Continues to Play a Role

1 *Many Voices – One World. Communication and Society Today and Tomorrow*, London: UNESCO 1980.

2 Gerbner, Mowlana and Nordenstreng 1993.

3 Bernd Blöbaum, *Nachrichtenagenturen in den Nord–Süd-Beziehungen. Eine Studie zur Entwicklung, Struktur and Reform der Weltnachrichtenordnung*, Berlin: Spiess 1983, p. 29 ff.

4 Heinrich von Nussbaum, UN-Ordnung mit System, in: *medium* 9 (1979) 2, pp. 8–14.

5 Rosemary Righter, *Whose News? Politics, the Press and the Third World*, London and New York: Times 1978, p. 15.

6 Alexander Ludwig, Die Bedeutung der Neuen Weltinformationsordnung and ihre Bewertung in vier Tageszeitungen, in: *Publizistik* 29 (1984) 3–4, pp. 287–302.

7 *World Summit on the Information Society, Declaration of Principles*, Geneva 2003 – Tunis 2005, Document WSIS-03 and Geneva and Doc and 4-E, 12 December 2003, <www.itu.int> (1 March 2006).
8 World Summit on the Information Society, Plan of Action, Geneva 2003 – Tunis 2005, Document WSIS-03/Geneva/Doc/5-E, 12 December 2003, <www.itu.int> (1 March 2006).
9 Klaus Liebig, *Geistige Eigentumsrechte: Motor oder Bremse wirtschaftlicher Entwicklung? Entwicklungsländer und das TRIPS-Abkommen*, Bonn: Deutsches Institut für Entwicklungspolitik 2001.
10 Xing Fan, *China's WTO Accession and Its Telecom Liberalization*, <www.csis.org/ics/chinaswtoaccession.html> (28 March 2004).
11 Marc Raboy, Media policy in the new communications environment, in: Marc Raboy (ed.), *Global Media Policy in the New Millennium*, Luton: University of Luton Press 2002, p. 7 f.
12 Ibid.
13 Markus Behmer correctly highlights the lack of transparency typical of the categorizations and assessments of trends in media freedom across the world produced annually by the major NGOs *Freedom House* and *Reporters Without Borders*. These organizations publish neither the precise criteria, nor the information on which they base their work, let alone the system of classification and assessment underlying the categories. See also Markus Behmer, Pressefreiheit in der Dritten Welt – Was heißt 'Freiheit'?, in: Michael Haller (ed.), *Das freie Wort und seine Feinde*, Constance: UVK 2003, pp. 147–60. It is understandable for strategic reasons that many people wish to avoid triggering a worldwide debate on the classification of individual countries as 'free' or 'unfree', which is highly contentious in many cases. This would wreck the authority of the 'hit lists' and relieve the political pressure on authoritarian states. At the same time, however, the lack of transparency feeds critical questions about the legitimacy of the work of some large NGOs. What sense does it make, for example, to categorize Lebanon – certainly the country with the most free press in the Middle East – as having an 'unfree' media system, as did *Freedom House* in 2002, while classifying Jordan, a country in which laws controlling the press have been tightened repeatedly, as 'partly free'? Without transparent explanations, it is hard to avoid the impression that an American NGO had a less critical attitude towards Jordan, an ally of the US, than towards at that time Syrian-dominated Lebanon. Despite their limited use for scholarship, these data are the only continuous surveys and are widely accepted as providing an overall picture of trends in media freedom.
14 Verena Metze-Mangold, Gibt es globale Spielregeln für die Pressefreiheit?, in: Michael Haller (ed.), *Das freie Wort und seine Feinde*, Constance: UVK 2003, pp. 123–35.
15 Freimut Duve, Alexander Nitzsche and Ana Karlsreiter, The OSCE, Islam, and the Media, in: Kai Hafez (ed.), *Media Ethics in the Dialogue of Cultures. Journalistic Self-Regulation in Europe, the Arab World, and Muslim Asia*, Hamburg: Deutsches Orient-Institut 2003, pp. 249–64.

16 Seán Ó Siochrú, Bruce Girard and Amy Mahan, *Global Media Governance. A Beginner's Guide*, Lanham: Rowman & Littlefield 2002, for example p. 163 ff., 167. In the same vein, see: Dwayne Winseck, The WTO, Emerging Policy Regimes and the Political Economy of Transnational Communications, in: Marc Raboy (ed.), *Global Media Policy in the New Millennium*, Luton: University of Luton Press 2002, p. 33.

17 Protocol no. 32.

18 See Lutz M. Hagen (ed.), *Europäische Union and mediale Öffentlichkeit*, Cologne: van Halem 2004.

19 *Jordan Times*, 29 November 2001.

20 *Nord-Süd aktuell* 14 (2000) 3, p. 409.

21 Fatima Boutarkha, The Role of Journalism Associations and Trade Unions in the Democratic Transition of Morocco, in: Kai Hafez (ed.), *Media Ethics in the Dialogue of Cultures: Journalisic Self-Regulation in Europe, the Arab World, and Muslim Asia*, Hamburg: Deutsches Orient-Institut 2003, pp. 147–57; M. Rabah Abdellah, Journalists' Organizations and Associations of Self-Regulation in Algeria, in: Kai Hafez (ed.), *Media Ethics in the Dialogue of Cultures: Journalisic Self-Regulation in Europe, the Arab World, and Muslim Asia*, Hamburg: Deutsches Orient-Institut 2003, pp. 158–61.

Chapter 9   Media Capital – the Limits of Transnationalization

1 See, for example, Edward S. Herman and Robert W. McChesney, *The Global Media: The New Missionaries of Corporate Capitalism*, London and New York: Continuum 1997; Chris Barker, *Global Television: An Introduction*, Oxford: Blackwell 1997, pp. 58–67; Edward Comor, Media Corporations in the Age of Globalization, in: William B. Gudykunst and Bella Mody (eds), *Handbook of International and Intercultural Communication*, Thousand Oaks: Sage 2002, pp. 309–23.

2 Otfried Jarren and Werner A. Meier, Globalisierung der Medienlandschaft und ihre medienpolitische Bewältigung: Ende der Medienpolitik oder neue Gestaltungsformen auf regionaler und nationaler Ebene? in: Hauke Brunkhorst and Matthias Kettner (eds), *Globalisierung und Demokratie: Wirtschaft, Recht, Medien*, Frankfurt: Suhrkamp 2000, p. 361.

3 Preben Sepstrup and Anura Goonasekera, *TV Transnationalization in Europe and Asia: Reports and Papers on Mass Communication*, No. 109, Paris: UNESCO 1994.

4 Benjamin Compaine, Think Again – Global Media, in: *Foreign Policy* 133/2002, p. 21.

5 Herman and McChesney 1997.

6 Ibid., pp. 156–88. For similar views applied to the German-speaking countries, see Christiane Leidinger, *Medien – Herrschaft – Globalisierun: Folgenabschätzung zu Medieninhalten im Zuge transnationaler Konzentrationsprozesse*, Münster: Westfälisches Dampfboot 2003, p. 323 ff.

7 Herman and McChesney 1997, p. 156.

8 Ibid., p. 9.
9 <www.forbes.com> (1 March 2006).
10 Naomi Sakr, *Satellite Realms: Transnational Television, Globalization and the Middle East*, London and New York: I. B. Tauris 2001, p. 66 ff.
11 Douglas A. Boyd, Saudi Arabia's International Media Strategy: Influence through Multinational Ownership, in: Kai Hafez (ed.), *Mass Media, Politics, and Society in the Middle East*, Cresskill, NJ: Hampton 2001.
12 Tourya Guaaybess, Restructuring Television in Egypt: the Position of the State between Regional Supply and Local Demand, in: Kai Hafez (ed.), *Mass Media, Politics and Society in the Middle East*, Cresskill, NJ: Hampton 2001, pp. 61–76.
13 Sakr 2001, p. 97.
14 Herman and McChesney 1997, pp. 162–6.
15 John Sinclair, Mexico, Brazil, and the Latin World, in: John Sinclair, Elizabeth Jacka and Stuart Cunningham (eds), *New Patterns in Global Television: Peripheral Vision*, Oxford: Oxford University Press 1996c, pp. 33–68.
16 David Page and William Crawley, *Satellite over South Asia: Broadcasting Culture and the Public Interest*, New Delhi: Oxford University Press 2001, pp. 120–3, 126–30.
17 Manas Ray and Elizabeth Jacka, Indian Television: an Emerging Regional Force, in: John Sinclair, Elizabeth Jacka and Stuart Cunningham (ed.), *New Patterns in Global Television: Peripheral Vision*, Oxford: Oxford University Press 1996, p. 90.
18 Keith Negus, *Producing Pop: Culture and Conflict in the Popular Music Industry*, London: Arnold 1992, p. 1.
19 David Hendy, *Radio in the Global Age*, Cambridge: Polity 2000, p. 61.
20 Herman and McChesney 1997, p. 189.

Conclusion: Globalization – a Necessary Utopia

1 Michael Giesecke, *Von den Mythen der Buchkultur zu den Visionen der Informationsgesellschaft: Trendforschungen zur kulturellen Medienökologie*, Frankfurt: Suhrkamp 2002, p. 204.
2 Paul Hirst and Grahame Thompson, Globalization – a Necessary Myth? in: David Held and Anthony McGrew (eds), *The Global Transformations Reader: An Introduction to the Globalization Debate*, Cambridge: Polity 2000, pp. 98–105.

Bibliography

Abdellah, M. Rabah, Journalists' Organizations and Associations of Self-Regulation in Algeria, in: Kai Hafez (ed.), *Media Ethics in the Dialogue of Cultures: Journalistic Self-Regulation in Europe, the Arab World, and Muslim Asia*, Hamburg: Deutsches Orient-Institut 2003, pp. 158–61.

Aksoy, Asu and Kevin Robins, Thinking across Spaces. Transnational Television from Turkey, in: *European Journal of Cultural Studies* 3 (2000) 3, pp. 343–65.

Allensbacher Jahrbuch der Demoskopie 1984–1992, ed. by Elisabeth Noelle-Neumann and Renate Köcher, Munich: Verlag für Demoskopie 1993.

Ammon, Royce J., Global Television and the Shaping of World Politics. CNN, Telediplomacy, and Foreign Policy, Jefferson and London: McFarland & Co. 2001.

Anderson, Walter Truett, *All Connected Now: Life in the First Global Civilization*, Boulder: Westview 2004.

Ang, Ien, *Watching Dallas*, New York and London: Routledge 1985.

Asche, Helmut (ed.), *Dritte Welt für Journalisten. Zwischenbilanz eines Weiterbildungsangebotes, im Auftrag des Modellversuchs Journalisten-Weiterbildung an der Freien Universität Berlin [Third world for journalists. Provisional appraisal of a course in further education, commissioned by the pilot scheme 'Further Education for Journalists' at the Free University of Berlin]*, Saarbrücken and Fort Lauderdale: Breitenbach 1984.

Assmann, Jan, Kollektives Gedächtnis und kulturelle Identität [Collective memory and cultural identity], in: Jan Assmann and Tonio Hölscher (ed.), *Kultur und Gedächtnis*, Frankfurt: Suhrkamp 1988, pp. 9–19.

Ayish, Muhammad I., Foreign Voices as People's Choices. BBC Popularity in the Arab World, in: *Middle Eastern Studies* 3/1991, pp. 374–89.

Ayish, Muhammad I., Political Communication on Arab World Television: Evolving Patterns, in: *Political Communication* 19 (2002) 2, pp. 137–54.

Ayish, Muhammad I., *Arab World Television in the Age of Globalization. An*

Analysis of Emerging Political, Economic, Cultural and Technological Patterns, Hamburg: Deutsches Orient-Institut 2003.

Barker, Chris, *Global Television:An Introduction,* Oxford: Blackwell 1997.

Becker, Jörg, *Massenmedien im Nord–Süd-Konflikt [Mass media in the North–South conflict],* Frankfurt: Campus 1985.

Becker, Jörg, Internationaler Nachrichtenfluß: Eine Stellungnahme zum Aufsatz von Birgit Schenk [The international flow of news: a comment on the article by Birgit Schenk], in: *Rundfunk und Fernsehen* 36 (1988) 1, pp. 45–55.

Becker, Jörg, Die Ethnisierung der deutschen Medienlandschaft – türkische Medienkultur zwischen Assoziation und Dissoziation [Ethnicization of the German media landscape – Turkish media culture between association and dissociation], in: Christine Lieberknecht (ed.), *Der Staat in der Informationsgesellschaft.* 9. Ettersburger Gespräche, Erfurt: Ministry of Federal Affairs 1998, pp. 71–5.

Behmer, Markus, Pressefreiheit in der Dritten Welt – Was heißt 'Freiheit'? [Freedom of the press in the Third World – what does 'freedom' mean?], in: Michael Haller (ed.), *Das freie Wort und seine Feinde,* Constance: UVK 2003, pp. 147–60.

Beisheim, Marianne and Gregor Walter, 'Globalisierung' – Kinderkrankheiten eines Konzepts ['Globalization' – conceptual teething trouble], in: *Zeitschrift für internationale Beziehungen* 4 (1997) 1, pp. 153–80.

Bennett, W. Lance and David L. Paletz (ed.), *Taken by Storm: The Media, Public Opinion, and U.S. Foreign Policy in the Gulf War,* Chicago and London: University of Chicago Press 1991.

Blöbaum, Bernd, *Nachrichtenagenturen in den Nord–Süd-Beziehungen. Eine Studie zur Entwicklung, Struktur und Reform der Weltnachrichtenordnung [News agencies within North–South relations. A study of the development, structure and reform of the world news order],* Berlin: Spiess 1983.

Bocock, Robert, *Hegemony,* London and New York: Tavistock 1986.

Böhm, Andrea, Die mediale Täter-Opfer-Falle: Ausländer als Objekte journalistischer Begierde [The media's culprit-victim trap: foreigners as objects of journalistic desire], in: Christoph Butterwegge, Gudrun Hentges and Fatma Sarigöz (eds), *Medien und multikulturelle Gesellschaft,* Opladen: Leske und Budrich 1999, pp. 90–4.

Boutarkha, Fatima, The Role of Journalism Associations and Trade Unions in the Democratic Transition of Morocco, in: Kai Hafez (ed.), *Media Ethics in the Dialogue of Cultures: Journalistic Self-Regulation in Europe, the Arab World, and Muslim Asia,* Hamburg: Deutsches Orient-Institut 2003, pp. 147–57.

Boyd, Douglas A., Saudi Arabia's International Media Strategy: Influence through Multinational Ownership, in: Kai Hafez (ed.), *Mass Media, Politics, and Society in the Middle East,* Cresskill, NJ: Hampton 2001, pp. 43–60.

Brecht, Bertolt, Der Rundfunk als Kommunikationsapparat. Rede über die Funktion des Rundfunks [Radio as communicative apparatus. Speech on

the function of radio]; Vorschläge für den Intendanten des Rundfunks
[Suggestions for the Director General of radio]; Radio – eine vorsintflut-
liche Erfindung? [Radio – an antediluvian invention?], all in: *Werke*, vol. 21,
Schriften I, Berlin, 1989.

Brecht, Bertolt, Der Flug der Lindberghs. Ein Radiolehrstück für Knaben
und Mädchen [Lindbergh's flight. An educational radio play for boys and
girls], in: *Werke*, vol. 3, Stücke III, Berlin 1989.

Breidenbach, Joana and Ina Zukrigl, Tanz der Kulturen. Kulturelle Identität
in einer globalisierten Welt [The dance of cultures. Cultural identity in a
globalized world], Munich: Kunstmann 1998.

Breslin, Shaun, Christopher W. Hughes, Nicola Phillips and Ben Rosamund
(eds), *New Regionalisms in the Global Political Economy*, London and New
York: Routledge 2002.

Brown, Aggrey, In the Caribbean, a Complex Situation, in: *Media and
Democracy in Latin America and Caribbean*, Paris: UNESCO 1996, pp. 40–7.

Bucher, Hans-Jürgen, Internet und globale Kommunikation: Ansätze eines
Strukturwandels der Öffentlichkeit? [Internet and global communication:
The beginnings of the structural change of the public sphere?], in: Andreas
Hepp and Martin Löffelholz (eds), *Grundlagentexte zur transkulturellen
Kommunikation*, Constance: UTB 2002, pp. 500–30.

Bunt, Gary, *Virtually Islamic: Computer-Mediated Communication and Cyber-
Islamic Environments*, Cardiff: University of Wales Press 2000.

Burkhart, Grey E. and Susan Older, *The Information Revolution in the Middle
East*, St Monica: RAND Corp. 2003.

Butterwegge, Christoph, Kampf oder Dialog der Kulturen? Samuel P.
Huntingtons These vom 'Zusammenprall der Zivilisationen' [Battle or dialogue of cultures? Samuel P. Huntington's thesis of the 'Clash of
Civilizations'], in: *Zeitschrift für Migration und soziale Arbeit* 17 (1996) 2,
pp. 44–7.

Büttner, Friedemann, Islamischer Fundamentalismus: Politisierter
Traditionalismus oder revolutionärer Messianismus? [Islamic fundamen-
talism: politicized traditionalism or revolutionary Messianism?], in: Heiner
Bielefeldt and Wilhelm Heitmeyer (eds), *Politisierte Religion: Ursachen und
Erscheinungsformen des modernen Fundamentalismus*, Frankfurt : Suhrkamp
1998, pp. 188–210.

Castells, Manuel, *The Information Age*, 3 vols, Cambridge, MA and Oxford:
Blackwell 1996–97.

Chouikha, Larbi, Etatisation et pratique journalistique [State control and the
practice of journalism], in: *Revue tunisienne de communication* 22/1992,
pp. 37–46.

Cleaver, Harry M., The Zapatista Effect: The Internet and the Rise of an
Alternative Political Fabric, in: *Journal of International Affairs* 51 (1998) 2,
pp. 621–40.

Collins, Richard, *From Satellite to Single Market. New Communication
Technology and European Public Service Television*, London and New York:
Routledge 1998.

Comor, Edward, Media Corporations in the Age of Globalization, in: William B. Gudykunst and Bella Mody (eds), *Handbook of International and Intercultural Communication*, Thousand Oaks: Sage 2002, pp. 309–23.

Compaine, Benjamin, Think Again – Global Media, in: *Foreign Policy* 133/2002, pp. 20–28.

Cottle, Simon, Reporting the Rushdie Affair: a Case Study in the Orchestration of Public Opinion, in: *Race and Class* 32 (1991) 4, pp. 45–64.

Curran, James and Myung-Jin Park, Beyond Globalization Theory, in: Curran, James and Myung-Jin Park (eds), *De-Westernizing Media Studies*, London and New York: Routledge 2000, pp. 3–18.

DeLuca, Anthony R., *Politics, Diplomacy, and the Media: Gorbachev's Legacy in the West*, Westport and London: Praeger 1998.

Domke, David, *God Willing? Political Fundamentalism in the White House: the 'War on Terror' and the Echoing Press*, London and Ann Arbor: Pluto 2004.

Dritte Welt und Medienwelt. Entwicklungspolitik und das Bild der Dritten Welt in Presse, Hörfunk, Fernsehen, Eigenerhebungen und Sekundäranalysen des Zentrums für Kulturforschung, Bonn, [Third World and media world. Development policy and the image of the Third World in the press and on radio and television. Surveys and secondary analyses by the Centre for Cultural Research, Bonn], Bonn: Zentrums für Kulturforschung, Bonn, and Ministry for Economic Cooperation and Development 1983.

Duve, Freimut, Alexander Nitzsche and Ana Karlsreiter, The OSCE, Islam, and the Media, in: Kai Hafez (ed.), *Media Ethics in the Dialogue of Cultures: Journalistic Self-Regulation in Europe, the Arab World, and Muslim Asia*, Hamburg: Deutsches Orient-Institut 2003, pp. 249–64.

Eckhardt, Josef, Berichterstattung über die Dritte Welt im ARD-Programm und im Westdeutschen Fernsehen [Coverage of the Third World by ARD and on West German television], in: *Media Perspektiven* 12/1982, pp. 767–75.

Egloff, Daniel, Digitale Demokratie: *Mythos oder Realität? Auf den Spuren der demokratischen Aspekte des Internets und der Computerkultur [Digital democracy: myth or reality? On the trail of democratic aspects of the Internet and computer culture]*, Wiesbaden: Westdeutscher Verlag 2002.

El-Nawawy, Mohammed and Adel Iskandar, *Al-Jazeera: The Story of the Network that is Rattling Governments and Redefining Modern Journalism*, Cambridge, MA: Westview 2003.

Europe 2004. A Survey of Decision Makers and Leading Consumers, Harrow: Ipsos Media 2004.

Fandy, Mamoun, CyberResistance: Saudi Opposition between Globalization and Localization, in: *Comparative Studies of Society and History* 41 (1999) 1, pp. 124–47.

Fandy, Mamoun, Information Technology, Trust, and Social Change in the Arab World, in: *The Middle East Journal* 54 (2000) 3, pp. 379–98.

Ferguson, Marjorie, The Myth of Globalization, in: *European Journal of Communication* 7 (1992) 1, pp. 69–93.

Fernsehnutzung der türkischen Bevölkerung in Herne. Forschungsprojekt im Auftrag von KOMTECH [TV use among the Turkish community in Herne. Research project commissioned by KOMTECH], Solingen: KOMTECH 2001.

Galtung, Johan, Eine strukturelle Theorie des Imperialismus [A structural theory of imperialism], in: Dieter Senghaas (ed.), *Imperialismus und strukturelle Gewalt. Analysen über abhängige Reproduktion*, Frankfurt: Suhrkamp 1972, pp. 29–104.

Gerbner, George, Hamid Mowlana and Kaarle Nordenstreng (eds), *The Global Media Debate: its Rise, Fall, and Renewal*, Norwood, NJ: Ablex 1993.

Giddens, Anthony, *The Constitution of Society*, Cambridge: Polity 1984.

Giddens, Anthony, *The Nation-State and Violence*, Berkeley: University of California Press 1987.

Giesecke, Michael, *Von den Mythen der Buchkultur zu den Visionen der Informationsgesellschaft. Trendforschungen zur kulturellen Medienökologie [From the myths of book culture to visions of the Information Society. Researching trends in the cultural ecology of the media]*, Frankfurt: Suhrkamp 2002.

Gilboa, Eytan, The CNN Effect: The Search for a Communication Theory of International Relations, in: *Political Communication* 22 (2005) 1, pp. 27–44.

Gillespie, Marie, Local Uses of the Media: Negotiating Culture and Identity, in: Annabelle Sreberny-Mohammadi, Dwayne Winseck, Jim McKenna and Oliver Boyd-Barrett (eds), *Media in Global Context: A Reader*, London: Arnold 1997, pp. 323–37.

Glass, Daniel, *Die Dritte Welt in der Presse der Bundesrepublik Deutschland. Eine ideologiekritische Fallstudie [The Third World in the West German press. A case study based on ideological critique]*, Frankfurt: Haag und Herchen 1979.

Groebel, Jo, *Die Rolle des Auslandsrundfunks: Eine vergleichende Analyse der Erfahrungen und Trends in fünf Ländern [The role of international broadcasting: a comparative analysis of experiences and trends in five countries]*, Bonn: Friedrich-Ebert-Stiftung 2000.

Guaaybess, Tourya, Restructuring Television in Egypt: The Position of the State between Regional Supply and Local Demand, in: Kai Hafez (ed.), *Mass Media, Politics and Society in the Middle East*, Cresskill, NJ: Hampton 2001, pp. 61–76.

Gurevitch, Michael, Mark R. Levy and Itzhak Roeh, The Global Newsroom: Convergences and Diversities in the Globalization of Television News, in: Peter Dahlgren and Colin Sparks (eds), *Communication and Citizenship: Journalism and the Public Sphere*, London and New York: Routledge 1993, pp. 195–216.

Habermas, Jürgen, *Strukturwandel der Öffentlichkeit [The Structural Transformation of the Public Sphere]*, Frankfurt: Suhrkamp 1990 (Orig. 1962).

Hafez, Kai, Islam und Modernität in der *Washington Post* zur Zeit der Iranischen Revolution 1978–79 [Islam and modernity in the *Washington Post* at the time of the Iranian Revolution of 1978–79], in: *Asien, Afrika, Lateinamerika* 21 (1993) 4, pp. 373–81.

Hafez, Kai, Salman Rushdie im Kulturkonflikt. Zum Problem der transkulturellen Kommunikation in der deutschen Presseberichterstattung [Salman
Rushdie and cultural conflict. The problem of transcultural communication
in German press coverage], in: Orient 37 (1996a) 1, pp. 137–61.

Hafez, Kai, The Algerian Crisis as Portrayed in the German Press: Media
Coverage of Political Islam, in: Communications. The European Journal of
Communication Research 21 (1996b) 2, pp. 155–82.

Hafez, Kai, Öffentlichkeitsbilder des Islam. Kultur- und rassismustheoretische Grundlagen ihrer politikwissenschaftlichen Erforschung [Public
images of Islam from the perspective of political science research and its
basis in theories of culture and race], in: Siegfried Jäger, Helmut
Kellerhohn, Andreas Disselnkötter and Susanne Slobodzian (eds),
Evidenzen im Fluß. Demokratieverluste in Deutschland, Duisburg:
Duisburger Institut für Sprach- und Sozialforschung 1997a, pp. 188–204.

Hafez, Kai, Dialog mit dem Islam: Die Debatte über Medien und
Außenpolitik [Dialogue with Islam: The debate on media and foreign
policy], in: Die Brücke 93/1997b, pp. 56–9.

Hafez, Kai, Antisemitismus, Philosemitismus und Islamfeindlichkeit: ein
Vergleich ethnisch-religiöser Medienbilder [Anti-Semitism, philo-Semitism
and Islamophobia: a comparative analysis of ethnic-religious conceptions in
the media], in: Christoph Butterwegge, Gudrun Hentges and Fatma Sarigöz
(eds), Medien und multikulturelle Gesellschaft, Opladen: Leske und Budrich
1999a, pp. 122–35.

Hafez, Kai, International News Coverage and the Problems of Media
Globalization: In Search of a 'New Global-Local Nexus', in: Innovation.
The European Journal of Social Sciences 12 (1999b) 1, pp. 47–62.

Hafez, Kai, Islam and the West – the Clash of Politicized Perceptions, in: Kai
Hafez (ed.), The Islamic World and the West: An Introduction to Political
Cultures and International Relations, Leiden: Brill 2000, S. 3–18.

Hafez, Kai, Mass Media in the Middle East: Patterns of Societal Change, in:
Kai Hafez (ed.), Mass Media, Politics, and Society in the Middle East,
Cresskill, NJ: Hampton 2001a, pp. 1–20.

Hafez, Kai, The Ethics of Journalism: Comparison and Transformations in
the Islamic-Western Context, Schloss Bellevue, Berlin, 29–30 March
2001, in: Orient 42 (2001b) 3, pp. 403–15.

Hafez, Kai, Über den 'digitalen Graben'? Das Medien- und Kommunikationswesen in Asien, Afrika und Lateinamerika [Across the 'digital
divide'? The media and communication system in Asia, Africa and Latin
America], in: Asien Afrika Lateinamerika 29 (2001c) 6, pp. 545–53.

Hafez, Kai, Die politische Dimension der Auslandsberichterstattung [The political
dimensions of foreign reporting], 2 vols, Baden-Baden: Nomos 2002a.

Hafez, Kai, Türkische Mediennutzung in Deutschland: Hemmnis oder Chance der
gesellschaftlichen Integration: Eine qualitative Studie [Turkish media use in
Germany: hindrance to or opportunity for social integration: a qualitative study],
Berlin: Federal Press - and Information Office of the German Government
2002b.

Hafez, Kai, Editor's Preface, in: Hafez, Kai (ed.), *Media Ethics in the Dialogue of Cultures: Journalistic Self-Regulation in Europe, the Arab World and Muslim Asia*, Hamburg: Deutsches Orient-Institut 2003a, pp. 13–17.

Hafez, Kai, Auslandsrundfunk im 'Dialog der Kulturen': Konzeptionelle Überlegungen Zur Gestaltung der Programme der Deutschen Welle in der islamischen Welt, Abschlussbericht zum Evaluations- und Beratungsprojekt [International broadcasting in the 'dialogue of cultures': conceptual remarks on the design of *Deutsche Welle* programmes in the Islamic world. Final report on the evaluation and advisory project], Erfurt: University of Erfurt 2003b (unpublished).

Hafez, Kai, Arab Satellite Broadcasting – Democracy without Political Parties?, in: *Transnational Broadcasting Studies* 1 (2005) 2, pp. 275–97.

Hafez, Kai, Globalization, Regionalization and Democratization: The Interaction of Three Paradigms in the Field of Mass Communication, in: Bob Hackett (ed.), *Democratizing Global Media: One World, Many Struggles*, New York: Rowman & Littlefield 2005, pp. 145–63.

Hagen, Lutz M., *Informationsqualität von Nachrichten: Meßmethoden und ihre Anwendung auf die Dienste von Nachrichtenagenturen [The Quality of News Information: Methods of Measurement and their Application to News Agency Services]*, Opladen: Westdeutscher Verlag 1995, pp. 252–64.

Hagen, Lutz M., Ausländische Berichterstattung über Deutschland: Erste Ergebnisse der 'Foreign-News-Studie' über Umfang und Themen von Nachrichten über Deutschland in verschiedenen Ländern [Coverage of Germany abroad: Initial findings of the 'Foreign News Study' on the extent and thematic content of news on Germany in various countries], in: Siegfried Quandt and Wolfgang Gast (eds), *Deutschland im Dialog der Kulturen. Medien – Images – Verständigung*, Constance: UVK 1998, pp. 203–11.

Hagen, Lutz M. (ed.), *Europäische Union und mediale Öffentlichkeit [The European Union and the Public Sphere of the Media]*, Cologne: von Halem 2004.

Halavais, Alexander, National Borders on the World Wide Web, in: *New Media and Society* 2 (2000) 1, pp. 7–28.

Hall, Stuart, Who Needs 'Identity'? in Stuart Hall and Paul du Gay (eds), *Questions of Cultural Identity*, London: Sage 1996, pp. 1–17.

Hasebrink, Uwe and Anja Herzog, Mediennutzung im internationalen Vergleich [Media use from a comparative international perspective], in: *Internationales Handbuch Medien* 2004–5, Hans-Bredow-Institut, Baden-Baden: Nomos 2004, pp. 136–58.

Held, David, Anthony McGrew, David Goldblatt and Jonathan Perraton, Rethinking Globalization, in: David Held and Anthony McGrew (eds), *The Global Transformations Reader: An Introduction to the Globalization Debate*, Cambridge: Polity 2000, pp. 67–74.

Held, David and Anthony McGrew (eds), *The Global Transformation Reader: An Introduction to the Globalization Debate*, Cambridge: Polity 2003.

Hendy, David, *Radio in the Global Age*, Cambridge: Polity 2000.

Hepp, Andreas and Martin Löffelholz (eds), *Grundlagentexte zur transkul-*

turellen Kommunikation [Key Contributions to Transcultural Communication], Constance: UTB 2002.

Hepp, Andreas, Friedrich Krotz and Carsten Winter, Einleitung [Introduction], in: Hepp, Andreas, Friedrich Krotz and Carsten Winter (eds), *Globalisierung der Medienkommunikation. Eine Einführung*, Wiesbaden: Verlag für Sozialwissenschaften 2005, pp. 5–17.

Herman, Edward S. and Robert W. McChesney, *The Global Media: The New Missionaries of Corporate Capitalism*, London and New York: Continuum 1997.

Herzog-Massing, Herta, Decoding Dallas, in: *Society* 24 (1986) 1, pp. 74–7.

Hess, Stephen and Marvin Kalb (eds), *The Media and the War on Terrorism*, Washington, D.C.: Brookings Institution Press 2003.

Hippler, Jochen and Andrea Lueg (eds), *Feindbild Islam [Islam as the Enemy]*, Hamburg: Konkret 1993.

Hirst, Paul and Grahame Thompson, *Globalization in Question*, Cambridge: Polity 1999 (2nd edn).

Hirst, Paul and Grahame Thompson, Globalization – A Necessary Myth? in: David Held and Anthony McGrew (eds), *The Global Transformations Reader: An Introduction to the Globalization Debate*, Cambridge: Polity 2000, pp. 98–105.

Huntington, Samuel P., The Clash of Civilizations? in: *Foreign Affairs* 72 (1993) 3, pp. 22–49.

Huntington, Samuel P., The Clash of Civilizations and the Remaking of World Order, New York: Simon & Schuster 1996.

Jameson, Fredric, Preface, in: Fredric Jameson and Masao Miyoshi (eds), *The Cultures of Globalization*, Durham: Duke University Press 1998, pp. xi–xvi.

Jarren, Otfried and Werner A. Meier, Globalisierung der Medienlandschaft und ihre medienpolitische Bewältigung: Ende der Medienpolitik oder neue Gestaltungsformen auf regionaler und nationaler Ebene? [Globalization of the media landscape and how media policy is dealing with it: the end of media policy or new organizational forms at the regional and national level?], in: Hauke Brunkhorst and Matthias Kettner (eds), *Globalisierung und Demokratie. Wirtschaft, Recht, Medien*, Frankfurt: Suhrkamp 2000, pp. 347–68.

Joetze, Günter, Politische Grenzen der Globalisierung [The political limits of globalization], in: *Internationale Politik* 54 (1999) 6, pp. 53–8.

Jones, Adam, From Vanguard to Vanquished: The Tabloid Press in Jordan, in: *Political Communication* 19 (2002) 2, pp. 171–87.

Jung, Matthias, Thomas Niehr and Karin Böke, *Ausländer und Migranten im Spiegel der Presse: Ein diskurshistorisches Wörterbuch zur Einwanderung seit 1945 [Foreigners and migrants as reflected in the press: a discourse historical dictionary of immigration since 1945]*, Wiesbaden: Vandenhoek & Ruprecht 2000.

Kavoori, Anandam P., Trends in Global Media Reception, in: Daya Kishan Thussu (ed.), *Electronic Empires: Global Media and Local Resistance*, London: Arnold 1998, pp. 193–207.

Keohane, Robert O. and Joseph S. Nye, *Power and Interdependence: World Politics in Transition*, Boston and Toronto: Little, Brown 1977.

Kleinsteuber, Hans J., Auslandsrundfunk in der Kommunikationspolitik. Zwischen globaler Kommunikation und Dialog der Kulturen [International broadcasting in communication policies. Between global communication and dialogue of cultures], in: Andreas Hepp and Martin Löffelholz (eds), *Grundlagentexte zur transkulturellen Kommunikation*, Constance: UTB 2002, pp. 345–72.

Kleinsteuber, Hans J., Bausteine für einen dialogischen Journalismus: Zur Umsetzung des Prinzips 'Dialog der Kulturen' [The building blocks of a dialogic journalism: putting the principle of 'dialogue of cultures' into practice], in: Jörgen Klussmann (ed.), *Interkulturelle Kompetenz und Medienpraxis: Ein Handbuch*, Frankfurt: Brandes & Aspel 2004, pp. 41–68.

Klemm, Verena and Karin Hörner (eds), *Das Schwert des 'Experten'. Peter Scholl-Latours verzerrtes Araber- und Islambild [The sword of the 'expert'. Peter Scholl-Latour's distorted conception of Arabs and Islam]*, Heidelberg: Palmyra 1993.

Kraidy, Marwan M., Glocalisation: An International Communication Framework? in: *Journal of International Communication* 9 (2003) 2, pp. 29–49.

Kriener, Markus and Miriam Meckel, Internationale Kommunikation. Begriffe, Probleme, Referenzen [International communication. Concepts, problems, references], in: Kriener, Markus and Miriam Meckel (eds), *Internationale Kommunikation. Eine Einführung*, Opladen: Westdeutscher Verlag 1996, pp. 11–18.

Lagrange, Frederic, Al-Tarab, *Die Musik Ägyptens [The music of Egypt]*, preface by Rabih Abou-Khalil, Heidelberg: Palmyra 2000.

Lechner, Frank J. and John Boli (eds), *The Globalization Reader*, Oxford: Blackwell 2000.

Lee, Hyangjin, *Contemporary Korean Cinema: Identity, Culture, Politics*, Manchester and New York: Manchester University Press 2000.

Leggewie, Claus and Christian Maar (eds), *Internet und Politik. Von der Zuschauer- zur Beteiligungsdemokratie? [Internet and politics. From a viewers' to a participatory democracy?]*, Cologne: Bollmann 1998.

Lehmann, Ingrid A., Transatlantic Media Divide over Iraq, in: *Medien Tenor Forschungsbericht* No. 147, September 2004, pp. 66–9.

Leidinger, Christiane, *Medien – Herrschaft – Globalisierung: Folgenabschätzung zu Medieninhalten im Zuge transnationaler Konzentrationsprozesse [Media – Hegemony – Globalization: appraising the consequences of transnational processes of concentration for media content]*, Münster: Westfälisches Dampfboot 2003.

Leonard, Mark, Diplomacy by Other Means, in: *Foreign Policy* 132/2002, pp. 48–56.

Lieber, Robert J. and Ruth E. Weisberg, Globalization, Culture, and Identities in Crisis, in: *International Journal of Politics, Culture and Society* 16 (2002) 2, pp. 273–96.

Liebes, Tamar and Elihu Katz, *The Export of Meaning: Cross-Cultural Readings of* Dallas, New York and Oxford: Oxford University Press 1990.

Liebig, Klaus, *Geistige Eigentumsrechte: Motor oder Bremse wirtschaftlicher Entwicklung? Entwicklungsländer und das TRIPS-Abkommen [Are intellectual property rights stimulating or hindering economic development? Developing countries and the TRIPS Agreement]*, Bonn: Deutsches Institut für Entwicklungspolitik 2001.

Löffelholz, Martin, Krisen- und Kriegskommunikation als Forschungsfeld [Communication at times of crisis and war as a field of research], in: Löffelholz, Martin (ed.), *Krieg als Medienereignis II. Krisenkommunikation im 21. Jahrhundert*, Wiesbaden: Verlag für Sozialwissenschaften 2004, pp. 13–55.

Lohlker, Rüdiger, *Islam im Internet: Neue Formen der Religion im Cyberspace [Islam on the Internet. New forms of religion in cyberspace]*, Hamburg: Deutsches Orient-Institut 2001 (2nd edn).

Ludwig, Alexander, Die Bedeutung der Neuen Weltinformationsordnung und ihre Bewertung in vier Tageszeitungen [The significance of the New World Information Order and its evaluation in four daily newspapers], in: *Publizistik* 29 (1984) 3–4, pp. 287–302.

Luger, Kurt, Dritte-Welt-Berichterstattung: eine einzige Katastrophe? Die Konstruktion von Wirklichkeit in Theorie und Praxis [Coverage of the Third World: an out-and-out disaster? The construction of reality in theory and practice], in: *Die Dritte Welt in den Massenmedien*, Salzburg: Institut für Publizistik- und Kommunikationswissenschaft der Universität Salzburg 1985, pp. 5–25.

Luger, Kurt, Zwischen Katastrophen und Shangri La: Bilder von der Dritten Welt [Between catastrophes and Shangri-la: images of the Third World], in: *Dialog 16* (1989) 3, pp. 19–29.

Lull, James, Superkultur [Superculture], in: Andreas Hepp and Martin Löffelholz (eds), *Grundlagentexte zur transkulturellen Kommunikation*, Constance: UTB 2002, pp. 750–73.

Many Voices – One World. Communication and Society Today and Tomorrow, London: UNESCO 1980.

Maresch, Rudolf and Florian Roetzer, *Cyberhypes: Möglichkeiten und Grenzen des Internet [Cyberhype: The Potential and Limitations of the Internet]*, Frankfurt: Suhrkamp 2001.

Margolis, Michael and David Resnick, *Politics as Usual: The Cyberspace 'Revolution'*, Thousand Oaks: Sage 2000.

McLuhan, Marshall, *Understanding Media*, London: Sphere 1967.

Meckel, Miriam, Internationales als Restgröße? Struktur der Auslandsberichterstattung im Fernsehen [International affairs as leftovers? The structure of foreign reporting on television], in: Klaus Kamps and Miriam Meckel (eds), *Fernsehnachrichten. Prozesse, Strukturen, Funktionen*, Opladen: Westdeutscher Verlag 1998, pp. 257–74.

Metze-Mangold, Verena, Gibt es globale Spielregeln für die Pressefreiheit? [Are there global rules governing press freedom?], in: Michael Haller (ed.), *Das freie Wort und seine Feinde*, Constance: UVK 2003, pp. 123–35.

Meyer, Thomas, *Mediokratie: Die Kolonisierung der Politik durch die Medien*

[Mediacracy:The Colonisation of Politics by the Media], Frankfurt: Suhrkamp 2004.

Micklethwait, John and Adrian Wooldridge, *A Future Perfect: The Challenge and Hidden Promise of Globalization*, New York: Crown Business 2000.

Mikich, Sonia, Geistige Provinzialisierung: Eine Zustandsbeschreibung [Intellectual provincialism: the current state of affairs], in: Claudia Cippitelli and Axel Schwanenbeck (eds), *Nur Krisen, Kriege, Katastrophen? Auslandsberichterstattung im deutschen Fernsehen. Dokumentation der 21. Tutzinger Medientage*, Munich: Reinhard Fischer 2003, pp. 117–28.

Miles, Hugh, *Al-Jazeera, How Arab TV News Challenged the World*, London: Abacus 2005.

Miller, David (ed.), *Tell Me Lies: Propaganda and Media Distortion in the Attack on Iraq*, London and Stirling: Pluto 2004.

Millikowski, M., Zapping between Dutch and Turkish: Satellite Television and Amsterdam Turkish Migrants, in: *Migration and Identity*, London 1998.

Mishra, Vijay, *Bollywood Cinema: Temples of Desire*, New York and London: Routledge 2002.

Moisy, Claude, Myths about the Global Information Village, in: *Foreign Policy* 107/1997, pp. 78–87.

Morley, David and Kevin Robins, *Spaces of Identity: Global Media, Electronic Landscapes and Cultural Boundaries*, London and New York: Routledge 1995.

Mostefaoui, Belkacem, Ausländisches Fernsehen im Maghreb – ein Medium mit kulturellen und politischen Auswirkungen [Foreign television in the Maghreb – a medium with cultural and political consequences], in: *Wuquf* 10–11/1995–96, Hamburg 1997, pp. 425–55.

Mueller, John E., *War, Presidents, and Public Opinion*, New York: Wiley 1973.

Münker, Stefan and Alexander Roesler (eds), *Mythos Internet* [*The myth of the Internet*], Frankfurt: Suhrkamp 1997.

Mytton, Graham, A Billion Viewers Can't Be Right, in: *Intermedia* 19 (1991) 3, pp. 10–12.

Mytton, Graham, Global TV Audiences: How Many Are Actually Reached? Let's Be Honest. Nobody Yet Knows, in: *ESOMAR News Brief* 7 (1999) 7, pp. 18–19.

Naficy, Hamid, *The Making of Exile Cultures: Iranian Television in Los Angeles*, Minneapolis and London: University of Minnesota Press 1993.

Negus, Keith, *Producing Pop: Culture and Conflict in the Popular Music Industry*, London: Arnold 1992.

Noelle-Neumann, Elisabeth, Die öffentliche Meinung und die Wirkung der Massenmedien [Public opinion and the effect of the mass media], in: Jürgen Wilke (ed.), *Fortschritte der Publizistikwissenschaft*, Freiburg: Alber 1990, pp. 11–23.

Nye, Joseph S., *The Paradox of American Power: Why the World's only Superpower Can't Go It Alone*, New York and Oxford: Oxford University Press 2002.

O'Neil, Patrick H., Democratization and Mass Communication: What is the Link? in: Patrick H. O'Neil (ed.), *Communicating Democracy: The Media* and *Political Transitions*, Boulder and London: Lynne Rienner 1998, pp. 1–20.

Ohde, Christina, *Der Irre von Bagdad: Zur Konstruktion von Feindbildern in überregionalen deutschen Tageszeitungen während der Golfkrise 1990–91 [The lunatic of Baghdad: The construction of conceptions of the enemy in German national newspapers during the Gulf crisis of 1990–1991]*, Frankfurt: Peter Lang 1994.

One Year After: Media Comments on the First Anniversary of September 11, Paris: Panos Institute 2002.

Osland, Joyce S., Broadening the Debate: The Pros and Cons of Globalization, in: *Journal of Management Inquiry* 12 (2003) 2, pp. 137–54.

Ott, Dana and Melissa Rosser, The Electronic Republic? The Role of the Internet in Promoting Democracy in Africa, in: Peter Ferdinand (ed.), *The Internet, Democracy and Democratization*, London: Frank Cass 2000, pp. 137–56.

Page, David and William Crawley, *Satellite over South Asia: Broadcasting Culture and the Public Interest*, New Delhi: Oxford University Press 2001.

Parekh, Bikhu, The Rushdie Affair and the British Press, in: Dan Cohn-Sherbok (ed.), *The Salman Rushdie Controversy in Interreligious Perspective*, Lewiston: E. Mellen Press 1990, pp. 71–95.

Pintak, Lawrence, *Reflections in a Bloodshot Lens: America, Islam and the War of Ideas*, London: Pluto 2006.

Pocket World in Figures 2005, London: *The Economist* 2004.

Pool, Ithiel de Sola, *Technologies without Boundaries: On Telecommunications in a Global Age*, Cambridge, MA: Harvard University Press 1990.

Potter, David, David Goldblatt, Margaret Kiloh and Paul Lewis (eds), *Democratization*, Cambridge: Polity 1997.

Pusch, Barbara, Neue Muslimische Frauen in der Türkei. Einblicke in ihre Lebenswelt [New Muslim Women in Turkey. Insights into their life-world], in: Mechthild Rumpf, Ute Gerhard and Mechthild M. Jansen (eds), *Facetten islamischer Welten*. Geschlechterordnungen, Frauen und Menschenrechte in der Diskussion, Bielefeld: Transcript 2003, pp. 242–55.

Pütz, Wolfgang, *Das Italienbild in der deutschen Presse: Eine Untersuchung ausgewählter Tageszeitungen [The conception of Italy in the German press: A study of selected daily newspapers]*, Munich: Ölschläger 1993.

Raboy, Marc, Media Policy in the New Communications Environment, in: Raboy, Marc (ed.), *Global Media Policy in the New Millennium*, Luton: University of Luton Press 2002, pp. 3–16.

Raboy, Marc, Television and Deregulated Global Markets, in: John Sinclair (ed.), *Contemporary World Television*, London: BFI 2004, pp. 21–4.

Rager, Günther, *Publizistische Vielfalt im Lokalen [The diversity of local mass communication]*, Tübingen: Tübinger Vereinigung für Volkskunde 1982.

Rawan, Shir Mohammed, Traditionelle Kommunikation und moderne Massenmedien in Afghanistan [Traditional communication and modern mass media in Afghanistan], in: *Orient* 36 (1996) 3, pp. 495–509.

Ray, Manas and Elizabeth Jacka, Indian Television: An Emerging Regional

Force, in: John Sinclair, Elizabeth Jacka and Stuart Cunningham (eds), *New Patterns in Global Television: Peripheral Vision*, Oxford: Oxford University Press 1996, pp. 83–102.

Renckstorf, Karsten and Paul Hendriks Vettehen, Watching Foreign TV Channels, in: Karsten Renckstorf, Denis McQuail and Nicholas Jankowski (eds), *Media Use as Social Action: A European Approach to Audience Studies*, London: John Libbey 1996, pp. 103–12.

Reynolds, Amy and Brooke Barnett, 'America under Attack': CNN's Verbal and Visual Framing of September 11, in: Steven Chermak, Frankie Y. Bailey and Michelle Brown, *Media Representations of September 11*, Westport, CT and London: Praeger 2003, pp. 85–101.

Rhodes, Mark and Carole Chapelier, 'Balance-Seekers' and New Information Sources. Media Usage Patterns in the Middle East, in: Oliver Zöllner (ed.), *Beyond Borders: Research and International Broadcasting 2003*, Bonn: CIBAR 2004, pp. 78–87.

Richter, Emanuel, *Der Zerfall der Welteinheit: Vernunft und Globalisierung in der Moderne [The Collapse of Global Unity. Reason and Globalization in Modernity]*, Frankfurt and New York: Campus 1992.

Righter, Rosemary, *Whose News? Politics, the Press and the Third World*, London and New York: Times 1978.

Robertson, Roland, Globalization or Glocalization? in: *Journal of International Communication* 1 (1994a) 1, pp. 33–52.

Robertson, Roland, Mapping the Global Condition: Globalization as the Central Concept, in: Mike Featherstone (ed.), Global Culture: Nationalism, *Globalization and Modernity*, London and Newbury Park: Sage 1994b, pp. 15–30.

Robinson, Piers, *The CNN Effect: The Myth of News, Foreign Policy and Intervention*, London and New York: Routledge 2002.

Rondfeldt, David, *The Zapatista Social Netwar in Mexico*, prepared for the United States Army, Santa Monica, Cal.: Rand Arroyo Center 1998.

Sakr, Naomi, *Satellite Realms: Transnational Television, Globalization and the Middle East*, London and New York: I. B. Tauris 2001.

Schäfer, Peter, *Internet als politisches Kommunikationsmittel in Palästina [The Internet as a means of political communication in Palestine]*, Hamburg: Deutsches Orient-Institut 2004.

Schenk, Birgit, Die Struktur des internationalen Nachrichtenflusses: Analyse der empirischen Studien [The structure of the international flow of news: analysis of the empirical studies], in: *Rundfunk und Fernsehen* 35 (1987) 1, pp. 36–54.

Schenk, Birgit, Internationaler Nachrichtenfluß: Einige Anmerkungen zur Stellungnahme von Jörg Becker [The international flow of news: a response to the comments by Jörg Becker], in: *Rundfunk und Fernsehen* 36 (1988) 2, pp. 247–49.

Schirm, Stefan A., *Globalization and the New Regionalism: Global Markets, Domestic Politics and Regional Cooperation*, Cambridge: Polity 2002.

Schmiedel, Michael, Das Internet in der VR China – Ein Netz, zwei

Systeme? [The Internet in the PR China – one Net, two systems?], in: *Nord–Süd aktuell* 15 (2000) 3, pp. 501–12.

Schulz, Winfried, *Die Konstruktion von Realität in den Nachrichtenmedien. Analyse der aktuellen Berichterstattung [The construction of reality in the news media. An analysis of current reporting]*, Freiburg and Munich: Alber 1990 (2nd edn).

Schulze, Reinhard, Is there an Islamic Modernity?, in: Kai Hafez (ed.), *The Islamic World and the West: An Introduction to Political Cultures and International Relations*, Leiden: Brill 2000, pp. 21–32.

Schuster, Thomas, Staat und Medien. *Über die elektronische Konditionierung der Wirklichkeit [State and media. The electronic conditioning of reality]*, Frankfurt: Fischer Taschenbuch 1995.

Sepstrup, Preben and Anura Goonasekera, TV Transnationalization in Europe and Asia. *Reports and Papers on Mass Communication*, No. 109, Paris: UNESCO 1994.

Sikkink, Kathryn and Margaret E. Keck, *Activists beyond Borders: Advocacy Networks in International Politics*, Ithaca, NY: Cornell University Press 1998.

Sinclair, John, Elizabeth Jacka and Stuart Cunningham (eds), *New Patterns in Global Television. Peripheral Vision*, Oxford: Oxford University Press 1996a.

Sinclair, John, Elizabeth Jacka and Stuart Cunningham, Peripheral Vision, in: Sinclair, John, Elizabeth Jacka and Stuart Cunningham (eds), *New Patterns in Global Television: Peripheral Vision*, Oxford: Oxford University Press 1996b, pp. 1–32.

Sinclair, John, Mexico, Brazil, and the Latin World, in: John Sinclair, Elizabeth Jacka and Stuart Cunningham (eds), *New Patterns in Global Television: Peripheral Vision*, Oxford: Oxford University Press 1996c, pp. 33–68.

Siochrú, Seán Ó, Bruce Girard and Amy Mahan, *Global Media Governance: A Beginner's Guide*, Lanham: Rowman & Littlefield 2002.

Sparks, Colin, Is there a Global Public Sphere? in: Daya K. Thussu, *Electronic Empires: Global Media and Local Resistance*, London: Arnold 1998, pp. 108–24.

Sparks, Colins, The Global, the Local and the Public Sphere, in: Georgette Wang, Jan Servaes and Anura Goonasekera (eds), *The New Communications Landscape: Demystifying Media Globalization*, London and New York: Routledge 2000, pp. 74–95.

Sreberny-Mohammadi, Annabelle, Kaarle Nordenstreng, Robert Stevenson and Frank Ugboajah (eds), *Foreign News in the Media: International Reporting in 29 Countries*. Final Report Undertaken for UNESCO by the International Association for Mass Communication Research, Paris: UNESCO 1985.

Sreberny-Mohammadi, Annabelle, The Global and the Local in International Communications, in: James Curran and Michael Gurevitch (eds), *Mass Media and Society*, London: Arnold 1994a, pp. 177–203.

Sreberny-Mohammadi, Annabelle and Ali Mohammadi, *Small Media, Big Revolution: Communication, Culture, and the Iranian Revolution*, Minneapolis: University of Minnesota Press 1994b.

Sreberny-Mohammadi, Annabelle, Dwayne Winseck, Jim McKenna and Oliver Boyd-Barrett (eds), *Media in Global Context: A Reader*, London: Arnold 1997.

Staring, R. and S. Zorlu, Thuis voor de buis: Turkse migranten en satellitteevee [At Home in Front of the Box: Turkish migrants and satellite TV], in: *Migrantenstudies* 12 (1996) 4, pp. 211–21.

Stolz, Joelle, *Les Algériens regardent Dallas: Les Nouvelles Chaînes [Algerians watch Dallas. The New Chains]*, Paris: Presse Universitaire de France and Institut d'Études du Développment 1983.

Straubhaar, Joseph D., Distinguishing the Global, Regional and National Levels of World Television, in: Annabelle Sreberny-Mohammadi et al. (ed.), *Media in Global Context: A Reader*, New York: Arnold 1997, pp. 284–98.

Straubhaar, Joseph, Brazil: The Role of the State in World Television, in: Nancy Morris and Silvio Waisbord (eds), *Media and Globalization:Why the State Matters*, Lanham: Rowman & Littlefield 2001, pp. 133–53.

Strawson, John, Holy War in the Media: Images of Jihad, in: Steven Chermak, Frankie Y. Bailey and Michelle Brown, *Media Representations of September 11*, Westport, CT and London: Praeger 2003, pp. 17–28.

Suárez, Luis, Mass Communications and the Major Challenges, in: *Media and Democracy in Latin America and Caribbean*, Paris: UNESCO 1996, pp. 48–53.

Television 2004, *International Key Facts*, Cologne: IP/RTL Group 2004.

Ter Wal, Jessika (ed.), *Racism and Cultural Diversity in the Mass Media: An Overview of Research and Examples of Good Practice in the EU Member States, 1995–2000*, Vienna: European Monitoring Centre on Racism and Xenophobia, Vienna (EUMC) 2002.

The Honolulu Statement, The Mac Bride Round Table, Honolulu, Hawaii, 20–23 January 1994, in: Richard C. Vincent, Kaarle Nordenstreng and Michael Traber (eds), *Towards Equity in Global Communication. MacBride Update*, Cresskill, NJ: Hampton 1999, pp. 331–4.

Thiermeyer, Michael, *Internationalisierung von Film und Filmwirtschaft [The internationalization of film and the film economy]*, Cologne: Böhlau 1994.

Thomas, Bella, Was die Armen im Fernsehen anschauen: Die Auswirkungen westlichen Fernsehens auf Entwicklungsländer sind geringer als weithin angenommen [What the poor watch on TV: Western television is having less impact on developing countries than is generally assumed], in: *Überblick* 39 (2003) 4, pp. 14–24.

Thussu, Daya K., *Electronic Empires: Global Media and Local Resistance*, London: Arnold 1998.

Thussu, Daya Kishan and Des Freedman (eds), *War and the Media*, London: Sage 2003.

Tomlinson, John, Cultural Imperialism, in: Frank J. Lechner and John Boli (eds), *The Globalization Reader*, Oxford: Blackwell 2000, pp. 307–16.

Tomlinson, John, Globalisation and National Identity, in: John Sinclair (ed.), *Contemporary World Television*, London: BFI 2004, pp. 24–7.

Tsagarousianou, Roza, Damian Tambini and Cathy Brian (eds), *Cyberdemocracy: Technology, Cities and Civic Networks*, London and New York: Routledge 1998.

Tumber, Howard and Jerry Palmer, *Media at War: The Iraq Crisis*, London: Sage 2004.

Tunstall, Jeremy, Worldwide News Agencies – Private Wholesalers of Public Information, in: Jim Richstad and Michael H. Anderson (eds), *Crisis in International News: Policies and Prospects*, New York: Columbia University Press 1981, pp. 258–67.

U.S. International Broadcasting. *New Strategic Approach Focuses on Reaching Large Audiences but Lacks Measurable Program Objectives*, Washington: United States General Accounting Office 2003.

U.S. Public Diplomacy: State Department and the Broadcasting Board of Governors Expand Efforts in the Middle East but Face Significant Challenges, Washington: United States General Accounting Office 2004.

van de Donk, Wim, Brian D. Loader, Paul G. Nixon and Dieter Rucht (eds), *Cyberprotest: New Media, Citizens and Social Movements*, London and New York: Routledge 2004.

Volkmer, Ingrid, *News in the Global Sphere: A Study of CNN and its Impact on Global Communication*, Luton 1999.

von Nussbaum, Heinrich, UN-Ordnung mit System [The systematic UN (dis)order], in: *Medium* 9 (1979) 2, pp. 8–14.

von Wilamowitz-Moellendorff, Ulrich, *Türken in Deutschland: Einstellungen zu Staat und Gesellschaft [Turks in Germany: attitudes towards state and society]*, Sankt Augustin: Konrad-Adenauer-Stiftung 2001.

Waisbord, Silvio and Nancy Morris (eds), *Media and Globalization: Why the State Matters*, Lanham: Rowman & Littlefield 2001.

Wang, Georgette, Anura Goonasekera and Jan Servaes, *The New Communications Landscape: Demystifying Media Globalization*, London: Routledge 2000.

Weiß, Hans-Jürgen and Joachim Trebbe, *Mediennutzung und Integration der türkischen Bevölkerung in Deutschland: Ergebnisse einer Umfrage des Presse- und Informationsamtes der Bundesregierung [Media use and integration among the Turkish community in Germany: the findings of a survey by the Federal Press and Information Office]*, Berlin: Federal Information Office of the German Government 2001.

Wildermuth, Norbert, Satellite Television in India, in: Stefan Brüne (ed.), *Neue Medien und Öffentlichkeiten*, Vol. 2, Hamburg: Deutsches Orient-Institut 2000, pp. 212–37.

Wilding, Colin M., 151 Million Listeners – But what Does it Mean? Uses and Misuses of Global Audience Estimates, in: Oliver Zöllner (ed.), *An*

Essential Link with Audiences Worldwide. Research for International Broadcasting, Berlin: Vistas 2002, pp. 61–9.

Winseck, Dwayne, The WTO, Emerging Policy Regimes and the Political Economy of Transnational Communications, in: Marc Raboy (ed.), *Global Media Policy in the New Millennium*, Luton: University of Luton Press 2002, pp. 19–37.

Wöhlcke, Manfred, Lateinamerika in der Presse. *Inhaltsanalytische Untersuchung der Lateinamerika-Berichterstattung in folgenden Presseorganen: Die Welt, FAZ, NZZ, Handelsblatt, Le Monde, Neues Deutschland, Der Spiegel [Latin America in the press. A content analytical study of Latin America coverage in the following publications: Die Welt, FAZ, NZZ, Handelsblatt, Le Monde, Neues Deutschland, Der Spiegel]*, Stuttgart: Klett 1973.

Wolfsfeld, Gadi, *Media and Political Conflict: News from the Middle East*, Cambridge: Cambridge University Press 1997.

World Culture Report 2000. Cultural Diversity, Conflict and Pluralism, UNESCO, New York: UNESCO 2000.

Zagala, Samera, *'Kampf der Kulturen' – 'Krieg der Zivilisationen': Theorien zum Konflikt zwischen dem Westen und dem Islam in deutschen Nachrichtensendungen. Eine inhaltsanalytische Untersuchung ['Battle of Cultures', 'War of Civilisations': theories dealing with the conflict between the West and Islam in German news programmes. A content analytical study]*, MA thesis at the Institut für Journalistik, Universität Dortmund, Dortmund 2004.

Internet Sources

Auh, Taik-Sup, Promoting Multilingualism on the Internet: Korean Experience, <www.unesco.org/webworld/infoethics_2/eng/papers/paper_8.htm> (1 March 2006).

Cham, Mbye, Afrika globalisieren? Der afrikanische Film zwischen Négritude und Globalisierung [Globalizing Africa? The African film between négritude and globalization], <www.vsp.vernetzt.de/soz/000516.htm> (1 August 2004).

Contrasting War Coverage, in: *Middle East Economic Survey* 46 (2003) 14, <www.mees.com> (1 March 2006).

Dahl, Stephen, Communications and Culture Transformation: Cultural Diversity, Globalization and Cultural Convergence, <www.stephweb.com/capstone/capstone.shtml> (1 March 2006).

Deutsch–arabischer Mediendialog [German–Arab Media Dialogue], Institut für Auslandsbeziehungen, Beirut, May 2004, <www.ifa.de/dialoge/dbeirut_protokoll.html> (17 September 2005).

Deutsche Welle Director General Bettermann: Gesetzentwurf stärkt Unabhängigkeit des deutschen Auslandsrundfunks [Draft legislation strengthens independence of German international broadcasting], <www.dw-world.de> (28 August 2004).

Die Zukunft des Internets: Auf dem Weg zum 'Digitalen Realismus' [The future of the Internet: Towards 'digital realism'], <www.zukunftsinstitut.de> (1 March 2006).

Doing the Dissent Thing? <news.bbc.co.uk/1/hi/uk/2907599.stm> (1 March 2006).

Fan, Xing, China's WTO Accession and Its Telecom Liberalization, <www.csis.org/ics/chinaswtoaccession.html> (28 March 2005).

Forum Barcelona 2004, UNESCO <www.barcelona2004.org/eng/ banco_del_conocimiento/documentos/ficha.cfm?IdDoc=230> (1 March 2006).

Giddens, Anthony, Lecture 1 – Globalization, <www.news.bbc.co.uk/hi/english/static/events/reith_99/week1/week1.htm> (22 February 2006).

Global Internet Geography Database and Report: The Definitive Guide to Global Internet Backbones and Traffic, <www.telegeography.com> (30 July 2004).

Global Trends 2015: A Dialogue About the Future with Nongovernment Experts, <www.cia.gov/cia/reports/globaltrends2015> (1 March 2006).

Held, David, Anthony McGrew, David Goldblatt and Jonathan Perraton, Global Transformations, <www.polity.co.uk/global/executiv.htm#whatis> (1 March 2006).

Lebert, Marie, Multilingualism on the Web, <www.etudes-francaises.net/entretiens/multieng1.htm> (1 March 2006).

Lieberman, Evelyn S., Remarks at Al-Akhawayn University, April 5, 2000, <www.usembassy.ma/Themes/EconomicIssues/lieberman.htm> (23 December 2004).

Marr, Merissa, BBC Chief Attacks U.S. Media War Coverage, <www.veteransforpeace.org/BBC_chief_attacks_042403.htm> (1 March 2006).

Nach dem 11. September ist Attac nötiger denn je [After 11 September, attack is more necessary than ever], <www.attac.de/kongress/2010v.html> (1 March 2006).

Naureckas, Jim, When 'Doves' Lie: The New York Times Plays Down Anti-War Opinion, <www.fair.org/extra/0304/nyt-doves.html> (1 March 2006).

Offenbartl, Susanne, Globalisierung durch Vermittlungsmedien? Vortrag auf der Jahrestagung des Arbeitskreises universitäre Erwachsenenbildung (AUE) [Globalization through intermediary media? Presentation at the annual conference of the study group on adult education at university], 23–24 September 1999, Deutsches Institut für Erwachsenenbildung (DIE), Bonn, <www.die-frankfurt.de/esprid/dokumente/doc-1999/offen bart199_11.htm> (1 March 2006).

Peyman, Saloumeh, Iranian Exiles Use Satellite TV to Promote Change, <www.antiwar.com/ips/peyman.php?articleid=3811> (1 March 2006).

Rendall, Steve/Tara Broughel, Amplifying Officials, Squelching Dissent, <www.fair.org/extra/0305/warstudy.html> (1 March 2006).

Rucht, Dieter, NGOs, Internet und Globalisierung, Vortrag DGB-Bildungszentrum Hattingen [NGOs, Internet and globalization. Presentation at the DGB Education Centre, Hattingen], 23 January 2003, <www.hattingen.dgb-bildungswerk.de/doku/2003INK/20123_6Rucht_Internet_NGOs 6.html> (1 March 2006).

Rugh, William A., Comments on Radio Sawa and al Hurra Television, <www.foreign.senate.gov/testimony/2004/RughTestimony040429.pdf> (28 August 2004).

Ted Turner Calls Murdoch Warmonger, <www.thetruthseeker.co.uk/article. asp ?ID=727> (7 May 2003).

TV, Patriotism Helped Swing British Opinion on Iraq War, Agence France-Presse, <quickstart.clari.net/qs_se/webnews/wed/az/Qiraq-war-britain> (10 May 2003).

Wang, Ning, Chinese Cinema Challenged by Globalization: A Cultural and Intellectual Strategy, <www.culstudies.com/rendanews/displaynews.asp?id=1403> (1 March 2006).

World Summit on the Information Society, Declaration of Principles, Geneva 2003 – Tunis 2005, Document WSIS-03/Geneva/Doc/4-E, 12 December 2003, <www.itu.int> (1 March 2006).

World Summit on the Information Society, Plan of Action, Geneva 2003 – Tunis 2005, Document WSIS-03/Geneva/Doc/5-E, 12 December 2003, <www.itu.int> (1 March 2006).

Woznicki, Krystian, Die vierte Macht [The fourth power], 28 June 2004, <www.heise.de> (20 September 2004).

Index